EC/EU
FACT
BOOK

WITHDRAWN

THE LEARNING CENTRE
HAMMERSMITH AND WEST
LONDON COLLEGE
GLIDDON ROAD
LONDON W14 9BL

0181 741 1688

EC/EU FACT BOOK

A COMPLETE GUIDE

Sixth Edition

ALEX RONEY

KOGAN PAGE

While technically the term 'European Union' (EU) does not cover all aspects of the European Communities (EC) provisions, this book will use both the terms 'EC' and 'EU' widely to accord with political reality, and to follow current (albeit not strictly accurate) practice.

First published in 1990
Second edition 1991
Third edition 1993
Reprinted in 1994
Fourth edition 1995
Reprinted with revisions 1996
Fifth edition 1998
Sixth edition 2000

Kogan Page Limited
120 Pentonville Road
London N1 9JN

© Alex Roney, 1990, 1991, 1993, 1995, 1998, 2000

British Library Cataloguing in Publication Data

A CIP record for this book is available from the British Library.

ISBN 0 7494 3192 X

Typeset by Saxon Graphics Ltd, Derby
Printed in England by Clays Ltd, St Ives plc

303846

Contents

Foreword to the First and Second Editions

Businessmen are often bewildered when they look at the European scene. They want to know how the establishment of the single market in the European Community will affect their business. Will it open new opportunities or does it conceal hidden pitfalls? Their bewilderment will grow when they listen to some of the forecasters whose views are often contradictory: some are overoptimistic pro-Europeans and others gloomy anti-marketers. The ordinary businessman will conclude: 'Give me the facts and I will form my own view; I know best the potential of my business'.

This is exactly what this book sets out to do and, it has to be said, does so in a most successful manner. In the Preface the author states that it is always important to ask the right questions. Not only does she skillfully articulate the questions, which must be in the mind of many directors and managers, she also gives the right answers accurately, briefly and in lucid non-technical language.

It is obvious that only an author who combines complete mastery of the subject with great practical experience can present this complex matter in such an easily understandable form. Mrs Roney possesses the combination of these qualities. She is a lawyer of distinction, being a member of the English Bar and having worked at the Community in Brussels; and as Legal Counsellor of the London Chamber of Commerce and Industry for many years she has an unrivalled knowledge of the practical needs of business.

The main merit of this book is that, in addition to conveying essential information to the reader (in a manner which makes it a pleasure to read this book), it exhibits the modern outlook on European and international affairs which is necessary if British business is to survive in the stormy winds of world competition.

Professor Clive Schmitthoff

Author's note: I have asked that this Foreword be reprinted in this edition as my own small tribute to Professor Schmitthoff, who is now, sadly, deceased.

Foreword to the Third Edition

Businessmen who are not conversant with the institutions of the European Community often need quick answers to a wide range of highly practical questions. Finding the answers is all too often a difficult and time-consuming task. One of the many virtues of Alex Roney's *European Community Fact Book* is that it identifies the information needs of the business user and assembles, in a concise and easy to read form, a wealth of data covering all aspects of Community organization and policy.

The two previous editions of the *Fact Book* were widely welcomed. It has now been fully revised and updated in this new edition, which is a mine of information on Community institutions and activities. Whether the reader wishes to know the significance of the Single European Act or the enhanced role of the European Parliament; the measures taken to liberalize the provision of haulage services or the protection of passengers; the rules to open competition in public procurement contracts or the freedom to provide Community-wide banking services, the answers will be found in this book. Alex Roney, a valued colleague on the International Commercial Practice Committee of ICC United Kingdom, has drawn on her long experience as a member of the English Bar and Legal Counsellor to the London Chamber of Commerce and Industry, to provide an indispensable guide to the complexities of doing business in Europe. I have no doubt at all that this new edition will be received even more enthusiastically than its predecessors.

Professor Roy Goode Q.C.
St John's College
Oxford
May 1993

Foreword to the Sixth Edition

This fully revised and updated edition of Alex Roney's highly regarded guide to the Union is a welcome addition at this time of evolution and debate within the European Union. The Union is facing a wide range of fundamental issues, most obviously eastern enlargement, structural reforms and the development of the Economic and Monetary Union (EMU).

The question and answer format is a particularly helpful tool for assisting understanding. As with the earlier editions, the EC/EU Fact Book is lucid and the format is clear and concise. The book aims to provide readers with succinct answers in non-technical language. But perhaps of equal importance – it identifies some of the most important questions that citizens, business people and students should be considering.

The EU is so frequently the subject of misinformation. The Fact Book successfully aims to explain to the reader some of the issues involved, for example the development of the internal market. Alex Roney untangles the facts and leaves the reader to develop opinions.

Alex Roney is a lawyer, and an external examiner for South Bank University. She was for many years Legal Counsellor of the London

Chamber of Commerce and Industry. She has a thorough understanding of this complex subject matter, and great skill in presenting the main issues in an easily understandable form. The Fact Book gets straight to 'the heart of the matter' in identifying the main issues that concern business. She has an unrivalled knowledge not only of the practical needs of business but also of the needs of students, especially those studying business and management.

Dr Jill Preston
Director of Research and Professor of European Integration
Anglia Business School
Anglia Polytechnic University
Cambridge
January 2000

Preface to the Sixth Edition

Nationalism has different meanings for different people. It is a natural instinct to be proud of and to protect one's family, village, town, county and country. It should be a natural instinct to protect one's neighbours; and the question has to be asked: who are our neighbours now in this shrinking world of cross-border pollution and the Internet? Time zones and thousands of miles are immaterial to the Information Society, and business can work in 24-hour daytime shifts between here and Australia.

Where nationalism is dangerous is where it is not benign but aggressive – fighting the supporters of another football team, suggesting people from other nations are definitely worse and more untrustworthy than those from one's own group, and even countenancing 'ethnic cleansing' and serious fighting. It seems to be on the increase.

What is behind this flip side of nationalism? Maybe a lust for political power; maybe a (usually misguided or abused) religious fervour; maybe just a fear of losing jobs or an established standard of living or way of life. At its most basic it could be a desire to get back at a winning team or to triumph over the losers.

Sometimes EU policies can properly be regarded as misguided, and mistakes are made. Too often countries have to be cudgelled into complying with their obligations. Sometimes plans that look good on paper don't work in practice. Every EU citizen can make his or her views known and be part of the consultative process. There are always options to be considered when looking at EU policies – from enlargement to Economic and Monetary Union, from social and industrial initiatives to trade, defence and many others. It is vital to understand the basic structures and thinking behind developments. As always I have tried to be as up to date as possible, but is always wise to check with sources given as to the most recent provisions.

Although Great Britain and Northern Ireland constitute a small area becoming less unified as devolution creates further divisions, the EU as a whole is growing bigger, both as to the breadth of policies, and as to the number of Member States. It is trying to provide a workable umbrella. There are new close neighbours to trade with, and worldwide links with others – all to some extent dependent on each other for success.

The EU, and this must never be forgotten, grew from the roots of two World Wars. It is still aimed securely at preventing wars among the diverse peoples of Europe, and at promoting a better life for those citizens, peace and prosperity.

That is why I have written the sixth edition of this book

Alex Roney
January 2000

Acknowledgements

Already, information packs, booklets and indeed countless books have been written on this subject. In writing this book I have spoken to those with special knowledge and am grateful for their help. I would like to mention some organizations and people who have supplied material that has been particularly helpful for this edition. These include the Department of Trade and Industry; the Foreign and Commonwealth Office; Edward Smith of the Patent Office; the Ministry of Agriculture, Fisheries and Food; the Commission of the European Communities, in particular Aisling Doherty of the City of London EIC; and The European Parliament Information Office.

The publication *Europe* has been invaluable in my researches. I am also grateful to Geoff Collins of Ashings, Peter Eldridge and many others, not forgetting my husband Charles, who has had to put up with the long hours I have spent on this sixth edition.

Lastly, I would like to thank the London Chamber of Commerce and Industry Examinations Board, which has kindly sponsored this edition.

1 The European Community: its aims, size and structure

Some basic facts and data

What are the countries of the European Community (EC), now usually referred to as the European Union (EU)?

The popularly called 'EU' is often referred to as the 'EC' – the European Community – which under the Treaty on European Union (the Maastricht Treaty) replaced the terms 'European Economic Community', 'the Common Market', 'the Internal Market' (solely in the 1992 context) and the 'EEC' (European Economic Community).

There are currently 15 Member States: Austria, Belgium, Denmark, Finland, France, Germany, Greece, Ireland, Italy, Luxembourg, The Netherlands, Portugal, Spain, Sweden and the United Kingdom.

What is the population of the EU?

The EU's population is about 375.4 million. The world's population is now nearly 6 billion and is, according to UN estimates, likely to rise to about 8.9 billion by 2050, with 95 per cent of the population increase in developing countries. The EU population is greater than that in the former Soviet Union (approximately 280 million), Russia (145.6 million) and the United States (approximately 254 million), but less than China (over 1 billion).

What are the individual countries' populations?

The individual populations (in millions) of the Member States are as follows:

Austria	8.068
Belgium	10.2
Denmark	5.3

Finland	5.1
France	58.9
Germany	82
Greece	10.5
Ireland	3.7
Italy	57.6
Luxembourg	0.429
Netherlands	15.7
Portugal	9.9
Spain	39.4
Sweden	8.8
United Kingdom	59.2

The above are January 1999 EU population figures. In 1999 birth-rate increases were the lowest since 1945, but the number of people living in the EU increased by almost one million, with net immigration of about 717,000, to total 376.4 million in January 2000. Further population statistics may be obtained from Eurostat Publications (see Appendix III).

All these countries are now a single 'home' market. The completed market is both a challenge and a threat. To take up the challenge, and guard against the threat, you must understand the background, and know what is happening now.

The beginnings of the European Community

How did this link-up start?

A unified Europe is not a new idea. By AD 14 Augustus Caesar had consolidated a vast Roman Empire, with a single currency. Others like Charlemagne, Napoleon and Hitler have tried to create great European empires, albeit by force rather than by mutual agreement.

World War II showed the need to unify the peoples of Europe in a way that would minimize, but not destroy, the national patriotism that was felt to be a cause of both World Wars. Sir Winston Churchill looked towards a form of 'United States of Europe', and Jean Monnet, the head of the French Recovery Programme, and Robert Schuman, the French Foreign Minister, agreed that there was an urgent need to pool and hold under a single authority the steel and coal resources of western Europe, as these had been a significant cause of the wrangling between Germany and France in particular. The Allies were also concerned that restoration of West Germany's industrial power would lead to another resurgence of the nationalism that had sparked the previous two wars. Their plan, the Schuman Plan, led in 1951 to six countries (Belgium, France, West Germany, Italy, Luxembourg and The Netherlands) signing the Treaty of Paris, which set up the European Coal and Steel Community (ECSC) concerned with the pooling of production and consumption of coal and steel. The ECSC Treaty lapses in 2002 and coal and steel will be brought within Community competences, albeit as a separate sector.

The success of the ECSC led to attempts to create a European Defence Community (EDC), which finally led to the formation of the Western European Union (WEU) and the North Atlantic Treaty Organization (NATO), although the EDC itself was rejected by France.

In 1957, largely due to the efforts of Belgian Foreign Minister, Paul-Henri Spaak, on the same day the same six countries signed the Treaty of Rome, establishing the EEC (European Economic Community), better known as the Common Market, and the EURATOM Treaty (European Atomic Energy Community), designed to promote and supervise the development for peaceful uses of nuclear and atomic energy, which was recognized as an essential resource. Also recognized was the importance of international co-operation to ensure its safe use.

In 1965, common institutions for the three Communities were established, and became effective in 1967. They were known as the European Communities.

The Treaty of Rome has been amended to meet the needs of the Member States in seeking to achieve their goal of creating the European Community, by three further treaties to date, namely the Single European Act, the Treaty on European Union (Maastricht) and the Treaty for Europe (Amsterdam).

In 1973, the UK, Denmark and Ireland joined the original six countries, followed by Greece (in 1981) and then, in 1986, by Spain and Portugal. In 1990 the reunion of East and West Germany was achieved, which effectively added another state to the Community. On 1 January 1995, Austria, Finland and Sweden joined to make a European Community of 15.

What about the offshore islands in the Community?

None of these are individual members of the Community, so their respective positions and those of their citizens are governed by protocols annexed to the treaties. There are around 450 inhabited islands within the EU – around 5 per cent of its land mass.

Expansion

Have any other countries applied to join the EU?

The reunification of Germany added impetus towards greater political union in the EC. The break-up of the Soviet Union had a profound impact, with the resulting necessity and cost of assisting East European countries moving towards market economies, many of which are now applicant countries. There are many Europe, partnership and co-operation agreements with third countries, and the GATT (General Agreement on Tariffs and Trade) and World Trade Organization (WTO) agreements are having a significant impact on world trade.

At the time of writing the following countries have applied to join: Turkey (1987), Cyprus and Malta (1990), Liechtenstein (1992), Hungary and Poland (1994), Latvia, Slovakia, Estonia, Romania, Bulgaria and Lithuania (1995), and the Czech Republic and Slovenia (1996). Malta withdrew its membership application, but has reapplied. The Community is committed to a community of 25 and may even extend to 34 Member States. Romania is likely to start membership negotiations in 2000.

Bulgaria, Latvia, Lithuania, Romania and Slovakia have joined the first six applicants in accession negotiations. Turkey is being considered as a viable candidate for membership of the EU.

How are accessions achieved?

Not only is an absolute majority of the European Parliament, together with a unanimous vote of the Council of Ministers, necessary for a country to be accepted, but also all national legislatures of the Member States have to ratify accession treaties, as does the national legislature of the country concerned. Thus Norway, whose accession negotiations were successfully concluded, did not actually join the EC, as the people by national referendum decided to remain outside the Union, as did the Swiss electorate (even though its Government had previously applied to join). Iceland has not applied to join the EU, but like Norway is a member of the EEA (European Economic Area). The Customs Union with Turkey is working well, but concerns remain about Turkey's human rights record in connection with its application to join the EU.

Are there any prerequisites to joining the EU?

Yes, the European Council at Copenhagen in 1993 stipulated that requirements should include an applicant having respect for human and minority rights, democracy, free and fair elections, a secure rule of law with effective institutions, progress in economic reforms and good relations with its neighbouring states.

Is there an accession strategy?

Yes. The Essen European Council in 1994 adopted an accession strategy for associated countries wishing to process through to full membership of the EU. This built on Trade and Economic Co-operation agreements as stage one, through the Europe agreements as stage two, and then through co-operation with EU institutions and discussion of a pre-accession strategy towards full membership. The pre-accession strategy varies from applicant to applicant, but should lead to reforms to enable the applicant to function within the EU as a democratic market economy. It is given the technical assistance necessary and should be able then to proceed to adopt the *acquis communautaire*.

The Council, acting unanimously with the European Parliament (EP), must consent to opening accession negotiations. The Treaty of Accession with each country is then drafted, signed and ratified by the EU members, the EP and the applicant country.

The 1994 accession strategy was followed by further agreement on the process needed at the Madrid meeting in December 1995, which itself was endorsed by the Amsterdam Inter-Governmental Conference (IGC) conclusions in 1997. The Commission then presented *Agenda 2000: For a Stronger and Wider Union* (see below), which suggested the strategy needed for the EU to enable it to extend, particularly eastwards. Another IGC will be necessary to agree the internal EU institutional reforms needed for enlargement. Presently, arguments continue as to the position of applicant countries with regard to the Common Agricultural Policy rights and subsidies.

What is the position with regard to present applicants?

Association and Europe agreements have been concluded with all the applicant states. For example, Association agreements require states individually to meet major conditions:

- to be able to assume the obligations of the *acquis communautaire*;
- to be sufficiently stable to guarantee democracy, human rights, law and a respect for ethnic minorities;
- to have a market economy;
- to endorse the EU's objectives as regards Economic and Monetary Union (EMU);

- to have an economy strong enough to cope with the competitive rigours imposed by membership of the EU (and its liberated markets).

In addition, the EU itself must be able to absorb the new members and at the same time ensure that the momentum of European integration is not adversely affected.

Ten Central and Eastern European Countries (CEECs) have Accession partnerships (Bulgaria, the Czech Republic, Estonia, Hungary, Latvia, Lithuania, Poland, Romania, Slovenia and Slovakia) and these set out priority areas, together with provision for EU advice and financial assistance to help them to meet the membership criteria. An accession negotiation Web site gives further details (see Appendix III).

What is the acquis communautaire?

This is the shorthand term for the acceptance of the existing obligations of membership of the European Union that new members must take on, and which the Members of the EEA have agreed to accept.

What was in Agenda 2000: For a Stronger and Wider Union?

This 1997 document, endorsed by the Council, considered the challenges facing the EU in the new millennium and focused on the deepening of the EU and consolidating policies, on enlargement, and on setting the financial framework for the future. It also looked at the financial framework and support needed for 2000–06 to cushion the costs and economic impact of absorbing new Member States, which are causing significant concerns.

What about decision-making in the enlarged EU?

The Amsterdam Treaty went some way to amend the powers of the EP and reform decision-making procedures, but it is recognized that further constitutional reform will be needed to prevent stagnation when the new Members actually join, and a further IGC is planned to consider this. In October 1999 the Dehaene Committee, set up to consider changes needed, suggested various reforms including:

- qualified majority voting to be the general rule in the enlarged EU with a parallel extension of EP co-decision procedures;
- the division of the EU Treaty into two parts to facilitate amendments: a basic treaty with aims, citizens' rights and institutional

framework, which would be within the remit of an IGC; and provisions relating to the implementation of policy, which would be within the powers of the Council/EP;

- increased powers for the President of the Commission over Commissioners;
- efficiency reforms for the Council;
- greater flexibility to facilitate faster or slower progressions by Member States;
- inclusion of European defence policy in the agenda of the IGC as a matter where reform is needed;
- the urging of the Commission to draft a treaty on institutional reforms for negotiation by the end of 2000.

What are the official languages of the EU?

There are now 11 official languages (Danish, Dutch, English, Finnish, French, German, Greek, Italian, Portuguese, Spanish and Swedish) and 35 minority languages in the EU. The plenary meetings of the European Parliament and of the Council are in all the official languages. With the accession of the new countries there are likely to be 26 countries, with a possible 15 official languages.

Reports

What about the Cecchini Report and the Delors Committee Report?

This introductory chapter would not be complete without mentioning these reports. After the Single European Act 1986 came Paolo Cecchini's 1988 major study entitled *The European Challenge 1992: The Benefits of a Single Market*. He and his team considered the likely effects of the completion of the Internal Market and the unnecessary costs to European industry resulting from bureaucratic requirements, border controls and nationalistic protectionism. The work was a remarkable achievement and provided scientifically assembled evidence to encourage the swift completion of the Internal Market because it illustrated the likely gains that should accrue to the economies and peoples of Europe. The study stressed the need for business, through national governments, to make more constructive input into political and legislative policy, and encouraged the orchestration of policies at Community level.

The Delors Committee Report concerned the steps needed to achieve Economic and Monetary Union (EMU) in the EC (see Chapter 12).

What was the Sutherland Report 1992?

The Sutherland Report 1992 on *The Internal Market after 1992 – Meeting the Challenge*, stressed the need:

- to make internal market provisions effective in all Member States;
- to inform citizens of their rights and legal means of protection at national court level, including courts of appeal. Courts and experts should be given more training in Community legislation and in the operation of the 1968 Brussels Convention on the mutual recognition and enforcement of judgements;
- to codify Community legislation, because otherwise it is not easily accessible to the public;
- to protect by confidentiality those seeking redress in public procurement cases (as knowledge by the tenderer of a complaint by a bidder could affect the latter's chances of securing that contract, or later contracts);
- to subject all proposals for EC legislation to a rigorous practicality and usefulness audit;
- to ensure the Commission periodically evaluates the real impact of national and Community legislation;
- to ensure that, ideally, Directives should be drafted with the intention of making them directly applicable legislation, so that one text would be effective throughout the EC and inconsistencies avoided.

This last recommendation could be said to go against the principle of subsidiarity, which has become increasingly important since then, but most of these recommendations have been progressed effectively.

A 1996 survey over two years and a report by the Commission gave a positive result for the Single Market and its creation of an extra 900,000 jobs, but urged greater Community action and co-ordination in some areas.

What changes are expected in the near future?

The Amsterdam Treaty came into effect on 1 May 1999 following its formal signature in October 1997. The launch of the enlargement process to take in new Member States in accordance with the procedure agreed in December 1995 has started. The integration of the Schengen Secretariat into the General Secretariat of the Council, and adoption of Schengen provisions, are having an impact on movement of people in the EU. Albeit there are reservations for the UK and Ireland, both countries have agreed to co-operate in certain areas provided for under Schengen, such as identification of illegal immigrants. A further IGC is to be held to agree the constitutional changes necessary for an enlarged EU.

Economic and Monetary Union, the single currency and the 'Eurozone' or 'Euroland' have started in 11 of the 15 Member States, with only Greece, Sweden and the UK remaining outside it. Despite teething troubles, it is at the time of writing generally regarded as a successful venture. It will have an enormous impact on the countries trading within it, and on those outside. The burgeoning use of the Internet and electronic trade is likely to change the attitudes and expectations of citizens of the Member States, and the new round of trade liberalization talks in the World Trade Organization will reflect these changes.

The recently elected European Parliament, and the lately appointed Commission and Commission President, are likely to make changes both in EU policy and progression of proposals, but the impetus is towards inclusion rather than exclusion, as there is a perceived need to encourage stability – political, social and economic – in the continent of Europe.

2 The Treaty of Rome, the Single European Act, the Maastricht Treaty on European Union and the Amsterdam Treaty

Introduction

The best way to understand the impetus behind the European Union of today is to look at the progression illustrated in the most significant treaties – the most important being the Treaty of Rome – and the amendments made to them.

The Treaty of Rome 1957

What was the aim of the Treaty of Rome?

The Treaty of Rome is one of the treaties that forms the Community of European Member States known today as the EU. The main objective of the original Treaty was to achieve a single integrated market possessing the following features:

- free movement between Member States of goods, unimpeded by customs duties and quantitative restrictions;
- free movement of labour;
- free movement of services;
- free movement of capital;
- trade protection where appropriate against non-Member countries by way of a common external tariff, ie a customs barrier, so that the same duty would be levied on goods coming into the Community regardless of which Member State imported them.

How did the Treaty try to achieve this?

The text of the Rome Treaty was comprehensive, but its scope has now been significantly extended. A list of its constituent parts and titles is set out below, including some details only, to give an idea of the extent of the concept of the European Economic Community, which has been developed and changed into what is now known as the EU. The Treaty is divided into parts, titles and chapters, which have been amended by the Single European Act (SEA), the Treaty on European Union (TEU) and the Treaty for Europe (Amsterdam Treaty). General details of the amending treaties are indicated afterwards to show the progression.

Reference should be made to the different chapters of this book for more detailed explanations of the effects of the treaties on different policy areas.

The following list refers to the consolidated Treaty of Rome, ie it includes amendments made after 1957 by the other treaties.

Part I concerns principles. Article 2 indicates that:

> The Community shall have as its task, by establishing a common market and progressively approximating the economic policies of Member States, to promote throughout the Community a harmonious development of economic activities, a continuous and balanced expansion, an increase in stability, an accelerated raising of the standard of living and closer relations between the States belonging to it.

Part I states that the institutions – the European Parliament, Council, Commission, European Court of Justice and the Court of Auditors – shall exercise their powers under the treaties.

Part II establishes citizenship of the Union, defining it by stating that every person holding the nationality of a Member State shall be a citizen of the Union; providing that citizenship of the Union shall complement and not replace national citizenship, and that citizens have both rights and duties.

Part III sets out Community policies, under titles.

Title I concerns free movement of goods: the Customs Union, the elimination of customs duties between Member States, the setting up of the Common Customs Tariff and the free movement of goods together with the elimination of quantitative restrictions between Member States.

Title II provides the basic principles of Community policy relating to agriculture, including the common organization of agricultural markets.

Title III sets out the principles of free movement of persons, services, capital and payments, and includes the right of establishment. This section covers such matters as abolition of discrimination, and rights to equality for workers, and social policy provisions. Transport services are dealt with separately.

Title IV makes provision for the harmonization of visas, asylum, immigration and other policies relating to the free movement of persons in the context of establishing progressively an area of freedom, security and justice. This section relates to wide home affairs issues, ranging from judicial co-operation to the rights of asylum seekers.

Title V governs transport and the setting up of the framework for a common transport policy, including international transport and rights of non-resident carriers within the EU.

Title VI sets out the common rules on competition, taxation and the approximation of laws. This section includes provisions relating to state aids.

Title VII on economic and monetary policy and the European Central Bank states that the Community and the Member States must act in accordance with the principle of an open market economy; and relates to economic measures, providing that Member States must avoid excessive government deficits. It provides for a monetary policy and for the tasks of the European System of Central Banks (ESCB) and European Central Bank (ECB). It provides for arrangements relating to Economic and Monetary Union (EMU).

Title VIII on employment provides that Member States must work towards developing a co-ordinated strategy for employment, and particularly for promoting a skilled, trained and adaptable work-force, and labour markets responsive to economic change.

Title IX on common commercial policy encourages harmonization of trading policies and systems of Member States, particularly in the context of world trade and export aid.

Title X provides that customs co-operation must specifically be encouraged.

Title XI on social policy, education, vocational training and youth is wide, and encompasses the improvement of working conditions, equality, education and health and safety (see Chapter 16).

Title XII on culture emphasizes the importance of cultural diversity and the EU's common cultural heritage.

Title XIII brings public health considerations into all aspects of Community policy and action, encouraging co-operation between Member States, and with third countries.

Title XIV makes the promotion of consumer protection a duty of the Community, encompassing health, safety and economic interests of consumers, and the rights of consumers to information, education and to organize themselves to safeguard their interests. Consumer protection requirements must be taken into account in defining and implementing other Community policies and activities.

Title XV relates to the establishment and development of trans-European networks in transport, telecommunications and energy, and to ensuring their interoperability.

Title XVI on industry provides that the Member States and the Community shall ensure that the conditions necessary for the competitiveness of the Community's industry exist.

Title XVII on economic and social cohesion provides that the Community must aim to reduce disparities between the levels of development of the various regions, and can act to achieve progress towards economic and social cohesion through use of the various funds and means available for the purpose.

Title XVIII on research and technological development provides that the Community objective is to strengthen the scientific and technological bases of Community industry, and to encourage it to become more competitive at international level, while promoting co-operation between different research, educational (eg university) and other undertakings.

Title XIX on the environment is widely drawn, encompassing the preservation, protection and improvement of the quality of the environment, human health, prudent utilization of natural resources and promotion of international environmental protection measures. Specifically, the individual Member States can introduce measures more stringent than Community provisions (see Chapter 17).

Title XX on development co-operation (ie help for developing countries) encompasses not only the gradual integration of developing countries into the world economy, but also a campaign against poverty in those countries.

Part IV concerns the association of the overseas countries and territories that have special relations with Member States.

Part V sets out provisions governing the institutions of the Community, including the European Parliament (EP), the Council, the Commission, the Court of Justice, the Court of Auditors, the Economic and Social Committee, the Committee of the Regions and the European Investment Bank.

Part VI sets out general and final provisions.

How did matters develop in respect of the Four Freedoms and the Common Market?

The abolition of import tariffs between Member States was achieved by 1968 with the implementation of the Customs Union. As a result, no customs duties were payable inside the Community, and the Common Customs Tariff, administered by the European Commission, was set up to apply to imports from non-Member states (see Chapter 8).

Since 1 January 1993 internal customs barriers for goods have been down, although some checks are still being made for arms and narcotics control purposes. The documentation has been simplified, and the Single Market for goods has been generally achieved. However, some non-tariff barriers remained after that date with the continuance of:

- technical barriers (differences in technical, professional, labelling and other standards);
- public procurement policy barriers (although public procurement is subject to legislation, control is difficult);
- fiscal barriers (excise and VAT differences, although these are much reduced);
- some residence and work permit provisions (although changes have been made by the Amsterdam Treaty).

The existence of provisions impeding the freedoms meant that the cross-border movement of goods, money, people and services within the EU was (and is) still sometimes difficult despite efforts to liberate the different markets.

The Single European Act 1986

What was the background to the Single European Act (SEA)?

Disappointment that significant barriers remained, and the slow progress towards making the countries of Europe into a single trading entity or home market resulted in the proposal for European Union adopted by the European Parliament in 1984. This led to the Commission's White Paper 1985 setting out the provisions necessary to achieve the completion of the Internal Market. Its conclusions were endorsed by the heads of government meeting in 1985, when it was decided to make changes to facilitate and speed up the Community's decision-making processes. This resulted in the Single European Act 1986.

What was the Single European Act?

The Single European Act was a document signed in 1986 by the heads of state and plenipotentiaries, and later ratified by the parliaments of all Member States. It made the first post-signature amendments to the Treaty of Rome. The complete Act came into force in July 1987, although some sections took effect earlier. It was enacted in the UK in the European Communities (Amendment) Act 1986.

The SEA aimed to provide impetus towards achieving the objectives of the original EC treaties, which were:

- to transform the relations between Member States into a real European Union;
- to achieve a common foreign policy;
- to promote democracy;
- to speak with one voice;
- to protect the EC's freedoms and human rights;
- to extend common policies;
- to facilitate the Commission's exercise of its powers;
- to work towards economic integration via Economic and Monetary Union (EMU);
- to work towards the protection of the general and working environment.

Besides providing for speeding up the legislative process by introducing qualified majority voting, the SEA set out the common intention that the EC shall have as its objective to contribute together to making concrete progress towards European unity. It provided that the European Council should meet at least twice a year, to bring together the heads of state and of government of the Member States, the President of the Commission of the European Communities and the ministers for foreign affairs.

More famously the SEA set 1992 as the date fixed for the completion of the Single Market by including the declaration that: 'The Conference wishes by means of the provisions of Article 8A to express its firm political will to take, before 1 January 1993, the decisions necessary to implement the Commission's programme described in the 1985 White Paper on completing the Internal Market. Setting the date of 31 December 1992 does not create an automatic legal effect.'

What was needed to achieve this Internal (or Single) Market?

To achieve within a reasonable time the hundreds of harmonization and other provisions necessary to encourage the removal of the physical, technical and fiscal barriers to trade, the requirement that every Member State had to agree to each proposal needed to be diluted to enable relevant legislation to be made by a majority of the Member States. To avoid unfairness to the small countries, the original treaties were amended to allow qualified majority voting (QMV) by the Council of Ministers in a number of situations, and the powers of the European Parliament were strengthened.

When could qualified majority voting be used?

The SEA allowed QMV for introducing common standards, and

for harmonizing or standardizing legislation aimed at establishing and operating the unified market. Issues included the free movement of goods, services and capital, the common transport policy, changes to customs duties, freedom of establishment and the recognition of professional qualifications.

The Treaty on European Union (TEU or Maastricht) extended the list of 'QMV' matters to include various social measures (special provisions applying to the UK, which opted out, albeit it has now opted in under the New Labour Government) and regulations on the minimum standards regarding the environment. QMV was again extended by the Amsterdam Treaty (see below). Unanimity is still required in some areas such as direct taxation.

Was environmental protection in the original Rome Treaty?

No. Article 30 of the SEA specifically amended the Rome Treaty to insert more precise provisions to make environmental considerations a component of other policies, and this was extended in the TEU and in the Amsterdam Treaty.

What about national tactics to avoid the Single Market provisions?

Although Article 100A of the SEA enabled the principle of free movement to be suspended or even set aside on national grounds of health, or protection of the working or general environment, the Commission had to confirm that such suspension could not be just a ruse to provide a trade restriction. The European Court of Justice (ECJ) has jurisdiction to ensure no improper use is made of Article 100A.

Has the European Court of Justice helped to prevent improper barriers?

Yes. In the Cassis de Dijon case (1979), the European Court of Justice ruled that goods produced and placed legally on the market in one Member State could not be barred from importation by another Member State because they did not conform to the requirements of the importing country's own technical or commercial standards.

The Dassonville Judgement 1973 established that a trade regulation likely directly or indirectly to hinder trade within Member States would be treated like a quantitative restriction and so prohibited by Article 30 of the Treaty of Rome.

In the Keck Judgement 1993, the ECJ decided that certain

national selling arrangements, eg shop opening hours and advertising provisions that apply equally to domestic goods and goods coming from other Member States, should not be covered by the Article 30 prohibition. There have been further judgements since, and the situation is improving, but sometimes barriers are a problem, and work continues to identify and remove improper restrictions that hinder trade in goods or services.

What about Treaty amendments?

The Treaty on European Union (TEU) 1992 was for many the logical progression from the completed Internal Market. The TEU concerned institutional reform and political union, together with the necessary amendments to the Rome Treaty, extending majority voting and strengthening the European Parliament. It incorporated the principle of Economic and Monetary Union (EMU), including the issue of the single European currency and provisions relating to security.

Before looking at the detailed requirements of the Single European Act, the Treaty on European Union (often referred to as the Maastricht Treaty) and the Amsterdam Treaty, it is important to understand the present structure of the EU, the institutions through which it operates, its legislative procedures and its funding.

By December 1992, nearly all the Internal Market programme measures had been finalized or were the subject of consensus within the Council of Ministers, but many had not been transposed into legislation in *all* the Member States. The problem of delayed transposition led to the increased powers of the European Court of Justice set out in the Union Treaty, which enabled countries to be fined for breach of their obligations and so encouraged them to transpose into legislation the measures they had agreed to implement.

The Treaty on European Union 1992

This Treaty (also known as the TEU or Maastricht Agreement) 'marked a new stage in the process of creating an ever closer union among the peoples of Europe, where decisions are taken as closely as possible to the citizens'.

It resulted from two parallel Inter-Governmental Conferences (IGCs), which concluded in December 1991. The aim of ratification by the end of 1992 was impossible due to political difficulties, and Germany was the last country to ratify in November 1993, when the Treaty came into force. Significant opt-outs negotiated for the UK in respect of Economic and Monetary Union (EMU) and the Social Chapter were included in the protocols; and

Denmark's position was set out in the agreement of the European Council in 1992.

Much has been said about the TEU with regard to EMU and social legislation, yet possibly its most significant effect arose from the transfer of greater direct legislative power from the national legislative bodies to the Community institutions for a wide range of matters with cross-border effects, with national matters remaining in the competence of Member States.

What were the aims of the TEU?

The TEU common provisions and preamble set out the aims of the Treaty, which included:

- the promotion of an international identity leading possibly to a common defence policy;
- the establishment of a single currency in the context of Economic and Monetary Union (EMU);
- reinforcement of environmental protection;
- a fund to promote cohesion in the context of economic and social progress, including improvement in the quality of life;
- the establishment of a common citizenship;
- the facilitation of free movement of people, not forgetting their safety and security;
- the development of closer co-operation in justice and home affairs;
- an improvement in the effectiveness of the Community's institutions, in particular by reinforcing the powers of the European Parliament (EP);
- the reaffirmation of the principle of proper respect for human rights;
- the extension of Community competence to new policy areas where this is seen to be needed.

The Treaty provides that the European Council shall meet at least twice a year, and report after each meeting and annually to the European Parliament. This is intended to give political impetus to the Union.

The TEU therefore amended the Treaty of Rome as necessary, introduced new policy areas, strengthened the European Parliament and expanded the responsibilities of the EC.

What did the TEU provide in respect of economic and monetary policy?

Changes to the Treaty of Rome were necessary to give effect to the principle of European Monetary Union (EMU) and the thrust towards the single currency, because new institutions and an agreed timetable were necessary (see Chapter 12).

What were the new policy initiatives introduced by the TEU?

The new policy initiatives proposed in the TEU were numerous. For ease of reference, the main items were:

- the Cohesion Fund set up by 1 December 1993;
- the Committee of the Regions established under the Treaty, with advisory status and intended to ensure that the separate voices of the EU regions are heard;
- restatement of objectives relating to the environment, with qualified voting allowed except for fiscal provisions, town and country planning, land use and choice of energy sources;
- a determination to develop industry and make better use of research and development, and technological developments;
- a determination to improve public access to information available to EC institutions;
- the appointment by the European Parliament of an Ombudsman;
- the grant of powers to the European Court of Justice to fine Member States for non-compliance with its judgements;
- provisions relating to the formulation of defence policy;
- provisions to give the EU a subsidiary role in the promotion of culture;
- a prohibition on central banks reaching agreements on the overdrafts of public authorities. This is one of the most significant clauses of the Union Treaty, found in Article 104, and effective from 1 January 1994. It means that public deficits cannot be financed by printing money. Article 104a goes further to prohibit privileged access by administrations to financial markets.

What are the three pillars of the TEU?

The three pillars of the Union Treaty are three main elements, or areas.

The *first pillar* embraced all existing policies of the European Community under the previous treaties, ie the Single Market, transport policy, etc. The *second pillar* introduced a section on common foreign and security policy (CFSP). The *third pillar* included new areas of co-operation in terms of justice and home affairs, including co-operation in police and judicial matters.

Under the first pillar of Community activity it is generally the Commission that has the right to make proposals and initiate legislation. Under the other two this right is shared with the Member States, but the aim is co-operation rather than harmonization.

Were the powers of the European Community (or Union) widened?

Yes. The EC institutions were given a more active role in the following areas:

- the establishment of trans-European transport networks;
- telecommunications and energy networks;
- development co-operation and industrial policy;
- environmental protection;
- education and culture;
- research and development;
- consumer protection;
- the extension of co-operation in justice and home affairs;
- visa and immigration policy.

What does citizenship of the Union mean?

Citizenship of the European Union was given to every person holding the nationality of a Member State with rights:

- to move and reside freely within the territory of the Member States;
- to vote and to stand as a candidate at municipal elections in the Member State in which he or she resides, under the same conditions as nationals of that state;
- to vote and to stand as a candidate in elections to the European Parliament in the Member State in which he or she resides, under the same conditions as nationals of that state;
- to the protection of the consular or diplomatic authorities of any Member State if he or she is in a third country in which his or her own country is not represented;
- to petition the European Parliament or apply to the Ombudsman under the provisions of the Treaty.

The TEU was followed by a 1994 Directive enabling EU citizens to vote in local elections in the Member State of residence, even if not nationals of that state. A 1997 Commission report on EU citizenship underlined the need to improve awareness of the rights of citizenship in the EU among its citizens. The Amsterdam Treaty enabled citizens to take the EC institutions before the ECJ for actions breaching their fundamental rights as citizens.

What effect did the TEU have on the European Parliament?

The European Parliament is often perceived to be a democratic body with insufficient powers, so the TEU gave the EP the right to approve the body of Commissioners prior to their appointment, the power of assent for major international agreements, and further involvement in enacting legislation through a 'co-decision' or 'negative assent procedure' with the power unanimously to refuse Council common positions in some areas. Co-decision was further extended by the Amsterdam Treaty, and the co-operation procedure whereby the Council may unanimously overrule the EP's views was reduced, being replaced in all cases by co-decision except on EMU matters. In addition, not only does the body of Commissioners have to be approved by the EP, but so also now does the President of the Commission.

What about home affairs?

Under the inter-governmental provisions of the TEU, joint policies and action can be taken by the Council in the areas of asylum and immigration policy, and the crossing of external borders; the combating of fraud and drug addiction; judicial co-operation in civil and criminal matters; and police and customs co-operation. Sometimes proposals in these areas can be decided by QMV. The Commission is involved, but has limited powers in respect of criminal matters. The EP must be consulted and kept informed. These areas are affected by the Amsterdam Treaty. EUROPOL, essentially an information exchange system, was set up following the TEU.

What about social affairs, ie employment provisions?

As the UK *originally* opposed the TEU provisions relating to social policy, it was agreed that no change would be made to the relevant articles in the Treaty of Rome, as amended by the Single European Act. The compromise reached was set out in a Social Chapter protocol to the TEU whereby it was agreed that the (then) other 11, later 14, Member States could 'borrow' the Community institutions in order to seek to implement the Social Charter 1989 (from which the UK was also excluded). The aim remained to achieve unanimity, but where the UK refused, it dropped out of deliberations and decisions, and the others sought to pass measures by way of a special qualified majority. The legislation did not apply *per se* to the UK (albeit some provisions had to be applied by UK companies operating elsewhere in Europe and in the UK).

The situation has now changed as the UK Government asked to be included in applying social policy principles and discussions on Social Chapter and employment rights, so this was incorporated into the Amsterdam Treaty's title on employment.

The social provisions concerned matters such as the improvement of the working environment to protect employees' health and safety, working conditions, information for and consultation of employees, and integration of people excluded from the labour market.

What about foreign and security policy and defence?

These are vitally important in the context of political union. It is necessary to distinguish between foreign economic and trade relations and development co-operation (already the responsibility of the Community institutions) and the foreign and security policies that are looked at through the Organization for Security and Co-operation in Europe (OSCE) and the Common Foreign and Security Policy (CFSP) process. The TEU provided that joint decisions would be binding in Member States; but if no joint decision has been made, then a Member State remained free to act, but must inform the Council. The joint actions could relate to control of armaments and disarmament in Europe, or non-proliferation of nuclear armaments, or other economic aspects of security.

The Amsterdam Treaty extended the TEU to include peace-keeping and humanitarian operations so that these will be carried out by the Western European Union (WEU) together with some or all Member States as appropriate, and includes a system of constructive abstention for Member States when they do not wish to participate in a project, but do not object to it, so as to enable other Member States to continue with it.

As to defence, the WEU is being developed, and under the TEU, confirmed by the Amsterdam Treaty and as agreed by the ministers of the WEU countries, will eventually become the defence arm of the Union, with the formulation in due course of a defence policy (see Chapter 19).

The Amsterdam Treaty 1997

What is the aim of the Treaty for Europe (known as the Amsterdam Treaty)?

The 1996 Inter-Governmental Conference (IGC) concluded in 1997, and resulted in this Treaty for Europe. It was signed formally in October 1997 at Amsterdam, and came into effect as ratified on 1 May 1999. The institutional changes expected in the context of enlargement were deferred, but, as may be seen from the amendments noted above, the Amsterdam Treaty was surprisingly far-reaching, and clarified provisions relating to transparency and subsidiarity.

For ease of reference the main revisions of the treaties are listed again:

1. Because the Community is moving towards a joint foreign and security policy, the Amsterdam Treaty included a revised section on this to enable the European Council to decide on common strategies to be implemented by the EU in cases where the Member States share important interests. It provided for a policy planning and early warning unit for the EU, together with procedures to enable the Council to agree common strategies and to encourage closer co-operation between the EU and WEU. The Secretary General of the Council of Ministers now represents the EU in this area.

2. The Amsterdam Treaty included a new section on the development over five years of a new area of freedom, security and justice, bringing extra areas into the competence of the EU such as measures to combat crime, and to prevent and combat racism and xenophobia, and judicial co-operation in civil matters. The intention is to enhance co-operation between police and legal systems. The Treaty provided for the gradual introduction of common rules on immigration, asylum and visa policy, including definitions of shared criteria and conditions for granting refugee status, residence permits, short-term visas, etc. Council decisions on these matters will have to be unanimous, but in future international conventions in the areas of justice and home affairs may enter into force once ratified by half only instead of all of the Member States. An action plan to counter organized crime, and improvements to international co-operation to fight the growing drugs trade have already been approved by the European Council.

3. A protocol integrated the Schengen Acquis on the abolition of border controls as an obligation into the framework of the EU in such a way as to enable continuation of the Nordic Passport Union, while enabling the UK and Ireland to continue to operate their common travel area, and to retain their frontier controls. Thus Denmark, Ireland and the UK have special arrangements.

4. The Amsterdam Treaty incorporated the Social Chapter from the TEU, and provided for greater co-operation and incentives to promote employment both at national and at EU level. This change ended the UK's opt-out noted above.

5. The Member States agreed to co-ordinate their economic policies, concentrating on jobs and growth.
6. A Charter of Human Rights outlawing discrimination based on race, origin, religion, gender or sexual orientation, or age or disability, was agreed. Under a new article, the Council may take action by unanimity to combat such discrimination. There was also a reinforced commitment to eliminate inequalities between men and women, particularly as regards equal pay for equal work, or work of equal value. Sanctions for abuse of human rights will be imposable on the Member States.
7. As to administrative matters:
    i) the EU was granted legal personality so that it may negotiate as a single entity;
    ii) the EU is to be formally represented by the Secretary General of the Council of Ministers in respect of decision-making procedures;
    iii) under a Treaty protocol the numbers of Commissioners will be reduced to one per Member State when the EU is enlarged to over 20 members, necessitating a review of the institutions;
    iv) the authority of the President of the Commission within the organization was increased.
8. As to transparency: citizens were given rights to access documents of the Council of Ministers unless three countries opposed disclosure. Voting results where Council decisions have legal effects would be made public. There would be protection from misuse of personal data held by Community institutions. National parliaments would be encouraged and enabled to hold debates on Community legislative proposals, as a protocol provided for a six-week period between the tabling of a proposal and its being put forward for decision by the Council.
9. The Treaty provided for strengthened co-operation in areas such as public health, environmental protection, sustainable development and consumer protection.
10. Under the Amsterdam Treaty, the powers of the EP were strengthened. Decision-making was made simpler, with the assent procedure being used for cases of international agreements, Treaty decisions and new Members; the consultation procedures being followed in cases of the EP being consulted where unanimous decisions are required in Council; but the co-decision procedure being extended to include most areas of the (old) co-operation procedure, which will be retained for matters relating to EMU. Thus the EP will adopt deci-

sions jointly with the Council or reject proposals in areas such as transport policy, trans-European networks, research, development aid, employment policy, public health, equal opportunities and the fight against fraud. The Amsterdam Treaty also obliged the EP to draft regulations governing the conduct and duties of MEPs.

11. Qualified majority voting (QMV) was extended by the Treaty to some areas currently subject to unanimity, such as rights of establishment and research aid. The Treaty allowed QMV for various new areas such as employment guidelines, incentive measures, social exclusion, equal opportunities, public health, transparency, combating fraud and customs co-operation.

12. The Amsterdam Treaty included a new protocol on subsidiarity providing that:

    (a) Community action is only justified when the objective is both achievable by the Community and not achievable by the Member States acting alone;

    (b) the Community provision should be as simple as possible, leaving scope for flexibility in national implementation;

    (c) there should be figures to justify Community action if possible;

    (d) there should be wide consultation by the Commission, and impact assessment of the proposed legislation to ensure that it imposes the lowest possible burden, while still achieving its objective;

    (e) the Commission should produce an annual report on the application of the principles of subsidiarity and proportionality in Community provisions.

13. The fight against fraud should be helped by the rise in the status of the Court of Auditors, enabling the Council to adopt measures to ensure the Community budget is not used fraudulently, and strengthening co-operation between the national customs authorities in the Member States, eg by ensuring more co-ordinated legislation.

14. As to development of the EU: arguably one of the most important features of the Amsterdam Treaty is the acceptance in the Treaty that some Member States may progress faster than others towards unity, and that this should be possible, provided that the interests of those not co-operating are protected. Such progress is subject to specific conditions, in that it should not only serve the objectives of the Union, but also respect the principles set out in the treaties, and their institutional framework. This means that at least a majority of the Member States should be involved, but the

acquis communautaire should be unaffected. The progress should not affect the rights, competences, obligations and interests of Member States not participating, and should be open to all Member States, who should be allowed to join at any time. Lastly the provision should only be used as a last resort, and the co-operative action concerned is further restricted in the Treaty so as to protect the competence and powers of the Community, and to avoid discrimination concerning EU nationals or trade in the EU.

What voting is needed for closer co-operation proposals?

It should be noted that the Member States have to agree to authorize proposals for closer co-operation, by unanimous vote for second and third pillar matters, and by qualified majority vote in respect of first pillar areas.

Conclusion

The most politically indisputable problem in the EU at this time is the high level of unemployment and the resulting economic and social strains on the Member States, so the main thrust of Community activities at the moment internally is towards encouraging growth, reducing unemployment, and training the adaptable work-force needed to keep the EU competitive in the new century. The other preoccupations are enlargement, and the resulting strains put on the EU as a whole; the large number of asylum seekers and other immigrants into the EU and the resulting strains seem to be causing a rise in nationalism in some countries; and EMU, with its attendant costs and continuing unpredictable impact.

Since the Amsterdam Treaty came into effect in May 1999, discussions and action have continued on, for example, the European Employment Pact, the Broad Economic Policy Guidelines, the Charter of (citizens') Rights, institutional reform, the integration of environmental considerations into other policy areas, and EU defence policy. A further IGC is scheduled to start in 2000 to consider institutional and other changes then needed.

3 The institutions and consultative bodies of the EC/EU

The main institutions

There are five principal EC/EU institutions:

1. the Council of Ministers, now called the Council of the European Union;
2. the European Commission;
3. the European Parliament;
4. the Court of Justice;
5. the Court of Auditors.

These are supported by:

- the Economic and Social Committee;
- the Committee of the Regions.

There are also:

- the Committee of Permanent Representatives (COREPER);
- the European Investment Bank;
- the Consultative Committee;
- many other bodies closely linked to the institutions.

What is the European Council?

This should not be confused with the Council of the EU, which is composed of ministers. The European Council is the name given to the twice-yearly summit meetings that began in 1975, but which was formally recognized in the Single European Act 1986. It consists of the government heads of state of the Member States, assisted by their ministers for foreign affairs, together with the President of the European Commission. They discuss major political issues and policies. The President of the European Council briefs the European Parliament on the conclusions of each European Council meeting.

The Council of the EU (Council of Ministers)

What is the Council of the EU and where is it based?

It is made up of ministers representing the governments of the 15 Member States. The Council is based in Brussels (see Appendix III).

Does the Council have many staff?

Yes. It has about 2,400 staff, of which about 450 are translators or interpreters. It is assisted by various working parties and the Committee of Permanent Representatives (COREPER, see below).

How are the ministers chosen?

The ministers concerned are ministers of the Member States, and Council membership tends to depend on the subject under discussion. Thus, the Agriculture Minister attends meetings on important matters relating to his or her own subject; the Transport Minister may be called to discuss transport issues; and so on. At each meeting, each country has one representative, so Council meetings always have 15 members.

What are the forms of voting?

These are described in detail in Chapter 4. For most purposes (except for EMU matters), following the Amsterdam Treaty there have been three main decision-making procedures: assent, consultation and co-decision.

Which country holds the Presidency of the Council?

Each Member State assumes the Presidency of the Council for six-month periods. Rotation is in alphabetical order, based on the name of each Member State. The Presidency hosts the European Council and chairs the Council of the EU and the Committee of Permanent Representatives. It also represents Council positions to other EC institutions and to non-EU countries.

What is the Community Troika?

At ministerial level it is the present, the immediate past and immediate future Presidents of the Council, who work together as a team in some negotiations.

What is the Committee of Permanent Representatives (COREPER)?

Work for the Council of the EU is prepared by COREPER, the Committee of Permanent Representatives. This comprises the ambassadors to the Community of the Member States, plus their deputies and advisers, assisted by committees of national civil servants. COREPER is useful for lobbying and can provide up-to-date information on specific matters.

Does anyone else become involved in the work of the Council?

Yes. The European Commission also takes part in the work of the Council and may at any time amend or withdraw proposals (which it prepares). The Council is assisted by various working parties.

In 1995 the Council set up 225 committees, which considered 3,705 issues, producing 3,379 opinions.

With regard to EC, EU and EURATOM matters, the Council and the Commission are assisted by the Economic and Social Committee, while for European Coal and Steel Community (ECSC) affairs, the Council is assisted by the Consultative Committee. The Committee of the Regions assists with regard to regional and cultural affairs. The ECSC, Consultative Committee and Committee of the Regions are discussed later in this chapter.

The European Commission

What is it?

Also referred to as the Commission of the European Community or, simply, the Commission, this is really the executive civil service of the Community with a unique role.

There are 20 Commissioners (two each for France, Italy, Spain, the UK and Germany, and one each for the other smaller Member States). This number is likely to be reduced to one Commissioner per country whether large or small following further enlargement of the EU. The Commissioners are appointed by the governments of Member States, by 'common accord' with all Member States, but have a duty to discuss problems from an EU rather than a national perspective; and they must remain independent both of their governments and of the Council. Their term of office is five years, and their appointments must be approved by the European Parliament, who may only refuse or dismiss the Commission as a whole (ie not individuals). Since the Amsterdam Treaty the EP must formally approve the President of the Commission.

What is the role of the Commission?

This is described in the consolidated Treaty of Rome in Article 211, and its duties are generally as follows:

- to act as a watchdog, ie to ensure that Community legislation is applied and complied with;
- to plan policies that flow from the provisions of the treaties;
- to initiate or promote or participate in forming Community legislation;
- to take Member States to the European Court of Justice if they do not comply with Community legislation;
- to act as mediator when inter-governmental disputes between Member States arise;
- to legislate in its own right (within the limited powers given by the Treaty of Rome Article 86 (ex 90) in relation to competition policy), or when authorized by the Council of the EU (eg, in the administration of agricultural policy);
- to represent the Member States in international negotiations where required to do so under the treaties.

The Amsterdam Treaty widened the powers of the President of the Commission with regard to the appointment of Commissioners to their responsibilities, and further staffing and administration reforms are now in hand.

How does the Commission operate?

The Commission is led by a President, appointed for five years by common agreement of all Member States and with the approval of the EP. Each Commissioner is appointed by a Member State, and is allocated a policy area, which does not necessarily accord with a single directorate, and is supported by administrative departments, or Directorates General, which are mostly located in Brussels, although some are in Luxembourg. In the past these have generally been referred to by their numbers, eg DG IV. The organization of Directorates can change according to the style of the President of the Commission and current requirements. Directorates are listed at the end of this chapter.

In March 1999 the Commission had a staff of 15,832 not including consultants, and of these approximately 1,600 (plus 745 temporaries) are translators or interpreters. Thus, the EU civil service is rather smaller than the bureaucracy required to run a large city in the UK. Although the Commission is sometimes blamed for bad legislation, in fact, other than in very limited circumstances, the decisive view on policy or legislation rests with the Council of the EU (ie the relevant ministers of the Member States). The

Commission is open about work in progress, encouraging wide consultation. Greater access to information about their activities should help the public image of the EU institutions in general. The Commission publishes an annual report on the activities of the EU to the EP.

What is the importance of the Commission to citizens?

The Commission is of vital importance as a source of information, as a prime place to lobby for changes to current legislation and standards, and as a guardian of citizens' rights, as well as being the administrator of various funds and grants. A useful guide on access to Commission documents is published by the Commission.

How can the Commission be controlled?

The Commission is answerable to the EP, which can dismiss it by a vote of censure. Thus following growing concern, the EP recently formed a committee to investigate allegations of mismanagement, fraud and nepotism in the Commission. Although no direct involvement of the Commissioners in fraudulent activities was discovered, the committee's findings in early 1999 of collective responsibility for 'instances of fraud, irregularities or mismanagement in their services or areas of special responsibility' were such that the Commission resigned as a body. They continued to work to avoid disruption of the legislative timetable until the formal approval of the new Commission and its President, Mr Romano Prodi, by the European Parliament in September 1999. Since then considerable organizational restructuring of the Commission has been undertaken.

Even prior to the EP report, in early 1999 codes of conduct were agreed by the Commission to bar Commissioners from taking outside employment while in office, to require them to declare financial interests (both their own and those of partners) and to stress the importance of independence and transparency. Commissioners must comply with the codes of conduct, avoid conflicts of interest, may not hold any elected office while Commissioners, and may not accept gifts of more than a nominal sum. The codes also require clear divisions in the roles of Commissioners, their cabinets and other staff. The Commissioners have recently proposed that they give up some of their tax advantages, but retain others, in a bid to improve their image.

The European Parliament

The EP started as the Common Assembly for the European Coal

and Steel Community in 1952 with 78 members, and then became the Assembly for the (new) European Economic Community with 142 members and with Robert Schuman as President. In 1962 the title 'European Parliament' was adopted and, in 1970, its powers were increased and it was given budgetary resources. In 1973 it grew to 198 members with the accession of the UK, Denmark and Ireland, and now has 626 members. The Amsterdam Treaty limited its numbers to 700 in the context of enlargement. Its first direct elections with universal suffrage were in 1979.

What is the role of the European Parliament?

The European Parliament is an increasingly powerful institution, directly elected by the citizens of the EU. It participates in the legislative process. It may initiate legislation by requesting the Commission to prepare legislation on particular issues, and may itself lay down regulations and general conditions governing the performance and duties of its own members after seeking the opinion of the Commission and the approval of the Council.

The EP has supervisory powers and may, by a two-thirds majority vote of censure, dismiss the Commission as a body. It also has to approve the Commission's appointment. Depending on the procedure applicable, it has the right to be consulted on Commission proposals, to give its opinion and make amendments where appropriate. It has the power of assent, in that EP approval is necessary before any treaties or agreements can be concluded with third countries, which means it has to approve enlargement, for example.

Have the powers of the European Parliament been increased in stages?

Yes. In 1975 the EP was given extra powers over the budget, and a consultation procedure was introduced to increase its role in approving legislation with budgetary implications.

The SEA 1986 further increased the role of the European Parliament by introducing a new co-operation procedure allowing a qualified majority in various proposal areas. The words 'after consultation with the Assembly' were replaced by 'in co-operation with the European Parliament'.

The TEU 1992 gave the EP powers of co-decision-making with the Council, with a negative assent procedure and certain powers of rejection, besides the right to be consulted in many areas, for example with regard to rights of establishment and internal market issues.

The Amsterdam Treaty further extended its powers and the areas where the co-decision procedure is used.

Does the European Parliament have specialist committees?

Yes. The Parliament has about 20 specialist committees on different matters such as economic and monetary affairs, and industrial policy. They usually meet in Brussels and may request the appropriate member of the Commission to appear before a committee to explain the Commission's position. Besides this, individual MEPs can table written and oral questions to the Council and Commission.

Who are the representatives?

There are currently 626 MEPs (Members of the European Parliament – also referred to sometimes as Euro MPs or Deputies) directly elected in the Member States every five years. The electorate numbered about 289 million citizens in 1999. There is a President of the EP, 14 elected Vice-Presidents and five elected Quaestors. Like their UK counterparts, MEPs now have to complete a declaration of financial interests, or face sanctions. They receive a salary from their Member States (from 1 April 1999 in the UK this is about £47,000 per annum), which is subject to national taxation rules, a general expenditure allowance and a travel allowance. Difficulties remain, as it difficult to equalize pay and expenses for MEPs from the different countries.

How many MEPs represent each country?

Austria	21
Belgium	25
Denmark	16
Finland	16
France	87
Germany	99
Greece	25
Ireland	15
Italy	87
Luxembourg	6
Netherlands	31
Portugal	25
Spain	64
Sweden	22
UK	87

What about political groups?

MEPs do not sit in national delegations but in political groupings.

To form an official political group in the EP it is necessary to have:

- 29 representatives if all are from a single Member State;
- 23 representatives if all are from two Member States;
- 18 representatives if all are from three Member States;
- 14 representatives if all are from four Member States.

The memberships of the main political groups at the moment are: Socialist Group: 180; European People's Party: 224; Liberal, Democratic and Reformist Group: 43; Green Group: 38. Full details can be obtained from the EP Information Office or from their Web site (http://www2.europarl.eu.int/election).

Does the Parliament have staff?

The Parliament's own staff numbers about 3,250 (plus about 550 temporaries), of whom approximately 680 are translators or interpreters. It is run by a Bureau including the President of the EP and 14 Vice-Presidents elected by secret ballot to serve for two and a half years.

What are the 'Assizes'?

These are periodic meetings between MPs in national parliaments and Euro MPs.

What is the 'Bureau'?

The Bureau consists of the President and the 14 elected Vice-Presidents of the European Parliament. The enlarged Bureau includes also the 10 leaders of the political groups, and often meets to discuss current issues.

What are European Parliamentary Committees of Enquiry?

These are committees set up by the EP to look at specific issues. There is also a Petitions Committee, which receives petitions from EU citizens. The petitions may be put before the EP or a relevant Community institution.

What is the role of the Parliamentary Ombudsman?

The TEU provided for a Parliamentary Ombudsman, appointed by the EP, to hear complaints (in confidence if necessary) concerning maladministration by any Community institution except

pendence must be beyond doubt'. They are appointe ' for six-year terms of office by the Council, acting unanimously after consulting the EP, and monitor the Community's budget. The Court examines the accounts of the Community, overseeing not only the general budget, lending and borrowing, but also 'off-budget' activities. It has responsibility for ensuring the legality and accuracy ɩ financial transactions and for ensuring the prudent managemenɩ of funds. The Court draws up an annual report recording its activities, but may also issue observations in special reports, or deliver opinions. For example, it condemned the EU programme on nuclear safety as both wasteful and ineffective. Its seat is Luxembourg (see Appendix III).

The Economic and Social Committee

The Economic and Social Committee (ECOSOC or ESC), which calls itself 'the Other Assembly', is made up of one-third each of representatives of trade unions, professional bodies and other interests appointed by the Council on the basis of proposals from national governments. It is made up of 222 members (24 each from France, Germany, Italy and the UK; 21 from Spain; 12 each from Austria, Belgium, Greece, The Netherlands, Portugal and Sweden; 9 each from Denmark, Finland and Ireland; and 6 from Luxembourg).

ECOSOC must be consulted and give opinions on proposals made by the Commission, before such proposals can go to the Council of Ministers. It may employ technical experts to consider proposals. Since 1972 it has been able to issue 'own-initiative opinions' on any subject that affects the Community. It is a useful place to lobby at an early stage for changes to proposals, and meets 10 times a year in Brussels.

Further information is available from the ECOSOC Secretariat in Brussels (see Appendix III).

The Committee of the Regions

This advisory body created by the TEU first met in February 1994, and meets in plenary session every 2–3 months in the EP building in Brussels. It has 222 members consisting of 24 each from France, Germany, Italy and the UK; 21 from Spain; 12 each from Austria, Belgium, Greece, The Netherlands, Portugal and Sweden; 9 each from Denmark, Finland and Ireland; and 6 from Luxembourg. Its secretariat employs about 70 people.

The members are representatives of local and regional authorities, and each has an alternate or deputy. They are appointed by the Council for four years, although the chairmanship of the Committee is for two years. Members have a duty to be independent in the performance of their duties, and may not serve simultaneously as MEPs.

What is the role of the Committee of the Regions?

It must be consulted on cross-border co-operation, regional policies, economic and social cohesion, trans-European networks, education, vocational training, public health and cultural policies; and on other matters deemed appropriate by the Council or Commission. It may also issue own-initiative opinions.

The Committee of the Regions should not be confused with the Assembly of European Regions, whose general assembly includes 400 representatives of 282 regions in 23 countries in Central, Eastern and Western Europe.

The European Coal and Steel Community and the Consultative Committee

The European Coal and Steel Community (ECSC) aims to support production, research and development and the restructuring needs of the coal and steel industries. The ECSC has its own funds, but its treaty, the Treaty of Paris, ends in 2002, so the area covered is to be included in the Rome Treaty as amended. The Commission is working towards the gradual inclusion of ECSC expenditure into the EC's general budget. It is suggested that the ECSC reserves in 2002 could form the nucleus of a guarantee fund for ECSC sectors.

The Consultative Committee has 96 members representing interested parties concerned with the coal and steel sector. It must be consulted on matters related to this sector and may also submit opinions on its own initiative.

European Political Co-operation (EPC)

EPC is not strictly an institution of the EU, but a recognized mechanism leading to common action by Member States in the area of foreign policy. It is effectively the conference of the foreign ministers of the EU Member States, and so works closely with the Western European Union (see Chapter 18).

The European Investment Bank

The EIB is the banking institution of the EU for long-term project finance. It was set up in 1958, and the consolidated Treaty of

Rome Articles 266–7 establish that the purpose of the EIB is to act as a facilitator by using its financial resources to achieve the steady development of the Common Market in the interest of the Community and to promote cohesion, assisted by the European Regional Development Fund, which facilitates financial provision for research and technological development. The EIB can often help where the size of a project is such that an individual Member State or region cannot itself fund it. It is particularly valuable in projects in less developed regions, but also assists in the implementation of EU development policy and in the distribution of funds under various agreements such as the Lomé Convention (discussed in Chapter 18). It is one of the largest lending and borrowing institutions in the world.

Its shareholders are the Member States of the EU, and its board of directors, nominated by the Member States, includes a minister (usually for finance) from each one.

How does it operate?

Although capital is subscribed by the EU members, the EIB also raises funds by borrowing on the international capital markets. As a bank, it is largely self-financing.

The EIB finances capital investment in various projects, for example for less-developed regions, infrastructure and transport projects, telecommunications, energy, advanced technology, environmental protection and tourism. It operates a funding for small business scheme through local banks, and assists with regard to the European growth initiative of the Council, and the European Investment Fund, which become operational in mid-1994, and takes a leading role in the EU job initiative action plans.

The bank operates on a non-profit-making basis, so loans tend to be at rates close to the EIB's cost of borrowing. The bank does not usually charge arrangement or other fees. It should not be confused with the European Bank for Reconstruction and Development (EBRD) (see Appendix I).

Further information concerning the EIB may be obtained from its offices in Luxembourg or London (see Appendix III).

The European Central Bank and the European Monetary Institute

See Chapter 12.

The Consumer Consultative Committee

The present Consultative Committee replaced the previous Consumers Consultative Council originally set up in 1973. It has

20 members, one from each Member State, and one from each of five organizations: the European Bureau of Consumer Unions (BEUC) representing consumer organizations; COFACE, representing family organizations; EUROCOOP representing consumer co-operatives; ETUC representing European trade unions; and IEIC, the European Inter Regional Consumer Institute. It serves as a forum for discussion and is involved by the Commission in consultation and drafting of new measures that impact on consumers.

Other agencies or bodies linked to the Commission

There are many other agencies or bodies linked to the Commission, some of which are listed below. Others are mentioned elsewhere in this book.

The European Centre for the Development of Vocational Training (CEDEFOP)

This was set up in 1975, and is sited in Thessaloniki in Greece. It employs about 80 people, and its aims are to promote and develop common vocational and in-service training policies by offering experience and information exchange. It starts its own pilot projects, produces seminars and publishes useful material.

European Training Foundation

Established by Council Regulation in 1990 and sited in Turin, it has a work-force of about 290. Its purpose is to contribute to the development of initial and continuing vocational training systems in various Central and East European countries and the newly independent states. It covers management and retraining as well as mobility schemes. It works closely with CEDEFOP.

The European Environment Agency

The Agency, set up by a 1990 Regulation with a staff of 50, is situated in Copenhagen. It provides objective, reliable information and monitors the effects of actions taken. It enables the EU to take proper measures, and to inform the public adequately.

The EU Technological Institute of the Joint Research Centre

Based in Seville, Spain, this body studies and evaluates Commission research policy options.

The European Assembly for Science and Technology

This comprises 100 representatives of the scientific sector, and assists the Commission in planning and implementing research and technological development policy.

The European Agency for the Evaluation of Medicinal Compounds.

This body, operational since January 1995, is sited in London and employs about 200 personnel.

The Food and Veterinary Office (previously called the Office for Veterinary and Plant Inspection and Control)

This is technically attached to the Commission and is located in Ireland.

The European Monitoring Centre for Drugs and Drug Addiction

Set up by a 1993 Regulation, this is sited in Lisbon. It provides statistical, documentary and technical information to enable European-level action to be properly targeted, and promotes co-operation and data exchange with organizations in Europe and elsewhere.

The European Police Office (EUROPOL) and the Europol Drugs Unit

Set up under the TEU, it provides an umbrella to facilitate police co-operation and information exchange to prevent or combat drug trafficking, terrorism and other forms of international crime. It is situated in The Hague, The Netherlands.

The European Foundation for the Improvement of Living and Working Conditions

This Foundation, set up by a 1975 Regulation, is in Dublin. It aims to contribute to the establishment of better living and working conditions by the dissemination of knowledge.

The Translation Centre for Bodies of the European Union

This is based in Luxembourg, and is intended to service the needs of the new institutions, and eventually to be self-financing.

European Commission Information Users Committee

This is set up as part of the reform of communication policy with 36 members overall, 18 of whom are high-level representatives of various user categories, eg consumers, media and socio-professional, and 18 of whom are from European-related media and academic users, each person acting in a personal capacity with four-year terms of office and two meetings per annum. Its periodic reports go to another strategic group, which decides on policy and its implementation.

The Office of Official Publications
This is sited in Luxembourg (see Appendix III).

The Task Force for Human Resources, Education, Training and Youth

The Euratom Supply Agency

The European Agency for Safety and Health at Work
This is sited in Bilbao.

The Office for the Harmonization in the Internal Market – Trade Marks, Designs and Models
This is sited in Alicante, Spain (see Chapter 14).

Directorates General and services of the European Commission

The composition and organization of the Commission has been subject to a radical overhaul and changes following the appointment of Romano Prodi in place of Jacques Santer, and the appointment of a new Commission in September 1999. The move is towards a closer relationship between the Commissioners and the departments they manage within their portfolios, and a move away from the numbering system for the Directorates General.

The list as constituted and listed at the time of writing on the Commission Web site at http://europa.eu.int/comm/dgs_en.htm is as follows:

- Secretariat General
- Legal Service
- Press and Communication
- Economic and Financial Affairs
- Enterprise
- Competition
- Employment and Social Affairs
- Agriculture
- Transport
- Environment
- Research
- Joint Research Centre
- Information Society
- Fisheries
- Internal Market
- Regional Policy

- Energy
- Taxation and Customs Union
- Education and Culture
- Health and Consumer Protection
- Justice and Home Affairs
- External Relations
- Trade
- Development
- Enlargement
- Common Service for External Relations
- Humanitarian Aid Office (ECHO)
- Eurostat
- Personnel and Administration
- Inspectorate General
- Budget
- Financial Control
- European Anti-Fraud Office
- Joint Interpreting and Conference Service
- Translation Service
- Publications Office.

The list of Commissioners and their portfolios is set out in Appendix V.

4 EC legislation, lobbying, justice and home affairs

Community law and procedures

Community law, properly made in accordance with the treaties, has priority over any conflicting law of a Member State. National courts must give effect to EC/EU legislation that has direct impact (eg regulations), the only exception being where the national legislation gives effect to an international convention that pre-dates the EC legislation. The European Court of Justice has ruled that national courts have an obligation to recognize and give effect to the supremacy of Community legislation and to interpret national laws in the context of the aims and wording of such Community legislation or provisions.

In what form are EC/EU rules set out?

There are the following kinds of instrument to establish law or policy in the EU:

- *Regulations.* These are directly enforceable laws, applicable and binding in the Member States. In other words, no local laws need be passed to give them force.
- *Directives.* These are legally binding and are addressed to the Member States, setting out the intended results of legislation, leaving it to the individual legislatures as to how these aims are to be achieved within a time limit. However, if they impose an obligation on a Member State (eg to implement the principle of equal pay for work of equal value), they may be effective even before they are actually implemented in the Member State concerned, if that State has not, for example, implemented them properly. Under the 'direct effect' principle, an unimplemented Directive may directly affect relations, particularly between Member States (including government agencies) and individuals. Until very recently, individuals or businesses were not affected by such Directives in relations between each other, but this is changing. Member States not only may be fined by the

ECJ, but also may be held liable in damages for loss caused to individuals or businesses due to failure to implement EC directives in time. This means it is important to watch not only national legislative developments, but also the implementation dates of EC legislation that might have become effective, but not yet implemented in a particular country.

- *Decisions.* These are addressed to Member States, or to an individual, or to a legal entity (for example, a company) and are binding on the addressee. They are used in particular to enforce competition policy.
- *Recommendations and opinions.* These are not legally binding, but they do have considerable political influence.
- *Notices.* These are not really legislation as such, nor do they have the force of law, but they are generally intended to provide guidance. Up to now they have usually been used to assist companies in the field of competition.
- *Inter-institutional agreements.* These enable the Council, Parliament and Commission to implement principles set out in the treaties or made by decisions of the institutions, eg concerning the detailed duties of the EP Ombudsman.
- *Conventions.* These are not Community law as such, but are effective among the EU countries acceding to them.
- *Agreements* between the EU and other countries, eg trade and co-operation or Europe agreements setting out various trade and other provisions between the EU and another country.

When is a matter the subject of Community legislation?

Because it was felt that too much Community legislation was being brought forward, in 1996 the Commission defined principles, criteria and requirements to be complied with at an early stage by new EC legislative proposals to ensure that only appropriate or necessary legislation is proceeded with. The procedure to be followed depends on the article of the Treaty under which the proposal is brought forward. Proposed legislation is also subject to the subsidiarity principle (see below).

What are the voting requirements for passing legislation?

There are various procedures depending on the importance of the subject under discussion, and they have developed since the Treaty of Rome because it became recognized that majority voting was the only way to progress legislation when so many Member States are involved.

The three kinds of voting require unanimity, or a simple majority, or a qualified majority (QMV). Unanimity is still required for various very important matters like the accession of new Member States, or amendments to treaties, or matters involving national interests.

An effective veto was introduced through the 'Luxembourg Compromise' of 1966, but its use has been restricted since July 1987.

The Council tries to reach a unanimous decision about proposals and policy presented by the Commission, but if disagreements occur, majority voting is possible on many issues. Where a qualified majority (QMV) is required, the votes are weighted by reference to the populations of the countries concerned. Thus, France, Germany, Italy and the UK have ten votes each, Spain has eight votes, Belgium, Greece, The Netherlands and Portugal have five votes each, Austria and Sweden have four votes each, Denmark, Finland and Ireland have three votes each and Luxembourg has two votes.

A qualified majority of 62 out of the 87 votes is acceptable for a wide range of matters, eg those relating to the completion of the Internal Market, such as the establishment of common standards.

The simple majority is 44 votes, and 71 per cent of votes cast are needed to pass proposals. The blocking minority is 26 votes.

What is the Ioannina Compromise?

This was an agreement reached in 1994 to deal with qualified majority voting difficulties following enlargement. It determined that when a Council decision is being made by a qualified majority, and Members of Council representing 23–25 votes indicate their intention to oppose such a decision by Council, then the Council must try to reach a decision by at least 65 votes within a reasonable time, and without prejudice to the compulsory time limits fixed by the treaties and derived provisions.

What are the different procedures for passing Community legislation?

There are the consultation, co-operation, co-decision and assent procedures.

What is the consultation procedure?

Under this procedure, introduced by the Treaty of Rome 1957, the Council consults the EP but is not obliged to take account of its views. Its use was extended by the Amsterdam Treaty to promote debate and transparency of legislation in, for example, matters relating to free movement defined in a new Article G, which are subject to unanimous Council decision, to some employment matters and to some international and intellectual property agreements.

The stages are as follows:

1. The Commission prepares and discusses a preliminary draft with government officials of Member States and other relevant bodies. It then adopts the proposal, which must then be published in the *Official Journal*.
2. Next, the Council of Ministers simultaneously seeks the opinions of the EP (which may suggest amendments) and ECOSOC. Both opinions are published in the *Official Journal*.
3. The draft then returns to the Commission, which may amend the proposal if appropriate, and may refer the new proposal to the European Parliament and ECOSOC.
4. The Commission then refers the amended proposal again to the Council, which refers it to one of its working parties to discuss the text and comment on it as appropriate.
5. It then goes to COREPER (the Committee of Permanent Representatives).
6. COREPER then returns the draft to the Council which, under the traditional consultation procedure, either (a) rejects it – so that it has to start again if it is to be approved, or (b) adopts it – and it is again published in the *Official Journal*.

What is the co-operation procedure?

This was the procedure introduced by the Single European Act 1986 with a strict time-scale, which added a stage but enables majority voting in specified areas. The EP was given more power, but the Council can still proceed without their agreement. The co-operation procedure was replaced by a simplified co-decision procedure with stricter time limits in all areas except four relating to EMU, by the Amsterdam Treaty.

The first stages of drafting are similar to the consultation procedure to the stage at which the proposal is presented to Council for final decision, and then the procedure is as follows:

1. If absolute agreement on the proposal is not achieved, the Council can adopt a common position by a qualified majority.
2. It then refers the proposal to the European Parliament (for second reading). The appropriate committee's opinions or recommendations are submitted to the full Parliament.

3. The Parliament then has three options. It can (a) within three months approve the position taken – in which case the proposal is sent straight back to the Council, which approves the legislation; or (b) take no position within three months of the Council's referral, in which case the Council adopts the legislation on its own terms; or (c) propose amendments by an absolute majority of its members. The proposal is then referred back to the Council, within one month, together with the Commission's views and possible amendments. Within three months, the Council must either approve it by a qualified majority or amend it unanimously. It is important to note that even if the Parliament's amendments are rejected by the Commission they can be reinstated by unanimous decision of the Council; and they can only be rejected by unanimous decision of Council.

4. If the European Parliament has rejected the Council position by an absolute majority, then the Council, within three months, can only adopt the legislation on second reading if members are unanimous. A one-month extension for the Council may be agreed, but if it still fails to reach a decision the proposal lapses. If adopted, it is published in the *Official Journal*.

What is the co-decision procedure (sometimes called the new co-operation procedure)?

The Union Treaty (ratified in 1993) introduced the co-decision procedure, which additionally provides for a third EP reading requiring a simple majority to support European Council common positions but, crucially, requires EP as well as Council consent before legislation is made.

Under the Amsterdam Treaty the co-decision procedure availability has been extended and is used for provisions relating to discrimination on grounds of nationality, free movement of citizens, social security for immigrant workers, right of establishment and training, some transport policy areas, some social policy and European Social Fund areas, research and development aid and Regional Fund implementing decisions, transparency, fraud prevention and customs, statistics, and the establishment of an independent advisory authority on data protection. In some cases these may be combined with a requirement for unanimity in Council (so that one Member State may veto proposals).

How does the Council/European Parliament co-decision procedure work?

It is complicated, but since the Amsterdam Treaty, which streamlined legislative procedures, it works in three ways, which are as follows (see also Appendix VIII):

1. (i) The Commission proposal is put to the European Parliament and the Council of Ministers.
   (ii)The EP gives its opinion (at first reading), which goes to Council.
   (iii)The Council may then adopt the draft (as and if amended by the EP) by a qualified majority, and the legislation is adopted (ie the legislation is passed).
2. The second procedure starts in the same way, but when the proposal is amended by the Council or the original unamended proposal is confirmed, it goes back to the EP as a common position from the Council, and the EP considers the common position (at second reading). Within three months the EP can:
   (a) approve the common position, which the Council can then adopt (ie legislation is passed);
   (b) not take any decision;
   (c) amend the common position; or
   (d) by an absolute majority reject the proposal.

If no amendments have been put by the EP, then the Council may adopt it as it is (ie legislation is passed). If the EP has proposed amendments, then within three months the Council may approve all the text proposed and adopt it (ie legislation is passed).

3. Under the third co-decision procedure:
   (i)   The Commission submits the proposal.
   (ii) The EP gives its opinion and may make amendments, which are sent to Council.
   (iii) Council adopts a common position, which goes back to the EP.
   (iv   The EP carries out the second reading, and within three months can (a) approve the common position (legislation is passed, as above), or (b) not take a decision, or (c) by an absolute majority of its members, reject the common position.
   (v)   If within three months the Council has not approved all the amendments suggested by the EP, then the Conciliation Committee is convened as quickly as possible within six weeks.

    (vi) The Conciliation Committee attempts to achieve agreement on the basis of both positions (ie EP's amendments and Council common position) within six weeks. If it achieves agreement, then the joint text may be approved by a simple majority by the EP, and by a qualified majority of the Council (ie legislation is passed). If the Conciliation Committee does not achieve agreement, the proposal is not adopted.

What is the assent procedure?

The assent procedure, used for international conventions and agreements on matters needing the unanimous agreement of Council, with the power of assent in the EP, which needs an absolute majority of MEPs, does not enable the EP to amend the Council position. Since the Amsterdam Treaty the assent procedure has been used for new treaty provisions, sanctions in the event of persistent breach of fundamental rights by a Member State, existing Treaty provisions, accessions, structural and cohesion funds, uniform electoral procedure and the conclusion of various international agreements.

What is the subsidiarity principle?

This has been much discussed and means the principle whereby action should be taken at Community level if the desired objectives cannot easily (or better) be achieved by national action by the Member States. The TEU set out the subsidiarity principle. The European Council of December 1992 stated it considered that the EU rested on the principle of subsidiarity, and set out guidelines, later supported by the Amsterdam Treaty, which required that the institutions of the Community should ensure that the guidelines (stated below) are complied with.

    Community action should only be contemplated in the following circumstances:

- There are transnational considerations that cannot be satisfactorily regulated by Member States.
- Lack of Community action would be in contravention of the Treaty.
- Community action would clearly be beneficial by reason of its effects and scale, ie the added value of Community action over national action.
- It is necessary to act to harmonize national norms, standards or legislation so as to achieve Treaty objectives, ie a legitimate need for a new initiative at Community level must be demonstrated.

What about the need to lighten the burden of bureaucracy?

The 1992 statement on subsidiarity stressed the following principles:

- Any action by the Community must always balance the need to keep down financial or administrative burdens on the Community, national governments, local authorities and citizens, against the benefit of the intended objective.
- Community measures should leave as much scope as possible for national decisions consistent with the particular provision, and care should be taken to respect well-established national arrangements and the organization and working of the legal systems of Member States.
- Whenever possible, minimum standards should be set at Community level, and Member States should be allowed to apply higher standards at national level.
- The form of action chosen should be as simple as possible, consistent with the need for legislation to be effective and enforceable. Thus, framework Directives were preferable to detailed Directives or regulations.
- When appropriate, co-ordination and co-operation between Member States should be encouraged rather than Community action taken. Where there is an area of shared competence, Community action should be the exception rather than the rule.
- When difficulties are localized, then the solution should also be local and not extended to other Member States.

Have these principles been taken on board?

Yes. Following a Commission review on adapting certain Community rules to the subsidiarity principle, in 1996 the Simpler Legislation for the Single Market (SLIM) initiative was launched to simplify rules and procedures, and weed out obsolete legislation. In compliance with the subsidiarity principles, some proposals for Directives have been withdrawn, and the volume of new proposals has fallen dramatically.

What about rights of appeal against Community legislation?

There is a right of appeal (as to proper areas of competence) to the European Court of Justice, and Council and Commission provisions can be annulled by way of an action based on *ultra vires* (ie acts in excess of powers), infringement of the treaties, abuse of discretion, or procedural violation.

What about lobbying?

This is important if you want to ensure that EC legislation takes account of your needs as a citizen, of your sector or your business. Consultation procedures are more open, so you should be able to get relevant documents. Whereas big businesses are professional about lobbying, and often use the services of professional lobbyists, this option is not always available for the individual or smaller business.

A Code of Conduct for Lobbyists is in hand, which sets out minimum professional standards in respect of relations with MEPs. It concentrates on transparency, and compliance with the prohibition on giving gifts or benefits to an MEP, who must register interests as appropriate.

Much depends on the matter in hand, but the first stops for individuals are usually their MP, MEP and possibly the Commission itself. In respect of regional matters they should not forget their regional representative on the Committee of the Regions. For business matters, they should use their trade or professional association, and inform the relevant government department such as the Department of Trade and Industry. They should contact the national standards authority in respect of European or international standards. The Ombudsman should not be forgotten if there is a situation involving institutional mismanagement, for example. In both the EP and the national parliaments there are specialist committees whose members take particular interest in specific subjects. The office of their country's Permanent Representative could also be helpful, as could their national member on the various consultative committees.

Above all, it is always most important to be well briefed about the matters in hand, and the proposals under discussion that relate to it. Sources of information are referred to throughout this book, and the Commission and its information offices are always helpful, but note should also be taken of the Internet Computer System, which has a EUROPASERVER that gives a great deal of information.

What is the Citizens First initiative?

This is an initiative by the Commission to inform citizens, and promote understanding of the EU and its relevance to every citizen. There are Citizens First information lines and guides published in various languages, including Welsh and Gaelic, which can also refer people to the relevant organization or Internet Web sites for available information. The Dialogue with Citizens initiative aims to raise awareness of citizenship rights (freephone in the UK 0800 581 591).

What is the effect on the citizens of Community legislation?

This depends on the area of impact, and individual perceptions. The following chapters will explain the thrust of legislation, which follows policy. However, although some people are wary of Community rather than national legislation, the subsidiarity principle taken to its logical conclusion could cause more problems than it solves, because the advantage of Community legislation for individuals, businesses and transnational enterprises is the relative ease of discovering precisely the rules that apply. If there is scope to apply rules in a 'general' way in different countries, then it remains necessary to discover detailed provisions, with the costs that entails. Specific provisions do at least mean that the general expectations of people as to their legal position are more often met.

What about consolidation?

In 1992 there was agreement between the institutions on the procedure to consolidate Community legislation, as one of the identified problems of business and individuals is understanding the increasingly complicated texts. The Commission has started to produce updated texts that include amendments.

Note must be taken of ECJ decisions, which can have far-reaching effects; and of the legislative shift away from national legislative bodies.

Justice and home affairs

This comes under the third inter-governmental pillar of the TEU, which brought co-operation in the fields of justice and home affairs within the responsibility of the Council so that there is now a Justice and Home Affairs Council. Some measures only require a qualified majority in respect of common actions. The Commission has a joint right of initiative with Member States in matters not concerning crime; and the EP must be consulted.

The Amsterdam Treaty brought extra areas into the competence of the Community by agreeing the introduction of an area of freedom, security and justice in the EU over five years, specifically stating that common rules on immigration, asylum, visa policy, refugee status, residence permits and other related matters will be introduced gradually. The European Council Summit in October 1999 confirmed the aim of creating an area of freedom, justice and security, with a 10-point plan. This plan was aimed at countering organized crime and inhibiting money laundering, co-ordinating procedures for asylum seekers, and achieving common definitions of offences in relation to such matters as human trafficking and sexual exploitation of children, drug trafficking, and technology-based and financial crime. It also covered relevant sanctions, together with better co-operation between police and prosecuting authorities in the Member States.

Council agreement on these matters has to be unanimous (ie any country can veto the development), but in future international conventions in the area of justice and home affairs may enter into force when ratified by half only instead of all the Member States.

What subjects are included in the area of justice and home affairs?

Subjects covered include:

- asylum policy;
- controls and rules of entry for persons crossing external borders from third countries;
- immigration policy, and policy regarding nationals of third countries, including residence, family rights and access to jobs, and illegal immigration;
- combating drug addiction;
- combating fraud on an international scale;
- judicial co-operation in civil matters;
- judicial co-operation in criminal matters;
- customs co-operation;
- police co-operation for the purposes of preventing and combating drug trafficking, terrorism and other forms of serious international crime – the European Information System (EIS) and the Europol Drugs Unit come within this area;
- extradition policy – an EU Extradition of Criminals Treaty signed in 1996 will come into effect when ratified by Member States.

What about immigration and visa requirements?

Immigration is a difficult area. In view of the serious unemployment problem in the EU, in June 1994 the Council defined a restrictive immigration policy for the EU and EEA, with implementation by 1 January 1996. This stated:

- Requests for admission to work can only be allowed where the post cannot be filled by a national or lawful permanent resident who already forms part of the work-force.

- Third-country nationals can in restricted circumstances be admitted temporarily for a fixed duration, eg frontier workers, key personnel and seasonal workers.
- Third-country nationals must have prior authorization to be admitted.
- Extensions of stay will be closely controlled.

A 1991 communication listed four areas of co-operation: identification of illegal immigrants, prevention of illegal immigration, definition of minimum standards of treatment and facilitation of repatriation. The TEU included immigration and asylum as areas of co-operation between Member States.

The External Borders Convention has yet to be ratified, but visa requirements for third-country nationals are already decided by qualified majority. Some bilateral accords have been signed with third countries, guaranteeing non-discrimination for non-EU citizens in terms of access to work and social security benefits.

What about rights of asylum and extradition?

Asylum policies cause difficulties, particularly in times of high unemployment or many refugees. The EU is moving towards a common asylum system based on the Dublin Convention 1990, which seeks to ensure that asylum seekers are properly processed at the point of entry; and a similar convention is under discussion with other European countries. The EURODAC system has been set up to deal with fraudulent or multiple asylum requests. A convention on simplified extradition procedures signed in 1995 between the EU Member States is improving legal co-operation, but the person to be extradited must agree to his or her extradition before its use. The Amsterdam Treaty includes a protocol on asylum for nationals of Member States, and EU provisions on asylum are under discussion. An action programme supports the integration of refugees, with some finance available to assist with both the reception and repatriation of asylum seekers and displaced persons.

What about the Schengen Agreement (or Schengen Acquis)?

The External Borders Convention should not be confused with the Schengen Agreement. This was signed in 1985 and implemented by the Schengen Convention signed in 1990 and subsequent accession protocols and agreements, which came into effect in seven member countries in 1995. It is incorporated for the other Member States by the Amsterdam Treaty into the EU's institutional framework, with special provisions for the UK and Ireland (to maintain border controls on people) and Denmark (see Chapter 8).

What about the fight against drugs?

The European Observatory on Drugs and Addicts was created in 1993 to assist the EU with information and research. Plans to counter organized crime, and improvements to international co-operation to counter the growing drugs trade, have been approved by the European Council. A five-year action plan proposed in May 1999 is aimed at reducing drug demand, stopping supplies and improving international co-operation. The European Monitoring Centre for Drugs produces an annual report. As stated above, new initiatives are being undertaken following European Council agreement in October 1999.

What about cross-border crime?

In principle, crime is a national matter, but in practice criminals do not respect borders, so mechanisms for co-operation have been developed. The Council of Europe has had a European Committee on Problems of Crime (CDPC) for many years, and there are at least 15 conventions with protocols, guidelines, explanatory reports, recommendations and resolutions dealing with such diverse subjects as traffic offences, firearms, and money laundering. The details cover mutual assistance, inter-state co-operation, extradition, enforcement of foreign criminal judgements, suppression of terrorism and compensation for victims.

International organized crime was the subject of research and an interim Commission report in 1994. An action plan for co-operation has been approved and in 1999 the Octopus 2 scheme, backed by both the EU and the Council of Europe, provided training for Central and Eastern European countries to help them counter organized crime and corruption.

What about Europol?

Europol, with an information exchange system between European police forces, is sited in The Hague. The Europol Convention deals with institutional provisions and the remit of the ECJ in this regard, together with the formal extension of the unit to fight terrorism.

The European Drugs Unit (EDU) has the remit to fight illegal trade in radioactive substances and nuclear materials, the smuggling of persons and vehicles, as well as the trafficking of women and children for sexual purposes. A strategy to combat trafficking in women for sexual exploitation was adopted in 1996, and Council joint action in the fight against trafficking in human beings and the sexual exploitation of children was agreed in 1997.

What about fraud?

The high cost to the Community budget of fraud (ECU 1.3 billion or 1.6 per cent of the overall Community budget in 1996) led the Commission to step up initiatives. The EU anti-fraud unit (UCLAF) has been replaced by the EU Fraud Prevention Office, which is independent of the Community institutions. Penalties have been increased, and task forces will investigate high-risk sectors. There is greater co-operation between Member States and customs and police authorities, and legislation and systems are being improved to cut waste and mismanagement in accordance with the Sound and Efficient Management (SEM) 2000 initiative. The computerized system for transit procedures should help with transit fraud. Greater clawback of defrauded monies and greater judicial co-operation should also help. It should be noted that the Member States themselves are the greatest losers from fraud. There is a confidential freephone number in each Member State to enable people to inform the authorities of their suspicions relating to fraud. In the UK this is: 0800 963 595.

What about corruption?

In May 1997 EU ministers signed a convention on corruption to make involvement in corruption by EU or Member States' officials a criminal offence. A protocol on bribery has been signed but not yet ratified.

What about human rights in the EU and elsewhere?

The EU is stated to be founded on the principles of liberty, democracy, respect for human rights and fundamental freedoms, and the rule of law. Human rights have long been taken into account by EU institutions as being part of the European heritage. The Single European Act referred to the European Convention on Human Rights 1950 – a Council of Europe convention – to which all EU Member States have acceded. The TEU included a statement of the fundamental rights – including voting rights and freedom of movement – of all citizens of the Union, ie all citizens of the Member States. Discussions continue as to the formulation of a Charter of Rights for EU citizens. The Amsterdam Treaty strengthened and set out the fundamental rights of citizens, specifically empowering them to take European institutions before the ECJ for breach of these rights, and provided for Member States to be penalized if found guilty of a serious and persistent breach.

Do agreements with third countries take the importance of human rights into account?

Yes. Human rights are specifically referred to in various aid and trade agreements such as the Lomé Convention. In the context of EPC (European Political Co-operation) the Community actively supports the promotion and protection of human rights and fundamental freedoms not only in Europe but elsewhere in the world.

What about racism and xenophobia?

A joint declaration on racism and xenophobia by the European Parliament, the Council and the Commission has been followed up by various resolutions. The Advisory Committee set up by the European Council to advise on racism and xenophobia made various suggestions aimed at countering these problems. Following agreement in 1996, five categories of racist behaviour became criminal offences in all EU states. The Amsterdam Treaty specifically outlaws racial discrimination and enables the Council by unanimous agreement to take action to combat racial or other improper discrimination. It has been followed up by an action plan mainstreaming the fight against racism into all EU policies and programmes, promoting best practice and strengthening information initiatives.

What about rabies?

The fight against rabies continues with vaccination programmes, and the Commission is creating a 100-kilometre vaccination barrier zone on the eastern borders of the EU. A 'pet passport' scheme to enable vaccinated animals to travel in and out of the UK was operational from 28 February 2000.

Does the Community have a policy on sport?

Discussions continue as to whether sport should be specifically included in the treaties, given that it is both a cultural and an economic activity, and the declaration adopted at the time of the Amsterdam Treaty states: 'The Conference emphasizes the social significance of sport, in particular its role in forging identity and bringing people together. The Conference therefore calls on the bodies of the European Union to listen to sports associations when important questions affecting sport are at issue. In this connection special consideration should be given to the particular characteristics of amateur sport.'

The EU is working with the International Olympic Committee to set up a world anti-doping agency.

What about cross-border access to justice?

It remains confusing and difficult for individuals or enterprises seeking cross-border redress for faulty goods or services, or breach of contract. The Commission produced a useful Green Paper in 1993 on access to justice and the settlement of consumer disputes, detailing the different judicial and non-judicial methods of dispute resolution in the courts of the different Member States, and work continues to facilitate cross-border access to justice. In February 2000, a Green Paper on legal and cross-border cases was published. There is the Brussels Convention 1968 on the reciprocal enforcement of judgements (extended by the Brussels II Treaty signed by EU ministers in 1998 on divorce and legal separation matters), and the parallel Lugano Convention; and there is a 1997 convention to facilitate cross-border exchange of documents in civil and commercial court cases. Work continues on a convention to promote legal assistance between countries to deal with criminal cases. Translation difficulties and expenses are difficult to overcome, but the general advice is always to take appropriate, probably local, professional advice.

5 The budget and the different EC/EU funds

The budget
What is the budgetary procedure?

The Commission first drafts a preliminary annual Community budget. This is sent to the Council, which can adopt it or amend it by qualified majority. The (possibly amended) draft budget then goes to the EP, which can adopt it or propose amendments. The budget is then re-examined by the Council, which can accept it by at least a qualified majority, or amend it again. Then it goes back for a second reading to the EP, which can finally accept it, or reject it. However, the European Council has great influence, eg in 1999 it agreed the Agenda 2000 package of reforms, which should stabilize Common Agricultural Policy (CAP) spending until 2006.

How much is the budget?

The preliminary spending plans for 2000–2006, now approved as the budget for 2000 by the EP, is for expenditures totalling ECU 93.8 billion in commitments, with a payments ceiling of ECU 91.3 billion being an average of 1.13 per cent of GNP of Member States. Commitment appropriations are expenditure obligations for the year ahead, and payment appropriations are obligations arising from previous years.

What are the priorities for future budget policy?

Stability of expenditure remains a first priority with commitments similar to 1999, and the emphasis on implementation of the Amsterdam Treaty obligations. Also noted is the need for pre-accession assistance for applicant countries, and the control of any increases in spending on CAP.

How is the budget financed?

Under the Agenda 2000 package, the financing framework of the

Community was agreed for 2000–06. This confirmed a budgetary resources limit overall of 1.27 per cent of Community GNP with the VAT contribution limit cut to 0.75 per cent in 2002 and 0.05 per cent in 2004. Most of this comes from VAT in the form of a levy on the gross value added of each Member State. The rest of the money is raised by customs duties on various goods, including agricultural products and sugar, and payments from Member States. There are also customs duties and agricultural levies on goods entering the Community. Thus, the budget is financed by 'own resources', ie revenues that the Community can raise, which are paid automatically into the budget.

Which countries pay, and which gain moneys?

The Commission report entitled *Financing the European Union*, published in October 1998, set out in some detail the net contributions and receipts of EU Member States concerning the EU budget. The data compared the different countries, and indicated that CAP spending had been dramatically cut. The contribution system relies on payments being related to a country's GNP *vis-à-vis* the EU as a whole. Thus Germany (which has 26 per cent of EU GNP) paid 28.2 per cent of budget costs, France (with 17.2 per cent of EU GNP) paid 17.5 per cent, the UK (with 16.1 per cent of EU GNP) paid 11.9 of budget costs (because of the rebate negotiated by Mrs Thatcher), and Italy (with 14.2 per cent of EU GNP) paid 11.5 per cent.

The various funds

How did the Cohesion Fund start?

The Cohesion Fund was started to assist less-developed Member States to achieve the convergence criteria required for Economic and Monetary Union (EMU). The Cohesion Fund with ECU 15.5 billion for 1993–99 for Spain, Ireland, Greece and Portugal was aimed chiefly at improving transport links and Community networks, and at achieving the required EU environmental standards. The Cohesion Fund and Structural Funds together support less-developed regions by helping economic and industrial development, employment, agriculture and fisheries, and environmental protection. This is achieved through grant aid and loan finance. The Commission has proposed that Ireland, Portugal and Spain be gradually withdrawn from Cohesion Fund finance (Ireland now has a higher per capita income than the UK).

What do the Structural Funds comprise?

These must be distinguished from the Cohesion Fund and are aimed at reducing regional disparities. They do not exclude any particular sector, whereas the Cohesion Fund is aimed at reducing economic disparities between Member States, but is limited to environment and transport infrastructures. The Structural Funds' expenditure will total ECU 213 billion for 2000–06.

The Structural Funds comprise:

- the European Regional Development Fund (ERDF);
- the European Social Fund (ESF);
- the European Agricultural Guidance and Guarantee Fund (EAGGF);
- the Financial Instrument for Fisheries.

The following six priority objectives have been set for the Structural Funds:

1. To promote the development and structural adjustment of less-developed regions in the EU. Objective 1 funds are aimed at the poorest regions, where GDP is up to 75% (inclusive) of the average in the EU.
2. To assist effectively those regions and border or frontier regions seriously affected by industrial decline.
3. To combat long-term unemployment.
4. To facilitate the occupational integration of young people.
5a. To assist production, processing and marketing structures in agriculture and forestry.
5b. To promote the development of rural areas.

To these have been added two more objectives, the most important being objective 6, introduced in 1995 to assist development in sparsely populated areas and aimed at helping the Nordic members.

Different areas or regions have priority for funds available under the various headings.

What is the purpose of the European Regional Development Fund?

As part of the Structural Funds, this assists regional development and the growth and adjustment of regional economies where there are structural deficits; and in the redevelopment of declining industrial regions with national regional policies. Much of the expenditure is for infrastructure projects. Applications are through integrated regional offices.

What about the European Social Fund?

The important European Social Fund was set up by the Treaty specifically to improve employment opportunities, mobility, vocational training, adaptability and standards of living of workers in the Community. It assists implementation of social policies with particular regard to combating general and youth unemployment, and encouraging vocational training and integration of young or 'excluded' people into the job market. Individual companies can sometimes apply.

When was the EAGGF set up?

The European Agricultural Guidance and Guarantee Fund was set up in 1962, and by 1995 the Agricultural and Fisheries Fund accounted for some 50 per cent of the budget, most of this going to guaranteeing farm prices and storage costs, but attempts at reforms continue to reduce this. In March 1999 it was agreed that CAP spending should be kept at an average of ECU 40.5 billion per year for 2000–06.

The EAGGF guidance section assists the modernization of agricultural infrastructure and supports farming in environmentally sensitive areas. Applications for grants or subsidies are through the national agricultural ministries.

Are there any other funds?

Yes, many. They include:

- *The European Monetary Co-operation Fund.* This fund, created in 1973, is intended primarily to keep account of short-term borrowing for support of national currencies. It also administers gold and silver reserves under the European Monetary System (EMS).
- *The New Community Instrument for Borrowing and Lending (NIC).* This was set up in 1978 to raise funds for the financing of structural investment projects through the European Investment Bank (EIB).
- *The European Development Fund.* This is not part of the general budget, and administers the Community's overseas financial aid under the Lomé Convention.
- *The European Coal and Steel Community (ECSC),* under the Convention that runs until 2002, and the *European Atomic Energy Community (EURATOM),* which is aimed at co-operation on peaceful uses of nuclear energy, are both sources of loan funds.

- *The European Financial Instrument for the Environment.* This is intended to cover investment expenses for environmental matters not covered by the Structural Funds or other programmes.
- *The Performance Reserve* is a reserve fund intended to be used to aid financing of Structural Fund projects of special merit in poorer regions.

There are a number of other funds concerned with, for example, development co-operation in various countries, and research and development.

What about the European Investment Fund (EIF)?

This was set up in the context of the European Growth initiative and is administered through the European Investment Bank. The EIF has an initial authorized capital of ECU 2 billion, 40 per cent of which is subscribed by EIB, 30 per cent from the Commission and 30 per cent from the private and public banks. Further information can be obtained from the European Investment Bank (see Appendix III).

What are Community Support Frameworks (CSFs)?

There is an agreed procedure for Member States submitting eligible development investment plans, including proposals for Community support under the Structural Funds. Community Support Frameworks are Commission guidelines on the use of Structural Funds in a state or region, and operational programmes based on them are used to improve infrastructure and tourism, to secure environmental improvements, to help small and medium-sized enterprises (SMEs) and to assist research and development. They give a summary of the individual sectoral measures to be undertaken within the framework of the CSFs. The Commission has produced information giving the broad outline as to contents of a programme, including the money involved and contact points for information.

What about other Commission initiatives?

The Commission can propose to the Member States on its own initiative a number of programmes that are aimed at correcting various regional imbalances within the framework of regional policy. Examples of these are:

- INTERREG to help border and outlying areas and external borders of the EU. The reform of the Structural Funds was partly in response to difficulties in administering this programme.

- REGIS to assist places such as the Canary Islands, Madeira and Guadeloupe.
- LEADER to assist innovative solutions for rural areas.
- The SME initiative to help small and medium-sized businesses to adapt to the Single Market.
- RETEX to assist textile regions, helping SMEs to improve management organization and skills.
- RESIDER to assist regions with reduced iron and steel production.
- REGEN to enable energy infrastructures to be constructed in regions of lagging development.
- KONVER to assist areas previously involved in defence to convert.
- PESCA to assist the restructuring of the fisheries sector.
- ADAPT to assist labour to adapt to industrial changes.
- RECHAR to support social and economic conversion in coal mining areas.
- URBAN to support new economic activities dealing with local employment, infrastructure and social health and security fields.
- The five-year Raphael Programme, and Culture 2000 support cultural heritage projects and encourage the dissemination of knowledge about European culture.
- EQUAL to combat inequality in the work-place.

There are other funds available for specific programmes, many of which are mentioned under the appropriate headings elsewhere in this book, eg the fifth Framework Programme for research, technological development and energy 1999–2003.

Why is it important to know about the Structural Funds?

It is important to know about the Structural Funds because it is possible to benefit from them, and they encourage employment. As the programmes now tend to be for longer periods, it is useful to establish at an early stage what opportunities are likely to arise in different regions. This is particularly relevant given the liberalization of public procurement, the importance given to employment creation and the perceived need to encourage SMEs to take part in public procurement contracts.

It has been suggested that Member States should have a more co-ordinated approach to structural reforms, to ensure cohesion in reforms of markets with regard to liberalization of service sectors, and to ensure social security and pension provisions remain adequate in the light of public spending controls.

What about fraud?

Fraud in connection with the various funds is seen as a serious problem. The Sound and Efficient Management 2000 initiative looked to improve anti-fraud checks and audit systems, and to scrutinize legislation to make it as fraud-proof as possible.

It has now been agreed that moneys paid out by the national bodies without sufficient guarantees of legitimacy or with unsatisfactory monitoring may be recovered by the Commission, which in 1999 was seeking to recover about ECU 493 million EU-wide. Of this about ECU 97.9 million was from France, and about ECU 49.5 million from the UK.

What about funds available for applicant countries?

PHARE and TACIS are two important programmes for applicant countries (see Chapter18).

Since 1995 PHARE's aim has been to help each applicant country to build a democratic, free enterprise economy to enable it to participate effectively in the Internal Market. There is a technical assistance information exchange in Brussels to help Central and Eastern European Countries (CEECs). TACIS is similar to PHARE, but is aimed at the newly independent states (NIS) and Mongolia.

In November 1998 two new budget instruments were agreed for countries preparing for EU membership:

1. ISPA pre-accession instrument 2000–06 with ECU 7 billion for Structural Funds.
2. SAPARD with ECU 500 million per year to help agricultural and rural development in applicant countries.

These will not affect the continuing PHARE programmes.

A European Agency for Reconstruction in Kosovo has been set up, which works with the United Nations (UN) and other agencies in the context of a reconstruction programme for Bosnia-Herzegovina.

More information can be obtained from the European Commission, the national ministries for agriculture, the Department of Trade and Industry (DTI) and national equivalents, Chambers of Commerce, the various European Information Centres, or the Web site http://www.cec.org.uk.

6 Harmonization of standards

Why is the harmonization of standards necessary?

Differing standards can constitute barriers to the free movement of goods within the EU, but harmonization of standards reduces these kinds of barrier, and common standards should eliminate them. The first steps were in 1961 with the formation of the European Standards Institute composed of: CENELEC (the European Committee for Electrotechnical Standardization) for electrical goods and equipment; CEN (the European Committee for Standardization) for other products; and ETSI (the European Telecommunications Standards Institute). All three include representatives from EEA and EFTA countries.

Was progress satisfactory?

Progress was not satisfactory at first, because negotiated standards had to be included in highly technical Directives, which then had to be implemented in the different Member States. In 1973 a different system was introduced for domestic electrical equipment – general safety standards requirements were agreed, and it was left to CENELEC to produce more detailed standards, which were then published in the *Official Journal*. Goods complying with these standards could then be marketed throughout the Community. This approach has since been widened to other goods.

What about new technical standards creating barriers?

The 1983 Directive on procedures for the provision of information in the fields of technical standards and regulations was designed to prevent new barriers. It required Member States to notify the Commission of proposals for new technical standards and regulations, and facilitated any necessary interventions by the Commission and other Member States. This promoted new European standards, and was extended in 1989 to cover extra areas (agricultural products, pharmaceuticals, foodstuffs and cosmetics). The next extension covered online and other information services, such as virtual shopping, interactive video entertainment, insurance, estate agency and legal or educational services online – but not broadcasting or banking.

A 1995 Council Decision required Member States to notify the Commission of any provisions that prevent the inter-state movement of products made or sold legally in another Member State.

In June 1999 further action to improve recognition of national standards in the EU was proposed. This included better monitoring of problems, publications and meetings to raise awareness, greater co-operation in Member States and better case management in Commission departments concerned.

How do CEN, CENELEC and ETSI operate?

They have their administrative headquarters in Brussels, but the main work is decentralized and carried out by the national standards institutes (the BSI in the UK), which work with intra-Community technical committees and working groups. It is beyond the scope of this book to list the standards concerned, but they include such matters as motor vehicles, toys, domestic electrical equipment and construction products, packaging, recycling and recovery standards.

What about international standards?

With the increase in global trade, international (ISO and IEC) standards have come to be adopted wherever possible. It is useful to note that there is an EU/EFTA arrangement (similar to the 1983 Directive) to notify new standards.

What about testing for certification outside the European country of origin?

Harmonized standards are leading to the mutual acceptance of other countries' certifications. Some European schemes exist within CEN, CENELEC and ETSI for various goods, and these are being expanded, and common criteria for assessing the competence of national certification and testing authorities are being published. In addition, the European Organization for Testing and Certification (EOTC) is recognized by EFTA as well as EU countries. Following the 1989 Commission programme entitled 'A Global Approach to Certification and Testing Quality Measures for Industrial Products', international standards are usually aimed for.

What about telecommunications and information technology?

Harmonization of technical standards and the application of competition provisions are the cornerstones of Community policy in this fast growing area. It is highly technical and new standards are being negotiated all the time, sometimes so fast that formal consultations are too slow and 'Publicly Available Standards' (PACs) are being developed to complement formal standards. The global aspect of this sector has led to industry-led agreed standards (see Chapter 15).

What about pharmaceuticals and medicinal products?

Since 1995 the European Medicines Evaluation Agency (EMEA) in London has enabled medicinal products for human or veterinary use to be given a single (and therefore swifter) central evaluation and market authorization valid throughout the EU. National authorities may only authorize use in their domestic market. Various strict provisions apply to the Agency's members, whether on the board or committee, eg they may not have any financial or other interests in the pharmaceutical industry that could affect their impartiality. Evaluations are given within a set time, and may be by majority decision. The EMEA has powers to check on good manufacturing, laboratory and clinical practice. It encourages co-operation between Member States, international organizations and third countries to improve medicinal safety. It is funded partly by the Community, and partly by fees paid.

Does CEN get involved in environmental protection?

Standards cover a wide range of subjects with environmental implications. For example, CEN is working on standards to improve waste packaging, recycling and recovery following the 1994 Directive, which requires methods for verifying the presence of heavy metals, emissions levels and marking.

What is CE marking?

This certifies compliance with various EU provisions, so that a product can be sold throughout the EU without further national standards assessments. The 1993 CE Marking Directive and Decision set out general harmonized conformity assessment procedures. This is a voluntary, but useful, system.

What is the overall effect of the harmonization of standards?

In the long term, harmonization broadens the available markets for goods and equipment. It eventually tends to raise standards overall, even though the recognized standard is often the product of negotiations, and so refers to minimums acceptable. Increasingly global standards apply. All this means increased competition, and so tends to drive down prices.

Further information concerning standards and how to obtain them may be obtained in the UK from the BSI, the Commission, the professional organizations of the product concerned and the DTI (see Appendix III).

7　Consumer protection policy

What is the consumer protection policy of the EU?

EU consumer protection policy aims to consider and protect the interests of EU consumers and their rights in matters within the competence of the Commission and Community legislation. It has impacted on harmonization measures since 1972 when the basic rights of consumers were set out, but it was not until the Single European Act (Article 100) that the protection of consumers (and the environment) was formally added to the Rome Treaty as a matter to be considered, and the consumer policy service was set up. The TEU made consumer protection a Community policy in its own right in 1993, and the Amsterdam Treaty (now in the consolidated version of the Treaty of Rome Article 153) states that consumer protection requirements must be taken into account in defining and implementing other policies and activities. This Article also provides that 'the Community shall contribute to protecting the health, safety and economic interests of consumers, as well as to promoting their right to information, education and to organize themselves in order to safeguard their interests'.

What are the basic rights of consumers?

These, set out in the first preliminary consumer programme and now incorporated in the United Nations' 1985 Guidelines on Consumer Protection, are:

- the right to protection of economic interests;
- the right to information and education;
- the right of representation and consultation;
- the right to protection of health and safety;
- the right to redress.

What sort of legislation is made because of consumer policy?

Many of the wide range of consumer protection provisions are closely linked to standards. These include Directives on food labelling, unit pricing, permissible colorants and additives, the composition and effect on health of food products, the levels of pesticide residues in food, and genetically modified food marking. Pharmaceuticals, cosmetics and motor cars are among products that are the subject of harmonized provisions governing standards and marketing practices.

Prices are monitored to avoid dual pricing policies, and safety is a prime factor. There are drafts, regulations or Directives on the use of asbestos in consumer goods; the approximation of legislation relating to the classification, packaging and labelling of dangerous substances (particularly aimed at domestic chemicals); on genetically modified organisms; on cement, tiles and other construction products; on the safety of gas appliances; on radioactive substances in household products; on electrical equipment safety and voltage, toy safety, and dangerous imitation products posing particular dangers to children; on consumer credit, and many others. Some of these are considered in detail later in this chapter.

Have any action plans been aimed at this sector?

Yes. Various initiatives and action plans have been aimed at encouraging:

- better consumer information and, more recently, education;
- better consumer protection;
- better consumer safety;
- better and cheaper access to justice, and more transparency in, for example, tele-purchasing and financial services;
- consumer confidence in the Internal Market;
- better cross-border payments systems;
- better health protection;
- improved quality, information and transparency in the provision of financial services, by public utilities, in the supply of essential services and with regard to 'the information society';
- the development of consumer policies in Eastern Europe and developing countries.

The Consumer Policy Action Plan for 1999–2001 seeks to ensure consumers have the right information, enabling them to make the right decisions. It encourages further inter-state co-operation, emphasizing the need to balance the interests of EU and other legislation with consumer interests, eg in the information society and CAP. It supports better consultation, a better level of health and safety, and action on the safety of services.

What about complaints about public administrations?

The TEU provided for an Ombudsman to hear complaints (in confidence if necessary) from any legal or physical person who is a resident or citizen of a Member State concerning maladministration by a Community body. He or she can seek out maladministration cases, and remedy them, or take cases before the European Parliament for scrutiny. Appointed by the EP, the Ombudsman is based in Strasbourg at the EP, and may be removed from office by the European Court of Justice (ECJ). EU citizens can write to the President of the EP if they believe a serious cause for complaint has arisen with regard to, for example, non-compliance by a Member State with the Treaties, but it is suggested that such letters are best routed through petitioners' local MEPs. Under the Amsterdam Treaty individuals may take the European institutions before the ECJ if they consider them to have acted in breach of their fundamental rights (which include human rights, and race and sex discrimination).

What about general consumer protection provisions?

There are many provisions or proposals, some of which are considered in more detail later in this chapter. For example:

- A 1976 cosmetics Directive introduced rules relating to the marking of ingredients and warnings. This has recently been amended to provide for the phasing out of cosmetics testing on animals.
- A 1985 Directive on sales away from business premises (doorstep selling) provided for cooling-off periods for consumers.
- A 1994 Directive on the sale of timeshares in properties also provided for cooling-off periods, with specific details concerning deposits, reflection time, withdrawal or termination, accurate descriptions of the property, period of rights sold, and the purchaser's right to choose the language of the contract.
- A 1997 Directive on distance selling introduced protective provisions relating to contracts 'made at a distance', eg through mail order, or via television or teletext.
- A 1998 (amended 1999) draft Directive on the distance selling of financial services includes minimum common protection standards, and is intended to complement the 1997 Directive.
- A 1997 Directive on cross-border payments or transfers gave rights to consumers (see Chapter 12).
- A 1997 Directive banned the use in cosmetics of animal tissue from animals at risk from BSE.

What about consumer health?

Human health protection considerations influence much EU consumer legislation and many programmes. The requirement to provide for Community action to complement national initiatives is set out in Article 152 of the consolidated Treaty of Rome, and is included in various programmes. For example, drinking and bathing water quality is the subject of provisions, and the Commission pursues infringing Member States. A Web site gives details of complying beaches. See Chapter 16 for health programmes, and Chapter 17 for provisions relating to, for example, use of growth-promoting hormones in animals.

A total ban on tobacco advertising from 2006 is being introduced with phased effect.

What about food safety?

Most recently the setting up of a European Food Agency, similar to the Medicines Agency, has been proposed. Bovine spongiform encephalopathy (BSE) problems led to a more robust approach by the Commission on food policy. A cross-department group of Commissioners for food health was set up in 1997 and a series of papers have been produced since. In April 1997 the Food and Veterinary Office (FVO) attached to the Consumer Policy and Consumer Health Directorate (DG XXIV) replaced the Office for Veterinary and Phytosanitary Control in the Agricultural Directorate General. The FVO carries out inspections not only in the Member States, but also in third countries seeking to export to the EU, to ensure compliance. The responsibility for implementation of the legislation remains with Member States, but the Commission monitors enforcement of a significant body of food safety rules that are designed to protect public health, animal health and welfare, and plant health. As it is intended to make producers ultimately responsible for food safety, stricter controls are increasingly being extended to all those involved in the food chain, and there is the possibility of product liability rules.

The 1997 Novel Food Regulation requires labelling of consumer products containing genetically modified (GM) crops. There are various proposals and provisions such as those limiting irradiation of foodstuffs and ingredients, and those covering the use of drugs in animal foodstuffs and the use of pesticides.

It is interesting to note that EU rules have to be considered in the light of WTO trade rules, and there have been recent rulings on, for example, the use of hormones to promote growth in meat production.

What about general safety provisions?

Besides those listed above, environmental protection schemes have significant health and safety aspects, and many of their standards are closely linked to consumer protection. Other standards include, for example, the Dangerous Preparations Directive 1990, which requires child-resistant packaging and tactile danger warnings for hazardous household chemicals.

What about product liability?

The 1985 Directive on Product Liability provides for the strict liability of manufacturers and others for defective products. This means that in some circumstances manufacturers and suppliers can be made liable for damage or injury caused by a product's defect without proof of fault, ie the complainant only has to show the damage, the defect and the link between the two, and the producer may be liable. The introduction of the 'development risks' defence, whereby if a manufacturer can show that the scientific and technical knowledge at the time the products were put into circulation was not such as to enable the existence of the defect to be discovered, was optional, so it is not an available defence in all Member States. Primary agricultural products and game that have not been processed are to be included within the scope of the directive from 4 December 2000 under a 1999 Directive.

New discussion of possible amendments to strengthen the Product Liability Directive are set out in a July 1999 Green Paper on liability for defective products.

The Product Liability Directive should not be confused with the 1977 Council of Europe 'Strasbourg' Convention on Product Liability covering personal injury and death. The Directive is applied slightly differently in the various Member States, but it should be noted that under it importers are deemed to be producers.

What about product safety?

The General Product Safety Directive 1992 on manufacturers' liability to customers for the safety of their products introduced a general obligation to put only safe products on the market. It also required all manufacturers to ensure that full information about the potential risks of their products is given, and that the Member States should have emergency procedures in place. A discussion paper *Review and Revision of Directive 92/59 EEC (the General Product Safety Directive)* was produced in June 1999. A Council Resolution 1998 concerns the quality of product operating instructions.

What about the exchange of cross-border information?

Information exchange is important to consumer protection, and is provided by the EHLASS (European Home and Leisure Accident Surveillance System) for Community information and statistics on accidents involving consumer products. RAPEX (the Rapid Exchange of Information System) relates to dangerous products. The European Network on Consumer Rights (COLINE) links various information centres with databases on national consumer rights.

What about doorstep selling?

The 1985 Directive on Sales Away from Business Premises – better known as the Doorstep Selling Directive – enables a seven-day cooling-off period for doorstep agreements involving more than a specified, small sum, to enable consumers to cancel.

What did the Distance Selling Directive 1997 provide?

It required minimum information to be given (although Member States may introduce more stringent provisions) and seven-day cooling-off periods for contracts negotiated 'at a distance', eg through post, mail order, television, telephone, fax, e-mail or teletext sales. It covered goods (which must be supplied within 30 days) and most services, excluding financial services, which are governed by separate provisions. It detailed rights to refunds and replacements, and enabled consumer organizations to pursue claims in the courts. The European Mail Order Traders Association has adopted a European Convention on Cross-Border Mail Order and Distant Sales.

What about distance selling of financial services?

A draft Directive, amended in 1999 and complementing the Distance Selling Directive, is intended to provide a protective framework for consumers for the distance selling of financial services. This would include a 14-day cooling-off period after, for example, insurance, banking or investment services are sold by telephone, post or Internet, and the period would be extended to 30 days for consumer pensions, mortgages or life insurance sales. Foreign exchange services would be excluded from the withdrawal right.

What about financial services generally?

There are around 50 Directives aimed at providers of financial services. Consumers are protected under the various insurance, banking and financial services Directives, including the Cross-Border Payments Directive 1997 (see Chapter 12).

What about consumer credit?

There have been various consumer credit Directives. They have covered such matters as harmonization of national provisions relating to consumer credit, a common method of calculation of the annual percentage rates of charge (APR), and authorization and control of those offering consumer credit or acting as intermediaries.

What about services generally?

Guidelines covering specific services provide for the establishment of compensation provisions by suppliers for consumers suffering from a fault in services that results in physical injury or damage to property, but not covering consequential economic damage; and urge the drafting of codes of practice.

The 1990 draft Directive on Liability of Suppliers of Defective Services, which would have imposed liability on service suppliers unless they could prove they were not at fault, was withdrawn, but an amended proposal might be introduced in the future. At the moment any victim of a defective service may have to prove negligence by the supplier in order to show liability. However it should be noted that some specific fields do have their own voluntary codes of practice, and it is worth asking advice from the relevant trade or professional organization.

What about travel?

The 1990 Directive on Package Trips, Package Holidays and Tours Sold or Put Up for Sale in the EC provides minimum protection for consumers. It specifies that brochures must be clear and provide key information. It controls price changes, and makes tour operators liable for services provided by their agents. It requires guarantees to be given to ensure reimbursement of travellers in the event of tour company insolvencies (see also Chapters 9 and 12). There are proposals to extend this. There are proposals or provisions on insurance for travellers, on visiting motorists and a regulation to improve compensation for travellers in air accidents. The liberalization of transport has lowered prices, particularly air fares. A 1986 recommendation urges minimum provisions for hotel fire safety.

What about the Unfair Contract or Abusive Terms Directive 1993?

This required Member States to ban the use of 'abusive' clauses in consumer contracts, ie broadly clauses that unfairly create an imbalance of rights between the parties to the detriment of the consumer. Any such clauses (eg the exclusion or limitation of liability by the seller or supplier for harm resulting to the consumer from an act or omission of the seller) are void, although the contract may stand without them. The Directive does not cover all consumer contracts (ie only standard, not individually negotiated contracts) and has been criticized for being too vague; but it enables organizations and individuals with a legitimate interest in protecting consumers under domestic legislation to challenge allegedly abusive clauses.

What about guarantees?

A 1999 Directive on Guarantees gives a consumer guarantee for a minimum of two years on goods bought anywhere in the EU, and must be implemented in 2001. Under it, consumers may have rights to have a faulty item repaired or replaced, or their money refunded, but account must be taken of the quality and performance of the goods and the price paid.

Is advertising affected by consumer protection policy?

Yes. The 1984 Misleading Advertising Directive aimed to protect consumers and business people from certain types of misleading advertising in the EU by requiring Member States to set up procedures to deal with false and misleading advertisements. The 1997 Comparative Advertising Directive amended the original Directive to permit comparative advertising subject to various conditions requiring, for example, advertisers to substantiate their claims, and not to denigrate or discredit rival brand names or trade marks. Other related provisions concern food claims, mail order or distance sales, and timeshare offers. There is a 1996 Resolution on male/female images in advertising.

A useful 1996 Green Paper, *A Single Market for Commercial Communications*, analysed differences in national regulatory frameworks for advertising, sponsorship, direct marketing, sales promotion and public relations generally. It aimed to establish how this sector could gain more from the Single Market, and to what extent consumers need extra protection.

The European Alliance for Standards in Advertising (EASA) includes representatives of all the self-regulating bodies in the EU and EFTA Member States, and seeks to co-ordinate systems and assist with complaints. It is situated in Brussels.

Further information concerning advertising can be obtained from national advertising standards bodies, or the Commission.

What about eco-labels?

These enable consumers to choose goods with the best environmental performance. The 1992 scheme required common assessment by competent bodies in each Member State of goods proposed as qualifying for these labels. However a new regulation is aimed at revitalizing the scheme, with a new body, the European Eco-labelling Organization (EEO), to link national bodies and establish ecological criteria.

What about data protection?

The electronic holding and transmission of data, which includes information relating to individuals, have assumed great importance given the vastly increased use of electronic databases. The Council of Europe Convention on Data Processing, although implemented in most Member States, was felt by some not to go far enough to meet Community needs. Now, however, there is a package of six Directives on data protection, the most important for consumers being the 1995 Personal Data Protection Directive, which established a regulatory framework to enable the free movement of personal data in the EU. It gives equivalent rights to a data subject no matter where the data are processed in the EU, and these should include: consent prior to any processing, communication or sale of data concerning him or her, and limitations on the use of personal data. Thus there is an obligation to collect personal data only for specified legitimate purposes, and to hold it only if it is relevant, accurate and up to date.

What about international data flows?

The proper privacy rights of individuals in respect of information concerning them and held by others continue to cause difficulties, particularly where there is international transmission of data. The Data Protection Directive 1998 enables any Member State to stop data flows of personal information going to countries with inadequate protection. A useful example of this is the continuing negotiations with the US, whose data protection rules are not so stringent as those in the EU. It seems likely that the US will agree to enable US companies to sign up to EU data protection principles, and provide 'safe harbours' for data flows between the EU and US.

What about the freedom of the press?

This is important to the individual both in terms of the supply of unhindered information to the public and in respect of personal privacy. A balance has to be achieved. It has not been an area for Community action as such, but the fundamental rights referred to in the Amsterdam Treaty could apply to the protection and confidentiality of journalists' sources, as could the European Convention on Human Rights. A Council of Europe Convention to prevent media concentrations is under discussion, as are possible EU restrictions to avoid multimedia concentrated ownership, which is perceived to be a danger to press freedom and independence.

What about access to justice?

Consumers undoubtedly need more information concerning rights of access to courts in the Member States, particularly where cross-border disputes arise, although costs, including translation expenses, are probably the biggest hurdle to claims. The Commission supports cross-border information centres, and has produced a *Guide to Legal Aid and Advice in the European Economic Area*, which covers the EU, Iceland and Norway. This is available on the Internet.

The Enforcement of Judgements Conventions assist in this area (see Chapter 20), and there is the Strasbourg Agreement on the transmission of applications for legal aid, but this has not been ratified by all Member States. The 1998 Directive on Injunctions for the Protection of Consumers' Interests will enable a national body in one Member State to take action in another, either itself or through its counterpart there, where it perceives a breach of various EU consumer protection provisions.

A 1998 Commission communication concerns improvements in access to legal or administrative systems in other Member States for consumers. A recommended claim form, together with seven recommended principles, is intended to facilitate out-of-court settlements.

Work continues to establish common procedures and facilitate cross-border actions, with encouragement for the use of alternative dispute procedures where appropriate (see Chapter 4).

What is the effect on consumers of the Rome Convention of June 1980 on the law applicable to contractual obligations?

This convention is applicable in most EU states (Belgium, Denmark, France, Germany, Ireland, Italy, Luxembourg, The Netherlands, and the UK) and provides that, other than for insurance contracts, a consumer will be protected by his or her own national mandatory protective provisions regardless of the choice of law clause in the contract concerned. If there is no choice of law clause (ie a clause stating that the contract is governed by the law of a specified country), then the law of the consumer's place of residence prevails provided that its provisions are in accordance with proper principles of public protection. This can be particularly important in disputes relating to banking and financial services.

What is the general effect of consumer protection provisions?

Many EU provisions include a strong element of consumer protection, not only in the measures detailed above, but in other areas such as the environment, sustainability, competition law, agricultural policy, and so on. As trade becomes increasingly global, so consumer interests have to be safeguarded more internationally; and the focus is also now on the safety of the citizen.

The 1999–2001 Consumer Programme focuses on greater consultation, and the consumer lobby is influential. The EU Consumer Committee consists of 20 representatives, one from each EU Member State and one each from five EU representative organizations: BEUC (consumer organizations), COFACE (family organizations), EuroCoop (consumer co-operatives), ETUC (Trade Unions) and IEIC (European Inter-Regional Consumer Institute).

Further information may be obtained from the European Commission (DG XXIV), the Consumers in the European Commission Group and the Bureau of European Consumer Organizations (BEUC) (see Appendix III).

8 Customs control, physical and technical barriers

Background

What was the background to the Single Market?

The Treaty of Rome, as amended, Article 23(1) states that 'The Community shall be based upon a customs union which shall cover all trade in goods and which shall involve the prohibition between Member States of customs duties on imports and exports and of all charges having equivalent effect, and the adoption of a common customs tariff in their relations with third countries.' Article 23(2) stated that this would apply to all products originating in the Member States, and products coming from third countries that are in free circulation in the Member States.

What is the effect of being in a customs union?

Countries within a customs union agree not to have any customs duties to act as barriers between them, and to have a common customs tariff for goods coming in from outside that area. This means that if goods originate in a customs area member country, or have been imported with duty paid in that country, then they can circulate freely within the rest of the customs union area.

How does this differ from a free trade area or zone?

In a free trade area or zone the international exchange of goods is unrestricted, and customs tariffs are only used to provide a source of revenue, and not as a barrier to trade. The World Trade Organization has definitions as to what constitutes a free trade agreement.

Where do the EU, EEA and Association Agreement countries stand?

The EU is a customs union. The EEA is more than a free trade area, but different external customs tariffs can be applied. Countries with EU Association Agreements are given reduced or no duty rates for the bulk of their goods, but some controls remain.

How did the EC Customs Union contribute to free movement of goods and people?

The elimination of customs barriers was seen as an important element in achieving the freedom of movement of people and goods. The Customs Union, however, with its abolition of customs duties between Member States and the common external tariff under which all Member States apply the same tariffs to goods coming from outside the EC, did not of itself provide the elimination of internal barriers to trade. These barriers were not being dissolved fast enough so, in 1985, the Commission published its comprehensive White Paper, *Completing the Internal Market*, and much has been done since.

What is 'Schengen'?

Some Member States did not think the European Community was moving fast enough on eliminating internal border controls, so in 1985 the original Schengen Accord was signed by five Member States. This was followed by a further Convention, the Schengen Agreement 1990, since agreed by all EU States (the UK and Ireland keeping special arrangements), which led to the effective elimination of internal border controls on people travelling between them, and to common visa and more stringent external border controls, all supported by a Schengen information system. The Amsterdam Treaty incorporated the Schengen Agreement into the EU's single institutional framework, with the Schengen Secretariat integrated into the General Secretariat of the Council. The special provisions enable the UK and Ireland to maintain border checks on people, and allow for the preservation of the Nordic Passport Union, so Norway and Iceland, which have accepted the 'Schengen Acquis', will also apply the agreement.

Why was the 1985 White Paper important?

It set out the timetable for achieving a European Community without frontiers – a truly integrated Single Market. It highlighted three main barriers: the physical barriers of frontier controls; the technical barriers of differing technical requirements; and the fiscal barriers of tax and duty provisions. In each case the action necessary for removing barriers, and the consequences of doing so by the end of 1992, were considered. A description of measures included in the Single Market Programme is set out in Appendix IV.

Problems and prospects

What is the position now?

The Single European Act 1986 (see Chapter 2) gave force to the White Paper. By 1993 the internal controls on goods, services and capital had been largely eliminated, although some problems remained, and in practice a few still remain. The ECJ has had a significant role in controlling remaining attempts to retain barriers or even to introduce new ones.

What about the free movement of people?

Some controls still remain for persons, and in some places such as the UK, for pets, and work continues on standard procedures and rights of immigrants, third-country nationals, visas and asylum seekers.

What about the need to maintain proper statistics concerning the movement of goods?

Detailed trade statistics are required and the Transit and Storage Statistics Between Member States Regulation 1992 originally set out the framework for collection of national statistical statements. Details are collected on a quarterly basis from VAT-registered traders. All such traders are required to provide summary figures of the total value of goods imported from and exported to other Member States as part of their normal VAT returns. The largest VAT-registered traders (ie, those representing the top 20 per cent by value of EC imports and exports) additionally complete monthly a new simplified statistical return (see Chapter 11). Because of the high degree of fraud connected with transit, a 1997 Council Regulation provided for closer co-ordination and harmonization of standards and methodology between Member States and the Statistical Office of the European Communities (EUROSTAT). This has been followed by efforts to update systems and procedures, and to negotiate a new transit convention with the EU's European partners.

What about excise duties?

Excise duties cause particular problems as they vary from country to country, and discussions continue to try to resolve them. The

FISCALIS programme is specifically aimed at increasing co-operation between authorities in Member States to fight VAT and excise duty fraud.

What about duty-free allowances?

Following the unanimous agreement of all Member States (including the UK) in 1991, the system of duty-free and duty-paid goods, and tax-free shopping for cross-border trips within the EU, was abolished by 30 June 1999, despite lobbying by ferry and air operators who argued that duty-free sales subsidized fares.

The provisions that came into force on 1 April 1994 with some exceptions, for trips between EU and third countries, remain. Further details of allowances are available from HM Customs and Excise (tel: 020 7202 4227; fax: 020 7202 4143).

What are the problems arising from removing customs posts?

The original reasons for frontier controls were military, fiscal, economic, commercial, health-related (health checks on food imports impose useful controls at an early point in the supply chain and reduce significantly the risks to public health) and statistical. National policing was facilitated as the free movement of illegal drugs, crime and undesirable people was hindered by customs checks. Now, in the context of the Citizens' Europe, various co-operation and information systems have been set up to control fraud, drugs, terrorism, trafficking in persons, etc. Firearms pose another problem, and the 1991 Directive on Control of the Acquisition and Possession of Weapons harmonizes rules as to licences and the carrying of arms. There are special provisions for explosives, radioactive substances, drugs and drug precursors (ie substances used to manufacture illegal drugs). Dual-use goods and technologies continue to pose problems, as do some agricultural products.

A Directive on restitution of cultural goods or art treasures illegally exported accompanies the regulation relating to the export of cultural goods. Measures relating to the illegal export of national treasures came into effect in 1993.

The abolition of frontier controls means each Community country has to rely far more on local domestic controls and regulations governing food production techniques and standards; and on the increased co-operation between the police forces and customs offices.

What is the European Information System?

This is linked to the External Borders Convention, and aimed at increasing co-operation between customs, police and judicial authorities in the EU and EEA. Co-operation between customs authorities is seen as vital to the fight against crime and terrorism. It should be noted that the SIS (Schengen Information System) is now operating effectively.

If you know of anyone who is smuggling or selling smuggled goods, there is a UK 24-hour confidential freephone number: 0800 901 901.

What is the role of customs officers now the internal borders are effectively opened?

In 1990 a Council statement indicated they:

- levy customs duties and Community agricultural levies on goods originating in third countries;
- levy national excise duties and VAT for imports;
- apply patent systems and Community and national quotas;
- apply zoosanitary and phytosanitary norms;
- collect international trade data;
- apply export restrictions;
- apply 'protective' restrictions, eg to prevent drug and arms smuggling.

The 1992 Mutual Customs Assistance (MAG92) Group was formed to promote even closer co-operation between Community customs. The MATTHAEUS and Tax Training Programmes enable cross-border work experience exchanges of customs officials.

What about VAT?

Differing VAT rates in the EU cause significant problems in spite of harmonization – all states agreed a 15 per cent minimum rate in 1992, and discussions continue on how best to reform the system. The 1996 Commission Green Paper, *A Common System of VAT*, proposed that there should be a single place of registration and taxation for enterprises; that taxation of all transactions should be based on the origin principle; that rates should be further harmonized; and that a new mechanism for collecting and redistributing VAT as between Member States should be set up. Discussions continue, and the technically transitional system continues to apply. Under this a declaration of EC imports is included in a business's periodical VAT return, and the information required varies according to the size of the enterprise. For an interim period, VAT continues to be payable in the country of sale, not origin (cars and distance sales are different, and VAT is payable in the country of registration or consumption). A common information system and EU co-operation in relation to VAT and excise duties (VIES) operates.

Do quotas cause a problem?

There are no inter-EU quantitative restrictions or quotas on goods. Quotas or quantitative restrictions remain, however, to protect the Community relative to third-country trade, but these are increasingly limited, due to the effect of World Trade Organization (WTO) agreements.

What is the Community attitude to customs controls?

The Community considers that these can constitute a significant economic constraint by imposing unnecessary burdens and costs on industry arising from formalities, and transport and handling charges for goods crossing frontiers, besides constituting a barrier to the free movement of persons and goods travelling within the EU. Negotiations have continued for many years to streamline formalities and cut the costs of intra-EU trade. Harmonization of the codes on information to be declared and other requirements has been achieved between Member States – and the harmonized system, *Tariff Intégré Communautaire* or Integrated Community Tariff (TARIC), and the Single Administrative Document (SAD), were the result. On 1 January 1993 all customs documentation for intra-EU trade was abolished, and on 29 March 1999 clearer customs transit rules simplifying EU procedures were adopted. The European Customs Code 1992 as amended sets out current customs legislation.

Why is the harmonized system sometimes referred to as the harmonized tariff?

The harmonized system is the tariff that came into effect on 1 January 1988, based on the harmonized commodity description and coding system that replaced the earlier classification system for goods. It set out thousands of codes, which identify products and enable correct customs classification for duty and other requirements. It seeks to satisfy not only customs requirements, but also freight statistics, insurance and other needs of international trade. It has world-wide application.

What is TARIC?

TARIC is the fully numeric, integrated customs tariff produced following revision of Community tariff requirements, which relates to most tariff measures that affect imports from non-EC countries and certain agricultural trade between Member States. TARIC takes account of statistical requirements. The system includes codes for goods, and is geared to enabling computers to read the coded information, facilitating the speedy handling of goods by customs authorities.

What is the Single Administrative Document (SAD)?

The customs procedure codes identify the regime under which goods are travelling, and all the information referred to in TARIC is included in the Single Administrative Document. The layout is designed in accordance with the United Nations layout key for international trade documents and part only of the SAD may be used in a segmented form, without any prior authorization, if in some circumstances no administrative document is in fact required.

The SAD as a multi-purpose document was a significant landmark in facilitating international trade but was abolished on 1 January 1993 for intra-Community trade. Since then it is only needed for goods not in free circulation in the EC, ie imports and exports from third countries.

What about warehousing and storage facilities?

There are harmonized arrangements throughout the EU whereby goods subject to duty may be admitted to a customs warehouse with duty suspension during storage or transfer from warehouse to warehouse, and with warehousing of excisable goods (alcohol, tobacco and mineral oils) being carried out by Tax Warehouses. The same applies to customs-free zones (areas where goods may be imported free of customs duties and VAT, to enable processing by the original importer within the zone, and then exported into the country concerned or re-exported to a third country when, of course, the goods attract the appropriate duty). Limited handling or processing of goods is allowed.

What are carnets?

There are several different kinds of carnet. The most generally used is the ATA carnet, an international customs document issued by chambers of commerce in most major countries throughout the world, which allows temporary importation of goods (for example, samples for exhibitions abroad) free passage through to their destination.

What does the Community Customs Code provide?

The Community Customs Code (1992) (as amended) sets out the general rules, regimes and procedures for goods traded between the EC and third countries, and includes such matters as customs appeal procedures. It collates all existing Community legislation governing trade with third countries, and the application of the Community's customs tariff. It also provides interpretation guidelines. The tariff quota was rationalized and simplified in 1997.

What about the Generalized System of Preferences (GSP)?

In 1994 the simplified regime for generalized tariff preferences in favour of developing countries until 1998 was approved. This has been simplified and improved since. The scope of countries included changes from time to time, thus some countries in Asia and elsewhere have been excluded, and GSP has been extended to some former USSR republics. The list is affected by WTO agreements.

What is the effect of minimal inter-state customs control?

The impact is significant. Transit times and expenses have been significantly reduced.

Since January 1992 the EU has been a single territory for the purposes of the TIR Convention (the Geneva Convention on International Road Transport) and the ATA (the Brussels Convention on the System of Temporary Entry), which facilitated internal frontier crossings.

Enterprises must monitor their markets throughout the EU more closely to check on counterfeits of their own products, which may be more difficult to prevent from circulating. If they sell imported food or pharmaceutical products, they may have to put in more effort to ensure compliance with proper requirements, bearing in mind national provisions may still differ, but they are likely to retain liability for defective products. In general, those trading within the EU (and EEA) benefit from the reduction in formalities, and year on year there has been a significant increase in intra-EU trade. It is expected that further downward pressure will be put on prices as the Euro becomes widely used in the Eurozone, with national differences in VAT rates, for example, becoming more visible.

9 Transport policy

What are the Community's aims with regard to transport policy?

The aims are to eliminate barriers and ensure the freedom to provide haulage and transport services (cross-border and internal), whether by road, sea, inland waterways or by air throughout the EU. Thus Article 71 of the consolidated Treaty of Rome indicates that common transport policy shall set out common rules applicable to international transport to or from the Member States, or passing through one or more of the Member States; the conditions under which non-resident carriers may operate transport services within a Member State; measures to improve transport safety; and any other appropriate provisions.

Transport accounts for over 7 per cent of community gross domestic product (GDP). Member States have been protective of their national carriers, but increased competition and better-organized haulage contractors are seen to reduce transport costs. Transport now consumes more energy than industry in the EU, over 80 per cent of which is for road transport.

What is combined or multi-modal transport?

This is where different forms of transport are used in transporting goods or people from one place to another. Its use is being encouraged by the Community in order to reduce pressures on road transport through the Pilot Actions for Combined Transport (PACT) Programme 1997–2001.

What is the Commission's role?

There have been many provisions relating to transport. The Commission encourages better co-ordinated infrastructure policies in the building of motorways and rail lines between Member States, and has instituted research projects to look at traffic control and hazards. Its competence in transport and safety was confirmed in the Union Treaty 1992, which emphasized the importance of a safe, effective transport infrastructure, taking into account environmental considerations.

The 1994 action plan indicated seven aims:

1. To guarantee correct implementation of Internal Market rules.
2. To establish an integrated transport system.
3. To act to protect the environment.
4. To reinforce safety and security.
5. To improve the protection of transport workers.
6. To work towards the elimination of bilateral agreements, and towards central negotiation of external agreements.
7. To support trans-European networks.

The Common Transport Policy Action Programme for 1998–2004 has priorities that reflect the aims above and include: improving market access and functioning of the transport market; further integrating the importance of the environment in transport initiatives; fair and efficient pricing in transport; safety and improving the quality of services; preparing for the future; and external relations.

There are various programmes such as DRIVE (to improve the management of transport demands), and EURET (to optimize network exploitation and transport logistics), as well as initiatives to promote safety.

What about trans-European networks (TENs)?

Master plans for TENs were first adopted in 1994 and covered land, sea and air infrastructure projects, together with a special funding mechanism through the European Investment Bank. Various priority projects have been started since then, and detailed maps can be obtained from the Commission. Private/public investment partnerships and joint ventures are encouraged to facilitate financing, and large sums have been spent. TENs have been extended to some Central and Eastern European countries.

What has the Commission done for passengers generally?

There are various provisions including the Package Travel Directive 1990, which aims to protect consumers whether travelling for business or private purposes, with precise rules governing the liability of tour operators, who have to accept legal responsibility for services offered. It requires accurate brochures, contracts that include essential terms, and guarantees to ensure reimbursement of travellers in the event of insolvencies.

There is a regulation relating to air transport, establishing common rules for repayment of passengers who have been 'overbooked' and cannot travel as arranged, and passengers are benefiting from the expected lower prices resulting from increased competition. A 1997 Directive increases the liability of air carriers in case of accident.

Various safety provisions apply, but it is generally the Member States that have to ensure there are properly enforced measures. There are provisions relating to vehicle and other insurance, and encouragement for access to public transport for persons with reduced mobility. Plans continue to develop the Citizens' Network (local and regional public passenger transport).

What are the provisions relating to travel insurance?

There have been various Directives to approximate the laws of Member States and impose duties on motor insurance bureaux to guarantee settlement of claims in their territory. These include cover for injury to property as well as personal injury, provision of single premium cover for use of motor vehicles throughout the EU, to ensure that Member States give an appropriate level of cover to car accident victims, and to ensure that liability for injury to passengers is also covered by insurance. There is a 1984 Tourist Directive on Insurance for the provision of assistance to persons travelling, and various conventions cover air and sea compensation provisions (see Chapter 12).

What about co-ordinating time changes?

The co-ordination of time in different Member States affects the transport sector more than any other. The 1997 Directive set the dates and times for the beginning and end of summer time until 2001. Work continues to harmonize times throughout the EU on a more permanent basis, and a further report is to be produced.

What have been the most significant barriers relating to liberalization of transport services?

The main barrier concerned restrictions on cabotage. Cabotage means the provision of an internal service, ie carrying goods or passengers within one EU country by an enterprise registered in another EU country. Elimination of this was regarded as essential to achieve a Single Market in transport.

Transport services are best explained sector by sector.

Road haulage

Since1 July 1998 road cabotage has been completely liberalized.

The 1988 Regulation on Liberalization of Road Haulage was followed by approval in 1990 of the principle of freedom to provide road transport services Community-wide, ie liberalization of road haulage with a system of Community licences aimed at abolishing inter-state road haulage permits. A gradual increase in road haulage authorization permit quotas preceded full liberalization of cabotage.

The EU countries without a toll system may eventually introduce the Euro-regional disk system with variable maximum duty rates for utility vehicles of over a specified tonnage, which will then be able to move freely in participating countries. The revenue to pay for the infrastructure and other costs will be fairly distributed in those countries, with special provisions for border regions.

EU Member States may impose infrastructure user charges for other vehicles, including private cars, and the EU countries that presently have a motorway user charge system may keep it. Since 1 January 1995 (with some derogations), Member States have applied (at least) a minimum tax on vehicles, and a 1998 White Paper on Transport Policy included the principle of payment according to use.

What about other areas?

The Commission has achieved considerable standardization; examples include drivers' hours; recognition of diplomas and qualifications of operators; mutual recognition of driving licences and a European driving licence valid throughout the EU; standards for truck lengths; and the reduction of speed limits for lorries and buses to conserve fuel. Negotiations continue to achieve a 'vehicle passport' by way of a harmonized vehicle registration certificate valid throughout the EU.

What about roadworthiness and safety?

Periodic roadworthiness tests are required for heavy goods vehicles, buses, light goods vehicles and private vehicles. Safety standards are being revised all the time. Recent provisions will require the phased introduction of new-style tachographs to monitor both time spent behind the wheel and speed for lorries and coaches to reduce tiredness causing accidents. Work continues on random roadside inspections of commercial vehicles.

What about the transport of dangerous goods?

The United Nations Recommendations on the Transport of Dangerous Goods (UN Recommendations) form the basis of the main European provisions relating to the transport of dangerous goods by road (ADR agreement) and rail (RID regulations), and international agreements for their transport by sea or air. ADR and RID are implemented in the EU by two framework Directives.

Road passenger transport

What is the position on passenger transport by road?

Since 1993 buses and coaches used to carry the same passengers throughout a journey or carrying workers and students in border areas (ie, 'closed door tours') have been able to operate entirely in another Member State, and since 1 January 1996 tourist coach cabotage has been allowed.

What about road safety?

Much is being done to increase the safety in road infrastructures with Community assistance through the TENs and regional development programmes.

Road safety policy is set against a background of approximately 44,000 deaths and 1.5 million people injured annually on EU roads in the late 1990s (a 14 per cent improvement on 1987 numbers). Seventy-five per cent of travel is by private car. Statistically, the UK is the safest country in the EU to drive in, and Portugal the most dangerous. There are various Directives and safety standards, eg on tyre treads, seat belts and speed limiters, and a Community database of road traffic accident statistics (CARE). An overall speed limit of 120 kilometres per hour, and 30 kilometres per hour in residential areas, remains under discussion. (Presently speed limits differ between Member States, sometimes even varying according to whether it is winter or summer.)

What is the effect of road transport policy?

The effect on road hauliers seems to be that if they are well organized they can take advantage of the liberalized market in road haulage, because they should be able to increase the utilization of their vehicles, and so, incidentally, reduce pollution and costs overall. However great distortions remain with regard to local fuel costs, for example, which are, particularly in the UK, causing national hauliers difficulties in respect of competitive pricing, thereby losing them customers to their EU competitors. Simpler customs and excise procedures shorten journey times, minimize delays and cut costs, but attempts to harmonize fiscal matters such as fuel taxation and motorway tolls should be watched. The proposals for eco-taxes could well impact harshly on road transport. Bilateral talks with Eastern European countries on increased market access and transit provision could have significant effects, as these countries' labour costs remain lower.

Further information with regard to road haulage may be obtained from the European Commission, the Road Haulage Association, the International Road Freight Office or the Freight Transport Association (see Appendix III).

Rail transport

What is the position on railway transport?

There is a perceived need to develop railway transport generally with a European network of high-speed trains, also covering EFTA and EU applicant countries. Thus European railway companies plan to build 30,000 km of high-speed track within the next 20 years.

The Community's long term strategy, adopted in 1991 was to provide:

- access for any railway operator to any railway infrastructure;
- that railways should be operated on commercial principles (and not be restricted to the operation of railway services);
- for aid to certain railway operations and to modify the rules governing the public service obligation under which states subsidize socially desirable, but uneconomic, railway lines;
- for the removal of historic debts; and
- for the separation of responsibility for the railway infrastructure from the operation of railway services so as to facilitate privatization, which itself is a national matter.

Much has been done since then. Measures or proposals include: the setting up of a single European rail authority; setting up railfreight freeways; the harmonization of standards of technical railway machinery (ie track gauges and equipment) to provide compatibility, so that trains, goods and passengers can move more easily across national borders; the breakdown of railway infrastructure capacities and taxes payable for use; the harmonization of licenses for rail operating companies; and the application of competition rules to rail transport. Proposals and provisions also define essential requirements in respect of health and safety, the environment, and customer protection.

In October 1999, the EU transport ministers agreed the strategy whereby access would be extended to the trans-European Freight railway network, and which should lead to full liberalization in the sector. This follows previous initiatives that built on the 1996 White Paper on Rail Strategies.

This had four priorities:

1. To reform railway finances.
2. To introduce market forces into rail by extending rights of access to infrastructures to new operators.
3. To consider the application of contracts with regard to non-commercial services between Member States and rail companies.
4. To create an integrated European rail network.

A 1999 Commission Communication and a draft directive dealt with various problems which prevent an integrated cross border network, for example operating systems, technical standards and signalling equipment. These problems will be addressed using financial cost assistance, ensuring a clear division between rail infrastructure management and rail service operations. The paper also included a definition of the trans-European Freight Network. The new proposals emphasized the need to encourage competitiveness and maintain high safety standards.

What about combined road-rail transport?

The regulation on combined road-rail transport enables hauliers to take goods to a train, pick them up in another Member State, and then take them on to their final destination. In addition an EC/United Nations agreement on road-rail transport, aimed at creating a legal framework for combined transport, was opened for signature in 1991. A 1992 Council Directive introduced tax relief provisions to encourage combined transport, seen as addressing road congestion and pollution.

What is the effect of rail transport policy?

Increasing competition in the rail transport sector should cut costs and increase efficiency, but this may be offset by increasing general and energy costs, and reductions in state subsidies. Nevertheless, encouragement of combined road-rail and inter-modal transport could benefit enterprises transporting goods across Europe.

It is interesting to note that a Community of European Railways has been formed, consisting of the general managers of the railway companies making up the railway network of the EU plus Norway and Switzerland. Their specific aim is to improve rail services Community-wide. Discussions limiting the concept of public service should be monitored.

Further information may be obtained from the European Commission, the British Railways Board, the Department of the Environment, Transport and the Regions (DETR), and the Freight Transport Association (see Appendix III).

Air transport

What is the Commission's attitude towards civil aviation and air transport?

The liberalization of civil air transport programme was complete by April 1997. There has been a series of liberalization measures, which gradually extended outwards from regional services, but this sector has to be looked at from a global perspective, with the competitiveness of the EU operators in mind. A Committee of Wise Men was set up who made recommendations as to proposals and progress in 1994, and their conclusions were adopted by the Council of Ministers. These were:

- Air safety rules should be harmonized internationally, and implemented.
- Support should be given to carriers to enable reductions in costs to enable them to remain competitive world-wide.
- Fair competition should be introduced, which should lead to reductions in customer costs.
- Liberalization of air transport should be facilitated by defining the state aid rules.

Since then action has been taken to strengthen the global competitiveness of EU civil aviation.

What is the position now?

Various provisions cover such matters as: fares; capacity-sharing – to set minimum capacity-sharing percentages to enable carriers to offer greater capacity to all airports (although bilateral arrangements allowing greater capacity-sharing were not affected); opening major routes to direct competition between airlines; and facilitating multi-stop services by combining routes. There are provisions concerning computer reservation systems, tariffs, ground handling services, licensing of national airlines, insurance requirements, air traffic management and airport charges, and complaints and hearings on air transport.

The Commission Report, *The European Aviation Industry: From Single Market to Worldwide Challenge*, published in May 1999, concluded that the Single Market in aviation is now achieved, and indicated that no further state aid can generally be justified. It also concluded that the result of the liberalization has been that prices have reduced and employment in the sector has increased by almost 490,000 in 1996. However, competition from third-country carriers remains significant.

What about the protection of services to peripheral regions?

Public service obligations may be imposed on airlines following consultation with the Commission and the parties involved.

What about air congestion and air safety?

Air congestion has placed pressure on air traffic control systems in the EU as major airports are already operating close to their maximum capacity. Flow management introduced for safety reasons causes delays and ill feeling. Particular attention is being paid to the harmonization and integration of the European Air Control and Management System under a 1994 Council Resolution, together with the development of global systems of satellite navigation, measures for transport security and the defence of EU interests *vis-à-vis* third countries. A 1996 Commission White Paper, *Freeing European Air Space*, was followed by proposals that EU states become members of a restructured Eurocontrol, the European Organization for the Safety of Air Navigation (established by an international convention in 1960 relating to co-operation for air safety navigation, whose membership includes the EU and some third countries).

Air safety is an area where harmonization of standards is moving ahead. There are calls for a Community Civil Aviation Authority, to cover certification of fitness to fly for planes, air traffic control, training and security. A Directive under discussion would increase international air safety checks, and employee working conditions are being considered, particularly in the context of flying times, as is a European system for reports of air incidents.

What about noise?

There are EC noise limitation provisions to prevent registration in EU states of aircraft that do not comply.

What about computer reservation systems and ground handling?

These are controlled by the European Civil Aviation Conference (an inter-governmental body of over 20 European states) rules, linked to an EC Council regulation on the use of computer reservation systems. There are common rules to compensate passengers denied boarding because of overbooking.

The 1999 Directive on the Liberalization of Ground Handling Services is to be progressively introduced.

What is the effect of air transport policy?

It is beneficial to the consumer, in that internal liberalization and international discussions relating to 'open skies' agreements should lead to lower fares and better services. Internationally agreed standards and monitoring should lead to greater safety.

Further information may be obtained from the European Commission, the DETR International Aviation Directorate and the Civil Aviation Authority (see Appendix III).

Maritime transport

Is there a common policy for maritime transport?

Sea shipping was originally excluded from the Treaty of Rome, although inland transport was included. However, about 90 per cent by volume of EU imports and exports are carried by sea, and recent environmental disasters caused by ships have led the Council to make a statement on maritime safety and the prevention of pollution, and the Commission to adopt a communication on safe seas. The maritime transport sector in the EU is in a time of crisis and decline, so the Council has urged the Commission to seek greater reciprocal access to ports in third countries, and more rigorously to enforce safety standards of third-country flagships sailing in Community waters. The policy is based on maintaining safety, know-how and capacity levels; and finally agreeing and implementing the EUROS shipping register. Two Commission communications, *A New Approach to Maritime Strategy 1996* and *External Relations in the Field of Maritime Transport*, look at the shipping industry and reciprocal access for EU shipping to third-country ports.

What about liberalization?

The Community's move towards liberalization is progressing.

Following four significant measures in 1986 (see below) and a 1992 Regulation on liberalization of maritime transport services in the EC, cabotage was made generally effective from 1 January 1993 between mainland ports in the EU, or from a mainland port to offshore installations. There is a phased programme of liberalization for some ports, with some Greek services enjoying exemptions until 1 January 2004. It should be noted that the State of Registry restrictions on the nationality of crews apply with the exception of island cabotage, where, for a transitional period, the host state can apply nationality requirements.

What were the original four measures?

They concerned: the Freedom to Provide Services Regulation for goods and passengers, both between Member States only and between Member States and third countries (ie not from port to port within one Member State); the Competition Regulation applying competition provisions to maritime transport, including liner shipping conferences (groups of shipping lines serving particular markets under joint agreements); the introduction of a procedure to control unfair pricing by non-Community shipowners and anti-dumping in relation to maritime transport, allowing a Community levy to be imposed on third-country carriers found to be implementing unfair pricing practices that adversely affected Community services; and a 1986 Council Regulation to institute a procedure to safeguard free access to ocean trade cargoes for Community ships. This reinforced the Community's negotiating position by enabling Community action to be taken to prevent attempts by non-EC countries to restrict the access of EC carriers to ocean trade.

What is the EUROS register?

This is a Community registration system for ships, with strict standards (EUROS), giving the right to fly the Community flag and to EU cabotage, ie the provision of services within the EU states for ships under 6,000 grt (gross recorded tonnage) flying EU flags.

Is the Commission looking at other aspects of shipping?

Yes. Measures agreed or under consideration include: the ability to transfer a ship's registry from one Member State to another, state subsidies for national shipping, ideas for improving the competitive position of Community shipping services and the use of waste reception facilities in ports.

It keeps under review other matters such as the shipment of hazardous waste, and collects information about third-country carriers by noting their shipping activity in various areas.

The whole area of maritime policy in Europe, taking into account the protection of the maritime environment, development of high-technology ships and the working of the mineral resources of the sea, is regarded as of increasing importance (see also under Environmental policy, Chapter 17).

There are various proposals and measures: on the implementation or updating of standards of ship safety; on pollution prevention and minimum living and working conditions on ships entering EU waters; on ship inspectors and minimum training levels for crews, and requirements that crew members can communicate with each other; and on mandatory inspection and monitoring in EU ports of a proportion of ships in respect of international maritime safety rules. In particular, the International Maritime Organization Code on Maritime Safety now applies in the EU. This covers such matters as safety policies, precautions, provisions and operational plans, together with a certificate of compliance issued by the flag state. It should be noted that negotiations continue in the World Trade Organization on liberalization of maritime transport.

Inland waterways

What regulations affect inland waterways?

A combined Road Haulage and Shipping by Inland Waterways Directive has been in force since 1987, which removed some restrictions for own-account road haulage operators. The Inland Waterways Cabotage 1991 Regulation set out the conditions for non-resident carriers transporting goods or passengers on inland waterways in Member States. This effectively allows any national of a Member State access to domestic inland waterway transport throughout the European Community. In 1989 a Regulation on Structural Improvements in Inland Waterway Transport was adopted. The role of inland waterways in the European mainland states, already important, is likely to grow significantly as trade with Eastern Europe increases.

There is a 1996 Regulation on Common Rules applicable to the transport of goods or passengers by inland waterways between Member States, which seeks to establish freedom to provide such services, various related proposals and provisions to reduce overcapacity and encourage investment in inland waterway terminals. There is a useful ship scrapping scheme.

What are the likely effects of the measures taken on maritime matters?

The general purpose of policies has been to reduce transport costs to everyone's benefit. The whole area of maritime inland, ocean-going and coastal transport is very specialized, and further information may be obtained from the General Council of British Shipping, the European Commission and the DETR (see Appendix III).

10 Competition and public procurement policy

Competition policy

What is competition policy?

This question is not as easy as it seems. I define it at its simplest as the policy to introduce procedures to control anti-competitive practices, or to control the abuse of market-dominant positions that tend to distort competition, and to improve the competitiveness of the EU globally. Competition control is by way of either preventing or regulating monopolies, by policing mergers, or by controlling agreements to carry out anti-competitive practices that distort trade in the Single Market, through legislation and decisions.

Please note that since implementation of the Amsterdam Treaty, the Article numbers that relate to competition policy have changed in the consolidated Treaty of Rome.

What is the Community's attitude towards competition policy?

Competition policy is regarded as a vital tool in the functioning of the Single Market in a changing economic environment.

The 1993 White Paper, *Growth, Competitiveness and Employment – The Challenges and Way Forward into the 21st Century*, set out long-term Community policies to achieve growth and competitiveness leading to greater employment. It urged the need to apply competition rules more rigorously to ensure proper working of the Internal Market, eg with regard to state aid, and to prevent abuses by large companies. Since then there have been various studies, proposals and provisions, and the progressive application of free-competition provisions to sectors where monopolies, frequently state aided, were normal, eg telecommunications and trans-European networks.

Has EU policy on state aid developed with the Single Market?

Yes. Rules controlling state aid are being progressively strength-ened, with new procedural rules being adopted in 1999. The Commission monitors national and regional aid policies to ensure compliance with Structural Fund, Internal Market and treaty rules. Restructuring aid rules have been revised, and there are pro-visions to encourage environmental improvement aid beneficial to citizens, but without anti-competitive implications. Aid to pro-mote cultural heritage and conservation, and the audio-visual sec-tor, and to support small and medium-sized firms, is encouraged.

The ban on operating aid to help 'lame duck' industries contin-ues and ECJ cases have confirmed that relevant aid should not be granted prior to Commission scrutiny to ensure compliance. There remains considerable dissatisfaction with the operation of state aid rules in the different Member States, and uncertainty as to the effect of the WTO codes on subsidies.

Is reform of the current system needed?

As the Competition Directorate of the Commission is felt to be over-stretched, the April 1999 White Paper proposed reforms to reduce its workload to enable it to investigate the worst abuses of competition laws.

Proposals seek to decentralize enforcement procedures, giving national competition authorities and courts joint responsibility with the Commission for implementation of Article 81 (formerly Article 85) of the Rome Treaty. There is already shared responsi-bility in respect of Article 82 (formerly Article 86) matters. Obligations regarding notification of agreements would be reduced under the proposals, which are projected to be in place by 2003.

It is interesting to note that since the UK's Competition Act 1998, all EU countries have domestic competition legislation based on the EU competition provisions.

What about competition policy and small and medium-sized enterprises (SMEs)?

The stated aim is to use competition policy to protect SMEs. To this end, the Commission may take action against: refusals to sup-ply products essential to the operations of an SME; the policy of charging low prices in order to squeeze out SMEs; otherwise improperly entering a market in a position of power and using that power improperly to squeeze out competition. The

Community has pinpointed the development and support of SMEs as central to the employment initiative and in this area the Commission encourages 'soft' state aid aimed at incentives, support for SMEs, staff mobility, training and R&D.

What is the attitude to public-private partnerships and concessions?

The Commission produced a consultation paper in early 1999 on transparency, competition and Single Market implications of such agreements.

What is the history of the Community's competition policy?

The Commission derives most of its powers in this area from Articles 81 (prohibition of anti-competitive practices and concerted practices) and 82 (abuse of dominant positions) together with Article 86 (formerly Article 90) of the Rome Treaty. Case law has extended and widely defined Community provisions. With regard to coal and steel, there were specific powers to control mergers in the original Treaty, and special competition rules apply in the fields of nuclear energy, agriculture and for some forms of transport. As Articles 81 and 82 are so important, the text is set out below. It should be noted that Community rules on competition (and state aid) were mirrored in the EEA Agreement, and the Commission works with the EEA Surveillance Authority (ESA) in this area within the context of a complicated set of rules.

Article 81 (formerly 85)
1. The following shall be prohibited as incompatible with the common market: all agreements between undertakings, decisions by associations of undertakings and concerted practices which may affect trade between Member States and which have as their object or effect the prevention, restriction or distortion of competition within the common market, and in particular those which:
   (a) directly or indirectly fix purchase or selling prices or any other trading conditions;
   (b) limit or control production, markets, technical development, or investment;
   (c) share markets or sources of supply;
   (d) apply dissimilar conditions to equivalent transactions with other trading parties, thereby placing them at a competitive disadvantage;
   (e) make the conclusion of contracts subject to acceptance by the other parties of supplementary obligations that, by their nature or according to commercial usage, have no connection with the subject of such contracts.

2. Any agreements or decisions prohibited pursuant to this Article shall be automatically void.
3. The provisions of paragraph 1 may, however, be declared inapplicable in the case of:
   - any agreement or category of agreements between undertakings
   - any decision or category of decisions by associations of undertakings
   - any concerted practice or category of concerted practices which contributes to improving the production or distribution of goods or to promoting technical or economic progress, while allowing consumers a fair share of the resulting benefits and which does not
   (a) impose on the undertakings concerned restrictions that are not indispensable to the attainment of these objectives;
   (b) afford such undertakings the possibility of eliminating competition in respect of a substantial part of the products in question.

Article 82 (formerly 86)
Any abuse by one or more undertakings of a dominant position within the common market or in a substantial part of it shall be prohibited as incompatible with the common market in so far as it may affect trade between Member States.

Such abuse may in particular, consist in:
(a) directly or indirectly imposing unfair purchase or selling prices or other unfair trading conditions;
(b) limiting production, markets or technical development to the prejudice of consumers;
(c) applying dissimilar conditions to equivalent transactions with other trading parties, thereby placing them at a competitive disadvantage;
(d) making the conclusion of contracts subject to acceptance by the other parties of supplementary obligations that, by their nature or according to commercial usage, have no connection with the subject of such contracts.

So what is the first distinction between Articles 81 and 82?

Generally Article 81 applies to agreements – written or verbal – between two businesses (which may, incidentally, be two companies in the same group provided they are operated separately) where such an agreement might affect trade between Member States.

Article 82 applies to companies that hold a dominant share of the market, and that abuse their dominant position in some way. The Commission explained how a relevant market should be defined for this purpose in its 1997 Notice.

What are horizontal and vertical agreements?

With regard to restrictive agreements, price fixing for example, it is important to understand the difference between horizontal and vertical agreements. Horizontal agreements are those between enterprises acting at the same level of trade, eg between different manufacturers of similar products (see the Dyestuffs case 1972 ECR). Vertical agreements occur where there are 'down the line' restrictions or agreements, eg where a manufacturer imposes price restraints on resale by wholesalers or retailers. A concerted practice is where two or more undertakings act, without any specific agreement, to co-operate in a practical way, eg by increasing their prices at the same time. It is sometimes difficult to distinguish a concerted practice from an agreement, but provisions are widely, rather than narrowly, construed.

Are some agreements that should come within the provisions exempt?

Yes. To mitigate the effects of these provisions, to direct the focus towards more important issues, and to limit the workload of the Commission, under a Council Regulation in 1965 the Commission was empowered to adopt block exemption regulations, which defined categories of agreement that could be exempted from the application of competition rules. There are various communications, notices, regulations and cases that assist, and the most recent regulations agreed in September 1999 provide that vertical restraints between producers and distributors that do not exceed a 30 per cent market share will come under a general block exemption and so will not need to be notified (see below). However, it is a very complex area, and expert legal advice is a necessity.

How do block exemptions work?

Block exemptions remove the need to notify or submit for scrutiny by the Commission agreements that are strictly within the competition provisions so that even if otherwise the agreements would be within the terms of Article 81, they are still valid and enforceable. The block exemptions are subject to time limits so as to ensure periodic revision. There are exemptions relating to exclusive purchasing and distribution agreements (important in the context of an estimated 100,000-plus exclusive distribution agreements, and over 500,000 exclusive purchasing agreements in the EU), as well as the special arrangements for vehicle sales, beer and petrol service stations and franchising. The Technology Transfer

Agreements Block Exemption Regulation 1996 replaced the previous patents and know-how block exemptions, and introduced significant changes with useful advice as to permissible clauses.

Vertical restraints were the subject of a 1998 White Paper, and two 1999 regulations provide for a new, reforming, broadly drafted block exemption by the Commission for all vertical restraints covering intermediate or finished products or services, provided the market share does not exceed 30 per cent. It also applies to certain retailers. One Regulation excludes restrictions such as resale price maintenance or other trade (eg territorial protection) clauses. The other Regulation exempts all qualifying vertical agreements from notifying prior to individual exemption, and enables retrospective exemption.

Export bans are particularly disliked by reason of their effect on EU trade and their anti-competitive aspects. For further information concerning block exemptions, see Chapter 14.

What about agreements of minor importance to EU trade?

In 1986 (amended in 1994) the Commission introduced guideline definitions in terms of market share and world-wide turnover in a notice on agreements of minor importance, which are generally excluded from Community competition control as being unlikely to affect trade significantly between Member States. Further provisions and guidance have been issued since.

Articles 81 and 82 appear to be very far-reaching. Is there much case law?

Yes, and this must be carefully analysed when agreements, whether formal or informal, that might come within its scope are being considered. The ECJ judgements in both the development and the interpretation of EC competition law have been significant. Thus for example in Brasserie du Pecheur-Factortame 1996 the ECJ held that a state might be liable in respect of damage caused by any breach of Community law regardless of the state body whose action or omission is responsible for the breach. Detailed guidelines with particular reference to state aid have been produced.

What are the sanctions to enforce competition provisions?

The Competition Directorate takes a robust attitude and penalizes those in breach of the competition provisions, with those abusing (not merely holding) a dominant position being fined sums running into millions of Euros. There are powers to fine heavily in cases of infringement, and fines have been imposed on companies (ranging from petrochemical and pharmaceutical manufacturers to toy manufacturers) for operating cartels, fixing common prices and conditions of sale, refusing to meet warranty claims on goods, infringements concerning parallel imports, and many other fields of competition provision breach. Large companies have to be particularly careful, and Member States are not immune from actions for infringement. For example, Audi (a Volkswagen subsidiary) was fined ECU 102 million for improperly ordering their Italian motor vehicle dealers not to sell to Austrians and Germans.

Recent investigations have involved Deutsche Post (in respect of cross-subsidies from monopoly profits) and Coca-Cola (in respect of loyalty payments). In July 1999 British Airways was fined ECU 6.8 million for abuse of their dominant position for wrongfully offering extra commission to travel agents who promoted BA services instead of those of competitor airlines. A new method of determining fines not linked to the turnover of the offending company was announced in December 1997, with fines more related to the gravity of the offence.

What about joint ventures?

To deal with this increasingly popular structure, the Commission widened the scope of applications for exemptions in 1994 by introducing a new short-form notification for joint ventures having only a minor impact within the EU, ie with a turnover or assets below ECU 100 million. The Commission guidelines clarified the distinction between joint ventures that are essentially mergers (concentrative joint ventures, and so dealt with under the merger regulation) and co-operative joint ventures, covered by Article 81. The provisions required more information to be given than previously. Further consultations continue concerning alterations to joint venture as well as to merger regulations, with procedural improvements suggested for co-operative joint ventures falling within Article 81.

What is the policy relating to merger control?

Enterprises planning a merger that might come within the competition provisions have to pre-notify the Commission. The 1989 Merger Control Regulation on the Control of Concentrations between Undertakings set out the provisions that enabled the Commission to control relevant mergers, stop them altogether, or even order that they be unscrambled where they breach competition provisions. Relevant mergers are those where resulting concentrations would have an effect on the Community. Other mergers are unaffected, ie those that do not affect adversely the market in the goods or services concerned. In any event a merger may be allowed if it would improve significantly the EU's competitive position relative to foreign competition, or if it would benefit consumers, or is in the public interest.

The Merger Regulation 1989 has been amended to simplify, explain and extend the rules. It now includes co-operative full function joint ventures (those whose lead to stand-alone undertakings) within the scope and procedures of the Merger Control Regulation.

What about take-overs?

Whereas control of take-overs is seen as meriting Community treatment, yet there has been difficulty in agreeing the rules that should apply. The latest draft Directive (based on UK provisions) on take-overs is a proposal for a European Parliament and Council Directive on Company Law concerning take-over bids, which provides minimum guidelines for the conduct of take-overs. It includes a framework of common principles and general requirements to be implemented through more detailed national rules as to protection of minority shareholders after the purchase, set time limits and information requirements, together with clarification as to which regulating authority should take jurisdiction in cross-border take-overs. It was blocked by Spain (displeased over continuing difficulties in respect of Gibraltar) in June 1999.

Do the competition provisions apply to publicly owned companies?

Publicly and privately owned companies are equally subject to competition rules, although sometimes restrictions on competition may be justified on public benefit grounds. Thus Article 86 of the Treaty extends the operations of Articles 81 and 82 to any action by Member States whereby either public or private enterprises are given exclusive or special rights. This means that the Commission has competition jurisdiction over grants (local or national), the write-off of losses for tax purposes, and state aids or subsidies of any sort where they are regarded as giving an unfair advantage to a particular sector with anti-competitive Community-wide effects. Proposals or amendments relating to state aid have to be notified to the Commission, and there is a special procedure to deal with these. The Commission may take action under Article 90 against

Member States if they grant exclusive or special rights to certain firms in breach of the competition rules, and can make decisions addressed to individual states, or even issue Directives (which are directed to all Member States).

Proper compliance with competition provisions in public procurement policies is seen as important in the Single Market. Competition provisions have been used to encourage harmonization in social affairs provisions and to encourage liberalization in, for example, the air and rail transport and telecommunication sectors; but dissatisfaction still remains as to the way in which some countries construe their competition obligations.

What if companies or individuals wish to complain about anti-competitive action?

They can write to the European Commission Directorate General of Competition, but it would be wise to take further advice first, ideally from a specialist in competition law, which is complex. The national competition authorities may help and, in the UK, the Department of Trade Action Single Market (tel: 020 7215 4212; fax: 020 7215 4489) is a useful first stop. Competition rules can be applied directly by national courts, and damages may then be available to the applicant. This is not the case where the complaint is made to the Commission for Commission action to be taken.

Does the European Court of Justice have a role to play in competition?

Yes. Those appealing against the Commission's decisions apply to the ECJ, which can confirm, increase, reduce or even cancel fines or penalties imposed by Commission decisions, or may force the Commission to act where it has not done so. The ECJ has interpreted the existing provisions widely, and case law must be watched closely. For example, the Court has held that an enterprise with a task of general public interest may be able to impose 'even an exclusion from all competition' clause if this is necessary to enable it to carry out its task (as in the D'Almeno ruling in the IJM Co case 1994, which concerned an exclusive purchase clause imposed by a regional electricity company).

The European Court of First Instance was set up principally to assist with the competition workload of the European Court, and a 1992 Directive helped by clarifying and extending the jurisdiction of national courts in matters other than transport, and coal and steel. Recent proposals for reform of the procedural system for competition cases are aimed at further decentralization.

Does the Commission have extra-territorial jurisdiction in respect of competition?

Essentially, competition provisions should be regarded as territorial in scope. However, the increasingly global economic aspects of trade have led to a perceived need to apply competition rules extra-territorially. This applies generally to third-country markets where anti-competitive practices effectively close them to EU enterprises, eg Japan and south-east Asia. National protective provisions are increasingly being considered in a global context at the WTO, which already has codes covering, for example, restrictive trade and public procurement practices, and an arbitration procedure for settling trade disputes. It should be noted that the European Court has ruled that the Commission may prosecute foreign companies for anti-competitive practices carried out outside the Community that have an adverse effect on trade, eg on markets or prices in Member States, *even if* they have no presence in the EU. The supply of goods from abroad has been taken to constitute a sufficient basis for jurisdiction to be taken. Enforcement of sanctions extra-territorially can be difficult, and extra-territorial jurisdiction is limited to the extent that it is permitted under international law, although some countries (eg the US) take a wide view in respect of their own authorities.

Public procurement policy

What is public procurement?

It is the purchase, under contract, of commodities, goods, works or services by public administrations. For the purpose of the Directives these include state, government or associations governed by public law, or similar bodies formed by regional or local authorities.

Public procurement is important because the Commission has estimated that such contracts – including those placed by state-owned companies – account for over 11.5 per cent of the total Community GDP (1996 figures); and in practice governments still tend to take a nationalistic view, giving large contracts to local firms, and using public purchasing as an economic tool to foster their domestic policies.

What is the EU's policy?

Agreed by all Member States, the EU policy is to open up public procurement, ie to encourage Member States to take tenders from firms throughout the Community, and to award contracts to the best contender (not necessarily from their own country). There are continuing difficulties in ensuring compliance with the public procurement provisions, because public procurement contracts are financially and politically sensitive issues. Various Commission reports, action plans and provisions have sought to solve these national preferences, which are now complicated by international considerations.

Is public procurement policy limited to the EU?

No. In 1979 the Community countries plus the European Free Trade Association (EFTA) countries, the USA, Canada, Japan, Israel, Hong Kong and Singapore signed the Agreement on Government Procurement (the GPA), which was intended to encourage international competition for supply. This was extended by a WTO Agreement on Government Procurement contracts within the WTO, which came into effect on 1 January 1996 in the present EC countries, the USA, Canada, Israel, Japan, Korea, Norway, Aruba, Liechtenstein and Switzerland, with others expected to join. It followed the EC rules closely, albeit with different thresholds, and covered procurement contracts for supplies, works and services by public bodies in the water, electricity, urban transport, airport and port sectors.

The EC public procurement rules extend to the countries of Central and Eastern Europe which have concluded Europe Agreements with the EU, who have immediate access to EU public procurement contracts; and the EU Member States will eventually have reciprocal access. Reciprocal agreements extend the EU public procurement provisions to the EFTA countries, except Switzerland, which is covered under the WTO agreements.

The European Bank for Reconstruction and Development, which provides finance for many large public procurement projects, has produced useful guidance entitled *Procurement Policies and Rules*.

What sort of EC public procurement Directives have been passed?

Rules were first detailed in the 1970s to encourage more open competition in public procurement contracts, which include contracts put out to tender by government departments and local authorities. Directives covered public supply (contracts for the rental, lease, purchase or hire purchase of goods worth more than a defined threshold), utilities contracts (energy, water, transport and telecommunications) and public works contracts (large building and engineering projects). Changes to value thresholds were by agreement of the Council as from 1 January 1998, and amendments were made to existing Directives in 1998 to co-ordinate procurement procedures of entities operating in the water, energy, transport and telecommunications sectors. Further changes are under discussion. It should be noted that contracts might also be covered by the GATT (General Agreement on Tariffs and Trade) or WTO agreement on government procurement.

Provisions set out three kinds of tender procedure – *open* (anyone can apply), *restricted* (pre-vetted applications only) and *negotiated* (chosen contractors only) – and indicate when each procedure should be used, advertising requirements, time limits, publication of results, the use of European standards and technical specifications, besides the strict award criteria. Member States have to report annually on contracts awarded by public bodies in their territory.

Public works may also be divided into 'priority' and 'residuary' categories, with different procedures applying.

What about complaints of unfairness or contested awards?

Directives also govern the various remedies and complaint procedures. Thus, for example, there are national appeals procedures for infringement cases, together with provisions for damages for victims for public works and supply contracts. Depending on the matter in hand, complaints can be made to or by the Commission, which may give a reasoned opinion or, ultimately, take the offending authority before the European Court.

Can any conclusions be drawn as to the effects of public procurement provisions?

Various Commission reports have reviewed progress, and suggested improvements, to encourage implementation of rules that are not always applied as they should be, and to increase access to information. The Commission Communication in March 1998 noted amendments to policy and provided for the use of framework contracts. The situation remains open for improvement, with the main difficulty often being that small companies cannot always monitor and tender for public procurement contracts despite efforts and grants to make these more available to them. However enterprises able to tender for public procurement contracts should monitor opportunities throughout the EU, the EEA and in the Government Procurement Agreement countries, because if their bid is more competitive, public bodies will find it difficult to prefer home-country applicants. Equally, previously safe home markets will be open to much wider competition from elsewhere. It is frequently expensive to make tenders, so potential tenderers must first thoroughly understand the different award procedures used (open, restricted or negotiated), as they are then more likely to be successful.

A close watch for appropriate invitations to tender may enable maximum time to be taken on preparation and therefore increase chances of success, so the Commission is presently studying ways of improving access to tender information. For example, there is a Common Procurement Vocabulary, which is a classification system to facilitate searches.

It is useful to know that the European standard for attestation was approved as CEN/CENELEC standard EN45503:1996 to award certificates of good procurement practice. Member States are being encouraged to appoint national attestors.

Further information concerning public supply and public works contracts may be obtained from: the European Commission, or its public procurement Web site (www.europa.eu.int/comm/dg15/en/pubproc/index.htm); *Tenders Electronic Daily*, the Official Publications Office of the EC, *Official Journal* ('S' Series), or the regional chamber of commerce (see Appendix III).

11 Taxation

Policy objectives

What are the EU's aims with regard to taxation?

The provisions governing Community taxation policy were originally set out in the Rome Treaty.

Article 90 (previously Article 95) prohibits internal discrimination in indirect or direct taxation between domestic products and similar products from other Member States; and bans Member States from imposing any internal taxation on the products of other Member States that would afford indirect protection to domestic products.

Repayment of internal taxation on exports must not exceed the internal taxation imposed on them whether directly or indirectly (Article 91).

Article 92 states that any tax charges and refunds on inter-EU imports and exports, and countervailing charges, have to be previously approved for a limited period by the Council acting on a qualified majority.

Article 93 concerns harmonization of turnover taxes, excise duties and other forms of indirect taxation to the extent necessary to ensure the establishment and functioning of the Single Market.

What are the more recent policy developments?

Most recently under discussion is a voluntary agreement and a draft code of conduct produced in October 1997 between Member States to end unfair taxation policies within the Member States. It is politically difficult to get formal approval for detailed EU controls, despite the fact that in 1996 the Council formally recognized the benefits of a comprehensive approach to taxation policy, and in a 1996 Report the Commission suggested that greater co-ordination of tax policies of EU countries would contribute to promoting growth and employment, and assist the environment. That report proposed four priorities:

1. Improving the functioning of the Single Market.
2. Controlling fiscal erosion.
3. Promoting employment.
4. Promoting respect for the environment (there has been some concern at the possible impact of 'eco-taxes').

These aims should be distinguished from the Community's previously established goals, which remain: to harmonize VAT, excise and other taxes so as to reduce the differences in indirect taxation rates in Member States. It is argued that without harmonization, no common 'playing field' can exist, and barriers remain. The Commission continues work on proposals that harmonize the bases of business taxation, in order to encourage cross-border investment and activity in the context of competitiveness, and to help SMEs.

Agreement on a common definition of what constitutes unfair or harmful tax competition is close, and would encompass lack of transparency, different treatment of residents and non-residents, and failure to comply with the OECD's standards on price transfers by multinationals.

As to the taxation of individuals, the twin policy principles seem to be to encourage mobility of labour, and to counter improper tax avoidance.

The practical and political impediments to harmonized taxation are enormous, and this is an area where unanimity is still required to pass permanent EU legislation.

What is the current position with regard to goods and services?

The Customs Union means that no tariffs may be imposed on Community goods within the EU, and sets out the common external tariff that all the Member States apply to imports of goods coming in from outside the Community. The Commission may impose anti-dumping duties in appropriate circumstances under the World Trade Organization (WTO) and GATT (General Agreement on Tariffs and Trade) anti-dumping codes.

WTO/GATT provisions include various agreements on trade, barriers and concessions with WTO signatory countries.

As noted above, Article 90 of the Rome Treaty states that member countries must not directly or indirectly impose any internal taxes on goods from other Member States, impose a higher tax burden than exists on their own similar domestic goods, or use internal taxes to protect their own domestic products relative to those of other Member States. This widely interpreted principle has been enforced by the European Court of Justice on a number of occasions.

Direct and corporate taxation

What about direct taxation?

A 1990 Directive abolished withholding taxes, and was aimed at eliminating the double taxation of dividends paid by a subsidiary in one country to its parent company in another Member State. A parent-subsidiary relationship exists where one company holds at least 25 per cent of the capital of a company in another Member State.

What did the Capital Movements Directive 1988 do?

This overrode domestic requirements for advance permission to be obtained for various transfers of ownership of share capital or other transactions in securities, where the movements of capital take place between residents of Member States. However, some transactions may have to be reported within six months to minimize any possible tax avoidance difficulties. There are proposals for an EU draft Directive that would impose a withholding tax on cross-border capital movements if the countries concerned do not share information on intra-EU capital flows.

What about transfer pricing disputes between taxing authorities in different states?

The 1990 Multilateral Arbitration Convention to resolve transfer pricing disputes between taxing authorities in different Member States came into effect on 1 January 1995. Specifically, it concerns the elimination of double taxation of companies established in different Member States, and introduces clear, but complicated rules for the settlement of conflicts between companies and tax authorities about the treatment of transfer prices and company profits.

What about SMEs?

The Commission has stated that it will not attempt harmonization of national tax systems for SMEs, but it has proposed guidelines to encourage:

- the improvement of the tax treatment of self-financing enterprises that are not companies with a share capital;
- the elimination of tax obstacles hindering the acquisition and use of venture capital;
- making SMEs taxable only in the place of their registered office when they operate across borders;
- facilitating transfers of ownership in the event of the death of the owner;
- simplifying provisions so as to avoid dual taxation.

What is the position on taxation of cross-border reorganizations?

Differing definitions for tax purposes of 'corporate profits' as well as differing tax rates still cause difficulties. The 1990 Directive on the common system of taxation applicable to mergers, divisions, transfers of assets and exchanges of shares concerning companies in different Member States provides that a merger or other relevant transaction should not give rise to the taxation of hidden reserves, or to any taxation of capital gains calculated by reference to the difference between the real value of the assets and liabilities transferred and their values for tax purposes. The tax interests of the state of the transferring company are protected. There are provisions relating to the gains of the receiving company, tax neutrality of shareholders and tax avoidance.

What about corporate profits of groups?

Differing rates and definitions for tax purposes of corporate profits mean that harmonization at EU level is difficult to achieve, but could be encouraged by an October 1999 ECJ decision ruling against the differing tax treatment of a German branch and a German subsidiary of Saint Gobain. The 1990 Directive relates to withholding taxes on dividends paid by subsidiaries in one Member State to parent companies in another. The Ruding Report 1992 – a major report by independent experts requested by the Commission on company taxation in the context of the Single Market – urged the need to eliminate discriminatory features of tax systems in Member States that impede cross-border investment and shareholding. It suggested a minimum level of statutory corporate tax rates, and the setting of common rules for determining the minimum tax base. The committee indicated that total harmonization in the short term was not achievable, but that a common system of corporate taxation should be a long-term goal and, in particular, that consideration should be given to how best to encourage investment and reinvestment in SMEs by using tax concessions. The Report has been reflected in recent thinking in the Community. However, it is important also to note the effect of the Capital Movements Directive, which concerns movements of capital taking place between residents of different Member States, as it can affect the situation where there is a transfer of ownership of share capital, for example.

What about income tax?

In 1993 the Commission issued a recommendation that fiscal

equality should be achieved in income taxes for residents and non-residents in the EU so as to encourage mobility of labour, as it is obviously unfair for a non-resident worker to pay different rates of tax from resident workers. Thus if a person earns at least 75 per cent of his total taxable income in a Member State, then he should receive the same tax treatment as a resident. The 'home' state could reserve the right to withhold benefits or certain advantages if these have been granted to him where he works. The recommendation covered employees, professionals, agricultural, commercial and industrial activities, and indicated that provisions should extend to taxation of savings. However, recommendations are of limited effectiveness.

What about withholding tax?

A proposal to impose a 20 per cent withholding tax on investment income, ie a tax that would operate as a tax on income from savings, is deeply unpopular, particularly in the UK where it is feared that it would, if implemented, have a severely adverse effect on the UK international bond market.

There are already some bilateral conventions that prevent double taxation of the same income in more than one state, but do not stop a state taxing an income source differently depending on who receives it. However the ECJ has usefully invoked the anti-discrimination articles of the Rome Treaty (39 and 43) to assist in this regard.

What about social security (ie national insurance in the UK) and other taxes?

The varying rates of taxation needed to service the different levels of social security expenditure and employee costs in the various Member States mean that these are unlikely to be harmonized in the near future, but bilateral agreements exist, and social security payments made out of the home state are governed by various provisions and developing case law (see Chapter 16).

Indirect taxation

What is being done with regard to indirect taxation?

Value Added Tax (VAT) is not simply a tax imposed in the EU, but is also imposed in many other countries around the world. Within the EU, however, the Commission has long been working on a harmonized system for VAT and excise duties, as VAT in particular is subject to many differing complex rules.

The sequence of general EC/EU legislation on VAT is outlined below.

In 1967 a Directive was adopted that required Member States to introduce VAT systems, and in 1977 a further Directive established a uniform basis of assessment.

In 1989 the Commission issued revised proposals for the approximation of VAT rates in Member States with a uniformly based, EU-wide system with only two rates. Reforms resulted in a transitional system in effect since 1 January 1993, which is likely to continue for the foreseeable future because proposals to move towards the definitive VAT regime, whereby the tax is payable at the ultimate destination of the goods or service, are causing some concern, as this system would unduly benefit Germany, which has the greatest population, and is the largest importer of goods from other EU countries.

A 1996 Directive set the minimum standard VAT rate at 15 per cent for a limited period, but this remains current, albeit reduced, and zero rates may be applicable in some countries (eg the UK). Various studies and proposals have been issued since, for example the 1996 Commission Green Paper, *A Common System of VAT – A Programme for the Single Market*, which reviewed the situation, and sought views. In 1998 the Commission proposed a Directive to standardize the rules governing input tax deduction. At the same time the Commission proposed a regulation to allow traders to deduct in their VAT returns input tax incurred in other EU countries. This proposal is intended to replace the discredited eighth Directive refund procedure. In other words the Commission has suggested a form of netting procedure to facilitate recovery of VAT on goods or services purchased in other EU countries by enterprises registered for VAT.

What about VAT on goods?

Since 1 January 1993, there have been effectively no customs posts and no customs documentation for intra-EC trade, so the idea of import and export has been replaced by the principle of acquisition and despatch, with the trader's own accounts providing the recovery mechanism for VAT.

How does this work?

In simple terms, traders' registrations for VAT may be used in a Community-wide context. If they are selling to other EU traders, they must check whether their customers are registered for VAT. If so, they obtain the customers' VAT numbers, and issue invoices in respect of the supply of the goods, ensuring that the supply is shown as being outside the scope of VAT in their own country. They should indicate their own and purchasers' VAT numbers on the invoices. They must complete their normal VAT returns showing the total of their EU supplies, and periodically make statements listing their customers in other EU countries, together with the customers' VAT numbers and the total value of sales to them in the relevant period.

Buying traders must declare the total of their intra-EU purchases in a separate box on their VAT returns, showing their liability for VAT on the purchases, and claim any relevant deductions.

What about VAT for transport services?

Provisions are complicated. There are various provisions and proposals in this area, including a 1994 VAT Simplification Directive on intra-EU transport services. This also simplified the rules relating to goods stored in customs warehouses, transport services, personal luggage, and goods delivered to international (mostly aid) bodies.

The place of taxation in intra-EC trade depends on a number of features such as the country of registration of the supplier and carrier, or even the customer.

What about purchases by private individuals?

These are taxed in the state of purchase, with a tax on transportation costs also levied there. There are various schemes for mail order and distance-selling purchases; for aircraft, boats and motor vehicles; and for special-category traders and institutions. It is interesting to note that the special system introduced for distance sales and for cars is intended to force the VAT to be accounted for in the country of destination, because people who buy cars and mail order products are not generally registered for VAT.

What about VAT on services?

Rules relating to VAT on services are very complicated. As a general rule, if the supplier and the customer are both registered for VAT and are in business in different EU countries, then the VAT is accounted for by the customer if the service is of a type that is supplied where it is received. This does not apply to services that are supplied where they are performed.

What VAT rates apply?

The national standard rates are listed below. Reduced rates occur in all countries except Denmark where, however, zero rates may be applied, as they are also in Belgium, Ireland, Italy, Spain and the UK. The standard VAT rates on 1 May 1999 were as follows:

Austria	20%
Belgium	21%
Denmark	25%
Finland	22%
France	20.6%
Germany	16%
Greece	18%
Ireland	21%
Italy	20%
Luxembourg	15%
Netherlands	17.5%
Portugal	17%
Spain	16%
Sweden	25%
UK	17.5%

How do Member States manage to control fraudulent VAT evasion?

The Administrative Co-operation Regulation 1992 provided for a special system of mutual assistance between the fiscal authorities of the EU Member States with automatic electronic exchange of information on intra-EC sales. The VIES computer network for customs authorities can match up purchases, sales and VAT numbers.

The 1979 Directive on mutual assistance extends to VAT and excise duties.

What about works of art and second-hand goods?

The seventh VAT Directive 1994 set out a regime for virtually all second-hand goods, works of art, antiques and collectors' items. The main elements of the new system are:

- Normal VAT rates apply except where reduced rates apply.
- Individual sales (ie between individuals) are informal and not subject to VAT.
- Business owners' or re-sellers' sales are subject to VAT on the profit margin.
- For important art objects from third countries, 5 per cent VAT is applied.
- A special system is set out for second-hand cars, which must be over six months old, or with a mileage of at least 6,000 kilometres.

Are there any other provisions or proposals relating to VAT?

Yes. Provisions are issued when agreement is achieved or changes make amendments necessary. Examples include provisions concerning: VAT regimes; goods and services expenditure on which VAT is not deductible; the stores kept by aircraft, international trains and ships; and gold, distinguishing between financial and industrial gold.

What about statistical data?

Boxes to indicate the figures for intra-Community trade are attached to the periodic VAT returns already used for movements within Member States. Only the top 20 per cent of Community firms (in terms of size) are required to fill them in (see Chapter 8).

Enterprises also have to complete ESLs (European Sales Listings), which are quarterly summaries by customer, VAT number and transaction value. Enterprises with an annual turnover of over £150,000 in the UK (the figure varies elsewhere) must provide more detailed supplementary sales declarations (SSDs) on a monthly basis to the VAT authorities.

What about excise duties?

As explained in Chapter 5 and Chapter 8, excise duties cause difficulties, and attempts by the Commission to harmonize provisions have been under way for many years. The 1992 Directive on the Holding, Movement and Control of Excise Goods provided that the movement of goods subject to excise duty, eg alcohol, essential oils and tobacco, will be under a duty suspension between bonded warehouses in the Member States that themselves authorize the warehouse-keepers. The goods attract duty when they come out of the system for consumption. The Directive also provided for methods of raising levies in the absence of border controls, and for a system of registered dealers operating outside the warehouse scheme.

What about excise duty rates?

In 1992 a Council Directive came into force to approximate the rates of taxation on cigarettes, tobacco, alcoholic drinks and mineral oils, and to provide minimum rates or rate bands for all products subject to excise duties (except some petroleum products with rate bands) from 1 January 1993. Since then Member States have been working towards achieving 'target rates'. These take into account other policies such as protection of the environment (eg unleaded petrol must be subject to lower tax rates than leaded petrol), energy, transport and health. A 1996 Directive on Biofuels gave the EU countries an option to reduce drastically excise duties on fuels of agricultural origin.

An expert Excise Committee may make recommendations to the Council as to necessary measures.

What about 'duty-free' travellers' concessions?

These were abolished for all journeys between EU Member States from 31 June 1999. However the lowest of the tax rates applicable in the country of departure or destination may be charged on goods bought in transit.

What about auditors and audits?

An obstacle to the valid comparison of accounts of enterprises in various EU countries is the differing quality of auditing and accounting standards. In May 1998 the Commission proposed reforms to improve the quality of statutory audits throughout the EU, and these remain under discussion.

What about enforcement?

A 1976 Directive concerns recovery procedures, and would be amended by a 1998 draft Directive targeted at those moving assets around the EU to avoid taxation. New draft Directives relate to obligations of authorities to disclose details of customers' accounts to other EU tax authorities, to corporation tax, interest payments and royalties.

What is the general effect of EU taxation provisions and proposals?

Inevitably the changing economic situation in different Member States means that harmonization of taxation is problematical. The general attitude has been to try to harmonize wherever convenient but, as stated earlier, the practical and economic difficulties remain great. Where simplification is achieved, it clearly benefits those buying and selling goods or services Community-wide. The harmonization of VAT and excise duties and procedures is seen as a vital component of the Single Market, but the rights of national governments to decide on when and how to collect revenue are jealously guarded. Concern about EU proposals to tax energy, polluting equipment and, more recently, IT equipment focuses on the extra burden put on production costs, which could affect the competitiveness of EU businesses *vis-à-vis* their third-country competitors. As the Euro becomes more generally used, so goods and services are likely to be marketed more throughout the Eurozone, and the different rates will become more transparent. It could be argued that this might well speed up the harmonization of rates rather more quickly than is achievable through political negotiations.

Further information may be obtained from the European Commission, the Inland Revenue and HM Customs and Excise (see Appendix III).

12 Economic and Monetary Union, capital movements and financial services

EMU, EMS and the ECU

What does Economic and Monetary Union (EMU) mean?

This is the system whereby a single currency is brought into effect in participating countries, with the currency managed centrally and members agreeing to keep within stated economic guidelines.

EMU and the single currency – called the 'Euro' – commenced on 1 January 1999 in the participating countries, ie in 11 of the 15 Member States. The area covered is often called the Eurozone, or Euro area.

The states currently participating in the Eurozone are: Austria, Belgium, Finland, France, Germany, Ireland, Italy, Luxembourg, The Netherlands, Portugal and Spain. Outside are Greece (which was unable to meet the criteria), Sweden, Denmark and the UK, which opted not to join at that time. Greece is likely to re-apply in March 2000.

To understand the functioning of EMU it is useful to list the progression that has led finally to the achievement of the Eurozone. It really started with the establishment of the European Monetary System (EMS).

What was the European Monetary System?

The EMS, launched on 5 December 1978, was intended to achieve monetary stability in the Community, have a stabilizing effect on international and economic monetary relations, and engender co-operation with a convergence of economic policy and performance in the Member States. The EMS was referred to in the SEA as important in the process leading towards EMU, and had two principal rules covering currency fluctuation margins and currency realignments by current accord.

The EMS covered four main areas: the Exchange Rate Mechanism (ERM), the European Currency Unit (ECU), the European Monetary Co-operation Fund (EMCF) and the Very Short Term Financial Facility (VSTF). A Member State could belong to the EMS without belonging to the ERM, which was introduced in 1972 (and was often referred to as 'the Snake'). The UK left the ERM in 1992 because of currency difficulties. Under the ERM, participating countries agreed to keep their currencies within an agreed fluctuation band.

Council agreement was reached in 1997 on a new mechanism to take the place of the EMS, ERM II, and on a resolution relating to commitments on implementation of two agreed Regulations on budgetary discipline, which together formed part of the Stability Pact needed to facilitate the Euro. Presently only Sweden and the UK are outside ERM II, so their currencies fluctuate freely against the Euro.

What was the ECU and how did it start?

The ECU began as a unit of account used as a uniform measure of value for budgetary purposes only. In 1975, it was decided to apportion specific currency quantities to form a 'basket' of Community member currencies and call it the European Unit of Account (EUA), later renaming it the ECU (European Currency Unit).

The yearly average value of the ECU in 1996 was £0.813798 in the UK. It was replaced by the Euro on a one-for-one basis in all contracts on1 January 1999.

What is the Community's policy on EMU?

EMU was the stated long-term aim of the Community. The Werner Report in the early 1970s called for closer economic and monetary links, and the EMS was specifically designed to limit currency fluctuations among Member States. In 1988, the European Council reaffirmed its view that in adopting the Single European Act, Member States had confirmed the objective of progressive realization of EMU. The Council asked Jacques Delors, President of the European Commission, to chair a committee to study and propose 'concrete stages leading towards this union'. The Delors Committee Report suggested a timetable leading to EMU that was reflected in the TEU, which clearly set out the decision to adopt EMU and a single currency, and was signed by the Member States in 1992. Both Denmark and the UK retained the right to opt out of EMU.

In December 1995 the European Council decided that the changeover to the single currency would begin on 1 January 1999 for those meeting the convergence criteria, and that the single currency would be called the Euro.

The introduction of Euro notes and coins is planned to start on 1 January 2002 with a six-month changeover period (although there is a proposal to limit this changeover time to six weeks). This means, by current plans, that national currencies and notes will have to be withdrawn by 1 June 2002.

What were the stages for the move towards EMU?

Arguably, the first step was taken in 1990, when the 1988 Directive on Liberalization of Capital Movements came into force in most EC countries, liberalization being achieved by 1994.

The first detailed timetable for EMU was agreed at the Maastricht Inter-Governmental Conference (IGC) in 1991. There were to be three stages, and these have broadly been followed.

Under *Stage I* all the national currencies became part of the European Monetary System, with realignments of exchange rates between currencies still possible, but with heavy reliance on other methods of adjustment. The composition of the ECU basket of currencies (see above) was then effectively frozen. Stage I was aimed at greater convergence of economic performance in Member States. The mandates of central banks were redefined to allow them to express non-binding majority opinions on the overall orientation of monetary and exchange rate policy and banking supervision. The Committee of Central Banks set up to promote central bank co-operation had worked well, but ceased on 1 January 1994 with the establishment of the European Monetary Institute (EMI). Multilateral monitoring of economic performance started.

Stage II as a transition period started on 1 January 1994, and moved through co-operation towards more collective decision-making and economic convergence, to ensure price stability, with the ultimate responsibility for economic and monetary policy still remaining with the national governments. The EMI was set up and sited in Frankfurt in 1994 to co-ordinate monetary union and to prepare for the creation of a European System of Central Banks (ESCB) in Stage III. In December 1995 the European Council decided that the changeover would begin on 1 January 1999 for those meeting the agreed convergence criteria.

Stage III began on 1 January 1999, and exchange rates between participating Member States meeting the convergence criteria were irrevocably fixed, the ERM II replacing the EMS. The single currency, called the Euro (European Council decisions of December 1995 and June 1996), was introduced as a currency in its own right, with central decision-making on matters relating to national budgets. The European Central Bank became fully operational on 1 January 1999, replacing the EMI, and now manages national reserves and takes responsibility for the single European monetary policy and market intervention in other currencies (although the Council of Ministers sets the Euro area exchange rate policy to be followed). It co-operates with the European System of Central Banks. The end of Stage III is scheduled for 2002 with the new currency and coins in place.

How was it decided which Member States form part of EMU and the single currency?

To join EMU, the Member States had to comply with the set convergence criteria, and want to join. However, a protocol to the TEU declared that the move towards union is 'irrevocable'.

EMU means that national economic policies have to be regarded as matters of common concern; economic developments have to be closely monitored by the Council of Ministers; excessive national budget deficits (over 3 per cent of GNP was the target set by TEU for those entering EMU) have to be avoided; and control is by way of the Stability and Growth Pact and its accompanying provisions.

What about the UK opt-out?

The UK opt-out clause was set out in a protocol to the TEU, providing that the UK is under no obligation to move to Stage III of EMU unless its government separately and specifically decides to do so. This means that for so long as the UK exercises its opt-out, the UK government:

- retains all authority over its own monetary and exchange rate policy, albeit following the start of EMU the UK agreed not to run an 'excessive' public deficit;
- may not vote in respect of EMU matters;
- may not appoint members to the European Central Bank board, and the Bank of England may not participate.

It should be noted that the UK, provided it satisfies convergence criteria, could change its notification after the deadline. Denmark is in a similar position.

What are the institutions of EMU?

The following institutions have a role in EMU:

- The *European Council*, acting unanimously or by qualified majority, is responsible for important EMU decisions.

- The *Council of Ministers* (usually the economic and finance ministers) is responsible for general policy matters, and reports on major issues to the European Council.
- The *European Commission* is responsible for proposing EMU policies to the Council, and assists with implementation and monitoring, but participates as adviser only in the Monetary Committee. It is the Community that carries out international negotiations on monetary issues, and consequent agreements are binding on the European Central Bank and on the Member States concerned. The Commission reports annually to the Council and the European Parliament.
- The *European Monetary Institute* was responsible for strengthening central bank co-operation and preparing for Stage III (eg by co-ordinating policies). Its 13 main tasks were set out in a protocol to the TEU. It had a general advisory function, prepared studies including a blueprint for the European Central Bank, and encouraged harmonization and preparation vital to enable EMU. It provided a forum for debate, and could act as an arbiter between countries. It was replaced by the European Central Bank.
- The *European Central Bank* (ECB) became fully operational on 1 January 1999 and took over from the EMI. Its executive board is appointed by agreement with the Member States and the Council after consultation with the European Parliament and the Governing Council of the ECB. This body consists of the executive board members, and the governors of the national central banks. It is legally accountable to the EP.
- The *European System of Central Banks* (ESCB) has taken over and is responsible for managing EMU. It is made up of the governors of the national central banks of the Member States of the EU and includes the ECB. The executive board members have eight-year terms of office, and national central bank governors five-year terms of office. Each member has a single vote, to protect the position and influence of small countries.
- The *European Parliament* must be kept informed, and its assent is needed for institutional changes.

What is the role of the European Central Bank?

The ECB is responsible for maintaining currency price stability and, in co-operation with the ESCB, for defining the general Community economic and monetary policy that the national central banks implement, although it is the Council of Ministers for the Euro area or Eurozone that sets the Eurozone exchange rate policy. The ECB is independent of national governments and has the exclusive right to authorize the use of Euro banknotes. It conducts foreign exchange operations, holds and manages official foreign reserves of Member States, and promotes the smooth running of payment systems.

What is the role of the European System of Central Banks (ESCB)?

The ESCB must define and implement the single monetary policy of the EU; conduct the foreign exchange operations according to instructions given by the Council of Ministers; and hold and manage the official reserves of the Member States in EMU.

What are the convergence criteria?

A Member State must fulfil the following criteria for a specified time:

1. It must have an inflation rate within one and a half percentage points of the average rate of the three states with the lowest inflation.
2. Its long-term interest rate must be within two percentage points of the average rate of the other Member States with the lowest long-term interest rates.
3. Its national debt must not exceed 60% of its gross national product (GNP).
4. Its national budget deficit must remain below 3% of its GNP.
5. For two years the currency must have remained within the fluctuation rate margin allowed by the ERM.

What is the Stability and Growth Pact?

In 1995 the European Council in Madrid confirmed the importance of ensuring budgetary discipline ahead of Stage III EMU by preventative and deterrent provisions. This led to agreement in December 1996 on the main elements of the Stability and Growth Pact, now set out in the Resolution of the European Council annexed to the Presidency conclusions of the 1996/7 IGC, and two Council Resolutions on:

1. surveillance and co-ordination of economic policies;
2. clarifying and speeding up the implementation of the excessive deficit procedure.

Under the resolution, the Member States committed themselves to a medium-term objective to be close to balance or in surplus, together with the action to achieve this; to meet their stability or convergence programmes; to act as appropriate to correct excessive deficits, unless there are special circumstances; and to act following notifications by the Council.

The Commission is authorized to act so as to facilitate the funding of the Stability and Growth Pact, to produce reports, opinions and recommendations to enable the Council to, for example, warn Member States; and to launch and apply an excessive deficit procedure. The Council can recommend that excessive deficits be corrected quickly, and impose financial sanctions (eg a non-interest-bearing deposit, which may be turned into a fine after two years) if the deficit is not corrected.

What will happen in respect of countries that do not initially join EMU?

They will be able to join late, and if that is relatively soon after the first tranche of countries, may even be able to use Euros by the deadline of 1 January 2002. It was agreed in 1996 that the revised exchange rate mechanism, ERM II, would continue, and that the system for joining late should be flexible and not undermine price stability in the Eurozone. Both Greece and Denmark are members of ERM II, but the UK and Sweden are not.

In the UK, current opinion concerning whether the UK should join EMU in the short term, the long term or at all swings with the current nationalistic, anti-Europe or pro-Euro media campaigns, and may well depend finally on the fate of cattle farmers, rather than the less emotive interests of big business.

What is the effect of EMU?

The effects of EMU in the Eurozone are far-reaching, and the subject of EU-wide studies. The availability of a single currency throughout Europe has obvious attractions (eg convenience, trade promotion, cutting cross-border transaction costs, pricing and monetary transparency), but some fears remain concerning loss of sovereignty and transition costs. The necessary central co-ordination of economic and monetary policy, and the withdrawal of the availability of using currency revaluations as an economic tool of government, present significant political and practical challenges, as individual governments have to co-operate.

At the time of writing, EMU seems to be working quite well and preparations for coins and banknotes are progressing. The design of these have proved to be a difficult task, as so many factors have had to be taken into account, such as national sensibilities, the needs of approximately 2 million blind or visually impaired people, security features, and machine-readable features to facilitate note-handling machines. The secure production of many billions of notes and coins also presents logistical problems. The Commission recommendations cover such matters as dual pricing and bank charges, and an EU Regulation of June 1997 made provisions for the legal impact of the change to the Euro to deal with contracts (standard terms and conditions, for example), and accounting questions.

However, financial transactions are increasingly achieved electronically, are fast and international. All Community countries are being encouraged to sign the Council of Europe Convention on Judicial Co-operation in the event of suspected large-scale fraud linked to crime or drug trafficking; and a single currency should help this by promoting transparency.

Will EMU be successful?

Whether EMU will be successful will in the end depend on political will, and whether the advantages of union outweigh the disadvantages of being unable to adapt national monetary policy (and currency values) to the fluctuating needs of participating Member States. The inevitable costs of supporting states in economic difficulties will fall to the more successful states, which will reflect in turn on the global competitiveness of those states. The advantages include promoting a united currency to rival the US dollar and the yen, lower transaction costs, more transparency and so more internal competition with lower prices, a more cohesive market, arguably greater competitiveness globally and less uncertainty.

What is important is that a close watch is kept on developments to ensure that enterprises and citizens are ready to cope with the inevitable changes.

Further information can be obtained from the Treasury, the European Commission and the Bank of England (see Appendix III).

Capital movements and financial services

Why are capital movements important?

As goods and people move more freely around the Community, so the movement of money or capital must be facilitated.

Is there a difference between abolition of exchange controls and liberalization of capital movements?

Yes. The liberalization of capital movements is a wider concept, incorporating not only exchange controls but also such matters as access to, and investment in, local stock markets.

How has the problem of liberalization of capital movements been tackled?

Two 1960s Directives liberalized movements of personal capital, commercial credit and direct investment, but many restrictions remained. A 1986 Directive liberalized capital movements in long-term commercial credit and transactions in securities not listed on a stock exchange, and abolished exchange controls on the admission of company securities of one Member State to the capital market of another. The 1988 Capital Movement Directive liberalized remaining EC capital movements to give individuals and enterprises complete freedom to open bank accounts anywhere in the EU. The remaining controls concerning current and deposit accounts, financial loans and credits, and investment in short-term securities have also been removed.

What is the importance of financial services to the Community?

Financial services account for an estimated 7 per cent of the GDP of the EU, and liberalization of financial services is an essential element of the Single European Market. The financial services market is becoming increasingly global, so the EU must be more efficient to meet the challenge of its US and Japanese competitors. The 1999 Commission paper, *Financial Services – Building a Framework for Action*, sets out the policy ideas for development of financial services legislation.

How has liberalization of financial services progressed?

The Community has followed a three-step approach:

1. To set key prudential standards.
2. To provide for 'home country' control of these standards.
3. To achieve mutual recognition and application of standards so that control in one country is accepted as adequate in another, along with the right of establishment in any Community country, ie the European 'passport' to providing services in any Member State.

This gives financial services providers and clients freedom to provide and use financial services under a regime whereby financial service institutions may, once authorized in their home state, establish activities and set up branches wherever they like in the Community, and offer their own financial services products freely throughout the EU, either within a state or across one or several frontiers, without the need to have an establishment anywhere other than in their own state or to have a local licence.

There is a wide degree of overlap in terms of regulation of financial services. It is important to note that each sector is very wide and specialist, so a choice has had to be made as regards the provisions mentioned. The global dimension and electronic commerce mean that progress in this area is fast, but national restrictions can still cause difficulties.

Banking and investment services

What about banking and investment services generally?

The Commission is seeking in its more recent reports and proposals to reflect the globalization of investment services. Thus the EU has many bilateral treaties dealing with rules for investments world-wide, and supports the development of international rules under the aegis of the World Trade Organization to open up the financial services markets world-wide in banking, investment and insurance.

There are many Directives concerning banks, securities and investment and insurance services that have the dual aim of consumer protection and liberalization of this sector. Only some of the main ones are listed below.

A Financial Services Action Plan published in May 1999 set out a five-year reform plan to update prudential and supervision requirements. It provided for the setting up of a Securities Advisory Body that would encourage co-operation between enforcement authorities, and a draft Directive on the use of cross-border collateral security required; it made suggestions as to the amendment of the Investment Services Directive; and proposed a common legal framework for integrated securities and derivatives markets.

What has been the Community's policy with regard to banking?

The Commission has worked towards harmonization in the banking sector for many years, seeking to liberalize the sector, improve consumer access, lower costs and streamline provisions.

The first banking Directive on banking services was the 1977 Directive on the Co-ordination of Laws, Regulations and Administrative Provisions Relating to the Taking Up and Pursuit of Business by Credit Institutions, these being defined broadly as including banks and building societies. A draft amendment would broaden this to include electronic money institutions. This Directive enabled a bank in one Member State to open a branch or offer banking services in any other Member State, provided it complied with the same conditions and supervisory requirements as those applying to local banks. This Directive did not remove some of the most significant restrictions, so the second Banking Directive 1989 was agreed.

What did the second Banking Directive 1989 do?

It removed the remaining barriers to full freedom of establishment for EC banking services, and facilitated a single banking licence so that a bank authorized in one country could establish branches or provide services anywhere in the Community without further authorization. In other words, it provided for mutual recognition of home country authorization by host and home countries.

The Directive included provisions enabling the Community to secure reciprocal access to third-country markets in this sector, but banks based in a non-EU country (with some exceptions) required local licences in each Member State in which they operate.

The minimum requirements for credit institutions required by the Directive included a minimum capital base, the disclosure of information on major shareholdings, the suitability of the 'controller' as defined in the Directive and of the institution's business plans, together with the level of involvement in non-banking activities. Control over securities activities, monitoring banks' liquidity positions, and any factors affecting the monetary policy of the host country became subject to host country and not home country control.

The Directive only related to minimum requirements, and Member States could have higher standards, although they had to recognize credit institutions operating in their country at lower standards, provided the latter met the EU minimum. The scope of the 1989 Directive was clarified in a July 1997 communication.

What other Directives and proposals are there?

Some of the more important of these are listed below:

- The 1983 Directive on Consolidated Supervision of Banks and Building Societies ensures that if one institution owns more than 25 per cent of another, then they will be supervised on a consolidated basis.
- The 1986 Directive on the Annual Accounts of Banks sets out the required format and content of the annual consolidated accounts of banks and other financial institutions, including building societies, that have their head office in the European Community.
- A 1985 Directive on Undertakings for Collective Investment and transferable securities, finally implemented in 1989,

enables an undertaking for collective investments (UCIT) (a unit trust or equivalent) authorized in one Member State to market units anywhere in the Community, provided it complies with local marketing regulations. This is now to be subject to amendment.

- There are various consumer credit Directives, from the 1987 Consumer Credit Directive, which provides a detailed list of minimum requirements throughout the Community, to the 1997 Directive, which provides revised formulae for the calculation of rates of interest.

- The Solvency Ratio Directive 1989 provides for strengthened solvency standards and capital adequacy and supervision procedures to protect depositors and investors. There are various 'own funds' Directives on capital adequacy of investment funds and credit institutions, which complement the Investment Services Directive and the second Banking Directive, so as to set out the minimum capital requirements for firms doing investment business in the European Community.

- There are various provisions to protect investors. Examples include the 1997 Directive on Investor Compensation Schemes, which provides that every EU member should have in place a compensation scheme to guarantee minimum repayments in the event of the insolvency of an authorized bank or investment firm, such schemes to be subject to home country supervisory requirements. It is similar to the Harmonization of Deposit Guarantee Systems Directive 1994, which is applicable to credit institutions.

- The 1996 Directive on Cross-Border Payments concerns transfers of up to ECU 50,000 and includes requirements for mandatory refunds of the first ECU 12,500 of sums lost during transfer. It also includes provisions to encourage efficiency.

- A 1989 Directive co-ordinates the requirements for the drawing up, scrutiny and distribution of the prospectus published when transferable securities are offered to the public for the first time, and there is a Directive on the mutual recognition of stock exchange listing particulars.

- The Insider Dealing Directive 1989 requires Member States to make insider dealing unlawful and to co-operate in exchanging information to enable enforcement of provisions.

- A Directive on Distance Selling of Financial Services is close to adoption at the time of writing.

- There are proposals on electronic money: on the harmonization of minimum rules; on the issue and organization of systems; and on the defining of electronic money in a technologically neutral way.

Other provisions in this area are beyond the scope of this book.

Work continues to encourage improvements in banking services, by encouraging electronic transfer and payment systems but simultaneously trying to counter dangers to consumers and fraud, ensuring cross-border payments are not subject to prohibitive charges and seeking to harmonize provisions relating to credit transfer arrangements.

What provisions relate particularly to investment services?

Many proposals that relate to banks also relate to investment services, such as the Insider Dealing Directive. The Commission has made various proposals concerning stock exchanges and general financial services. The most important of these are listed below:

- The Investment Services Directive 1993, which is similar to the second Banking Directive, provides that a home country licence should be recognized as authorization to offer services elsewhere in the Community in the fields of, for example, portfolio management and investment advice, brokerage, participation in securities issues and market-making.
- The Investment Services Indemnity Directive 1997 provides for an adequate minimum investor compensation fund of ECU 20,000 per investor in the event of the insolvency or default of an investment firm.
- The 1992 Directive on the Supervision of Credit Institutions on a Consolidated Basis requires that the supervisory role be carried out in the country where most of the company's transactions are made, irrespective of the country of headquarters.
- The 1989 Directives on prospectuses and recognition of listing particulars were amended in the 1994 second Listing Directive to simplify procedures for cross-border admission of securities to the various stock exchanges.
- The Disclosure of Major Shareholdings Directive 1988 requires those with major shareholdings in companies listed officially in the EC to disclose those holdings on acquisition or disposal.
- The Capital Adequacy for Credit and Investment Institutions Directive 1993 also applies to banks. It is aimed at consumer protection and imposes a framework of minimum capital requirements.

What about money laundering?

The Money Laundering Directive 1991 requires credit and financial institutions (including banks) to report suspicious transactions to the proper authorities, and to keep relevant records for five years to combat the processing of drug money. Proposals to extend this to the proceeds of other serious crimes, and to extend the client identification and reporting requirements to other sectors, eg casinos, estate agents and the legal profession, are under discussion. There is also a Council of Europe Convention on money laundering. Further initiatives to control it are under discussion in the drive against organized crime and drug trafficking.

What about global investments?

The Commission initiative to establish international as opposed to EU rules for foreign investments world-wide continues. There are currently about 600 bilateral treaties and a non-binding OECD code, and there is a perceived need for a dispute settlement procedure. As noted above, discussions continue with the WTO.

What about pensions?

These provide a huge investment market. It was reaffirmed in 1999 that provisions must be aimed at ensuring greater member protection, more efficient investment schemes for pension funds and more flexibility, together with less distortions in respect of cross-border pension payments.

What is the position with regard to insurance?

In principle, the completion of the Internal Market for insurance is achieved. There are specific measures covering the different insurance sectors, but they are beyond the scope of this book. They cover such matters as when host country control or home country control is required, the required annual and consolidated statements and accounts, technical reserves of, and significant shareholdings in, insurance companies, and the compulsory winding-up of insurance companies. There is a 1999 Directive on Supplementary Prudential Supervision of Insurance Undertakings, which sets out new rules, and should assist in insolvency assessments. There is also a regulation establishing a block exemption from the competition provisions for certain agreements between insurers, and consumer protection provisions generally and relating to the rules on insolvency margins of insurance companies.

What about motor insurance?

Motor insurance has been the subject of various Directives since 1973. These cover areas such as the assurance of civil liability resulting from the free movement of automobiles, which made insurance cover for all passengers compulsory, and the harmonization of national provisions for funds to compensate victims where vehicles are uninsured.

The Motor Insurance Services Directive 1990 extended home state control to motor vehicle liability insurance providers. A 1999 Commission Decision relates to the application of the 1972 Directive on the approximation of laws of Member States relating to insurance against civil liability in respect of the use of motor vehicles, and the obligation to insure against such liability, and there is a draft Directive on this.

What about export credit insurance in the EU?

Most member countries have national export credit insurance schemes, and most are either wholly owned by governments or supported through reinsurance by their national governments. They provide insurance cover against non-payment by a purchaser, caused by political or commercial difficulties, resulting in loss or even termination of an export contract. The bulk of business insured is for exports on short payment terms, but most schemes are able to insure major projects. State assistance for export credit insurance where there is commercial availability is increasingly frowned on as constituting unfair competition.

Further information may be obtained from the International Credit Assurance Association.

What about domestic sales?

Domestic sales can easily be insured against, for example credit risks, but credit insurance can be costly, especially in trades where defaults or insolvencies are common. As with export credit, there tends to be a dominant insurer in this field in each country.

It is interesting to note that catastrophe credit insurance schemes, especially designed for large companies, are a new and growing field.

What are the effects of liberalization in financial services generally?

Banks, investment and insurance companies may now establish themselves and advertise their services in any other Member State, although some practical difficulties remain. The result is that in the financial services sector many EU enterprises are taking an interest in, taking over or collaborating with local financial services companies in other EC countries. Wider choice should benefit users as competition leads to better services, but more care may be needed to assess accurately the increasingly varied services available. A Commission communication adopted in February 2000 explains the current thinking and ideas behind the freedom to provide services in the insurance sector. It can be found at http://europa.eu.int/comm/dg15.

13 Company law harmonization

Why are the European Commission's proposals for company law harmonization significant?

The harmonization of the company laws of Member States progressed steadily as an important part of the abolition of obstacles to the free movement of goods and services, and of the completion of the Internal Market, because it ensures that the expectations of individuals and enterprises dealing with companies in other Community countries are met. Simple legislation encourages cross-border activity.

While the big multinationals and public companies tend to hit the headlines, private companies constitute the vast majority of limited companies. In the UK in September 1999 there were 1,314,767 active companies listed on the 'live' register of the Registrar of Companies in Great Britain (ie not including Northern Ireland).

Although there are exceptions, most businesses in the UK begin life as unincorporated bodies, and, if they are successful, after the first three years or so they tend to convert to being a limited company. Limited company status brings privileges and duties, and the public does require some protection. Good companies legislation can assist corporate success, so corporate governance, and the extent to which simplification or adaptation of national provisions on the structure and organization of powers in public limited companies is desirable, are subjects of current EU studies and consultation. It is hoped to encouraged best practice, and an EU-wide study by Ernst and Young initiated by the Commission collated the rules in the various Member States, and made recommendations. It also considered the fifth Directive in this context.

Is it important to know the definitions of small and medium-sized enterprises (SMEs)?

Yes, because it may mean that a company can take advantage of EC measures to help SMEs.

The 1996 definition holds that an SME is an enterprise with up to 250 employees, which includes micro-enterprises, small and medium-sized enterprises. SMEs can be broken down further into:

- very small enterprises, also called micro-enterprises, with under 10 employees;
- small enterprises, of under 50 employees, with an annual turnover of under ECU 7 million, or a balance sheet total of up to ECU 5 million;
- medium-sized enterprises, of 50–250 employees, with an annual turnover below ECU 40 million, or a balance sheet total of up to ECU 27 million.

Directives and draft Directives

What did the first Council Directive 1968 on Company Law do?

It sought to harmonize safeguards, and provide for a system of disclosure by way of a companies register in each Member State, which must be open to the public, with a view to making companies equivalent throughout the Community. It provided that those contracting with a company should be protected against defects in its incorporation, limitations on its capacity or any internal restrictions on its directors, so enabling people in different Community countries to deal with registered companies without detailed enquiry.

What did the second Council Directive 1977 do?

This harmonized the classification of companies within Member States as either public or private companies (or their national equivalents). It imposed various requirements on public companies, for example minimum capital requirements, and requirements in respect of the maintenance or alteration of prescribed capital. These were designed to protect creditors and others dealing with the company by providing for a minimum level of protection. It was extended (in 1992) to strengthen and extend restrictions on public limited companies using their own companies or subsidiaries to acquire their own shares.

What do the third and sixth Directives (1978 and 1982) do?

These relate to uniform internal procedures and safeguards for mergers (third Directive), demergers or divisions (sixth Directive) of public limited companies, where they are situated in the same Member State. The aim is to protect minority shareholders and others who might be vulnerable. The Directives are important but, for example, the third Directive may be avoided, so if a merger is carried out by way of a take-over, the procedures will be unregulated under these Directives.

What is the purpose of the fourth (1978) Directive?

This harmonized the rules relating to the drawing up, auditing and publication of limited company accounts throughout the Community. Insurance companies are included in the 1991 Directive on Annual Accounts of Insurance Undertakings.

The fourth Directive permitted Member States to allow small companies to draw up abridged versions of balance sheets, profit and loss accounts and notes to the accounts. Member States could exempt small companies from publishing a profit and loss account within the directors' report, from publishing an audit report, or even from having their accounts audited. It was amended by the 1990 Directive amending the scope of the fourth and seventh Directives, and of the 1994 Directive that updated the thresholds for exemptions for small and medium-sized companies set out in the fourth Directive.

Under the fourth Directive medium-sized companies are required to draw up a full balance sheet, although Member States may allow an abridged version to be published. They may file an abridged profit and loss account and notes to the accounts.

What does the seventh Directive (1983) do?

This specifies how and when consolidated accounts should be prepared and published by companies with subsidiaries, or by groups, and is intended to complement the fourth Directive dealing with the accounts of individual companies. This has also been amended as to its scope of application.

What about partnerships?

The Partnerships Directive 1990 brought limited and unlimited partnerships with a limited company partner within the scope of the fourth and seventh Directives.

What are the proposals for a fifth Council Directive?

Proposals for a fifth Directive on the structure and management of public limited companies (PLCs) were issued in 1972, 1983 and

1991. Agreement is unlikely until after the European Company Statute is completed – if then – as it would affect all public limited companies, and provide for the introduction of a distinction between PLC directors responsible for management, and those responsible for 'supervision'. This distinction could be achieved either through a two-tier board (as is done in Germany) or, with the conventional UK single-tier board, by differentiating between the functions of 'executive' directors (managing) and 'non-executive' directors (supervising).

Why is the draft fifth Directive unpopular in some Member States?

It has been unpopular in the UK because it includes mandatory employee participation in company decision-making in PLCs employing over 1,000 staff in the EU either directly or in subsidiaries (plus optional provisions for employee participation by employees of other group companies that are not PLCs); and for the harmonization of laws for PLCs relating to the duties, liabilities, appointment and removal of directors, the powers of the general meeting, the rights of shareholders and minorities, and the approval of annual accounts. Some ideas set out in the fifth Directive were included in the Works Councils Directive 1994.

Another proposal for employee consultation was the Vredeling Draft Directive with some provisions similar in concept to those in the draft fifth Directive. It was similarly unpopular and appears to have been shelved (see Chapter 16).

What about employee participation in company profits?

This was the subject of the Pepper II report adopted by the Commission in 1997 on the promotion of participation by employed persons in profits and enterprise results including equity participation. The report considered the different provisions currently used in the EU and suggested that national frameworks to encourage this should be developed, and more co-operation and information exchange between Member States encouraged. Work continues in this area.

What about the draft ninth Directive 1984 on the conduct of groups of companies?

This Directive would provide a harmonized legal structure for the 'unified management' of a public limited company and any other undertaking that had a controlling interest in it, whether or not that undertaking was itself a company. It remains on the table but with a very low profile in favour of work on the European Company Statute (discussed below).

What is proposed in the draft tenth Directive 1985 on cross-border mergers of PLCs?

This would apply to mergers between public limited companies in different Member States. It relates to share exchange mergers and not to the take-over procedure that is more usual in the UK. It would incorporate many of the provisions from the third Directive, and also includes worker consultation proposals. A new text is under discussion.

What is the effect of the Regulation on the Preliminary Control of European Mergers 1989?

It strengthened and clarified the Commission's control of mergers with a 'European dimension'. The purpose of the regulation was to distinguish between mergers with a European dimension (which are the Commission's responsibility), and smaller national mergers (which remain under home country control).

The regulation includes detailed definitions and notifications requirements and was amended by a 1997 Regulation (see also Chapter 10).

What about the eleventh Directive 1989 on branch disclosure requirements?

This Directive concerned the harmonization and co-ordination of minimum financial disclosure to be made in the host Member State by branches of companies registered in other Member States, or outside the Community.

It was aimed at avoiding differences between Member States in the protection of shareholders and others with regard to the duties and obligations of branches and subsidiary companies.

What is the effect of the twelfth Directive 1989 on single-member private limited companies?

This Directive required Member States that did not already have such a system to introduce one to allow the setting up of a private limited company with only one member, as opposed to a minimum of two members (as previously required in the UK).

Member States had some discretion to make special provisions where a natural person is the sole member of several companies, and where the single member is another company or legal entity.

What is the position with regard to take-overs?

The thirteenth draft Directive was withdrawn, but its place was taken by a 1996 draft European Parliament and Council Directive on Company Law concerning take-over bids. This provides minimum guidelines for the conduct of take-overs, and includes a framework of common principles and general requirements to be implemented through more detailed national rules as to protection of minority shareholders after the purchase. It details time limits and information requirements, and provisions on the conduct of take-overs with a requirement that the target board must act in the interests of the company as a whole. At the time of writing it was close to approval, but again blocked by Spain, displeased by the continuing position of the UK with regard to Gibraltar.

Is the proposal for a European Company Statute really needed?

The Commission has long worked towards a European 'model company' that could be validly formed anywhere in Europe where companies in at least two Member States wish to come together. The first proposal was made in 1970. There are now two linked proposals: a 1991 draft regulation for a statute for a European company; and a 1991 draft Directive complementing the statute with regard to involvement of employees in the European company. Although the statute would only be an option (ie those wishing to form a company in the EU would not be obliged to use it), the proposals were originally unpopular in the UK because of the compulsory employee participation provisions (which, incidentally, were strongly supported by the European Parliament). The Netherlands is concerned about creditor protection aspects. However, agreement is now close.

Would the European Company Statute be used?

This rather depends on what precisely will be on offer. At present, the attitude of those experienced in forming companies outside their own country is that it is usually best to use the 'host' type of company because this engenders the most goodwill. However, it would enable companies in different Member States to join to create a more competitive unit, either by setting up a joint subsidiary, or by merging, or by creating a holding company under a single body of rules, and a single financial information system. Even single-member companies will be able to do this provided they have a branch or subsidiary in another Member State. A 1997 Report sought to resolve the employee participation deadlock by providing for the reference rules to apply only as a last resort where free negotiations between employers and employees or their representatives fail.

European Economic Interest Groupings (EEIGs)

These entities have been available since 1989. They are incorporated directly into European Community law, and are designed to facilitate trans-national co-operation, particularly between SMEs in various joint initiatives. Examples include research and development, the formation of a group able to tender for large contracts and computerized data processing (for production and for sales or purchasing purposes). An EEIG is intended not for integration (ie facilitating mergers and acquisitions) but for economic co-operation – to co-ordinate the specified activities of the members concerned. It should not make profits for itself, all profits being taxed through its members. It is an optional not a mandatory form, and mirrors a similar French entity. It is being increasingly used, and there are proposals to widen its provisions.

Who may form an EEIG?

Any person, company, organization or indeed university, registered in a Member State, may belong to an EEIG, which cannot itself employ more than 500 people. Members must come from at least two different Member States.

Are there any capital requirements?

No. This means that a party to it may contribute skill, for example, or may contribute by way of regular contributions. However, its members have joint and several liability for its debts, and the EEIG may sue and be sued in its state of registration, which must be a Member State, although its principal activity may be carried out elsewhere, even in a third country.

What law governs its operations?

This depends on what area of operations is concerned, but account must be taken of: Community law (for example, concerning its formation, management and competition policy); the law of its country of registration; and, where appropriate, the local law of the places where it operates (for example, as to employment provisions). The EEIG itself has full legal capacity. It can make contracts and so on and, in the event of defaults, as stated

above, the members have unlimited joint and several liability for
its debts.

What about European co-operatives, mutual societies and associations?

There is a proposed package of three regulations on these forms
of association, and three linked draft Directives with information
and consultation procedures intended to facilitate cross-border
operations. The package remains under discussion.

What about insolvency?

The provisions relating to insolvency are again being brought forward for discussion. A convention on insolvency proceedings,
signed in 1995, was intended to enable the principal procedures
to be undertaken where the debtors' main interests are located,
and secondary procedures where they own establishments or
property. A draft bankruptcy convention has been under discussion for some years.

What is covered by the eighth Council Directive 1984 on the qualification of auditors?

This Directive came into effect in 1990 and obliged Member
States to ensure that statutory audits are independent and properly carried out, and laid down minimum standards for the qualification and regulation of those authorized to audit company
accounts. This affects every company, as they have to check that
their accountant is properly authorized. It also affects every
accountant who carries out statutory audits.

It is increasingly being recognized that the scope and definitions
used by accountants in statutory audits need to be harmonized
EU-wide, and there are proposals and discussion on possible initiatives on statutory auditing, concentrating on achieving international standards; and on auditors, their training, role, position and
liability, with a view to moving towards a harmonized provision
to enable cross-border service provision of auditing services in the
EU, and to complement efforts towards international cohesion in
auditing.

Are there any further provisions or proposals relating to company law?

Yes. Examples include the Disclosure of Major Shareholdings
Directive 1988, which includes provisions for minimum rules for

disclosure of changes in shareholdings of companies listed on a stock exchange, and provisions on the liquidation of companies.

Further information may be obtained from the Department of Trade and Industry (Companies Division) or the European Commission (see Appendix III).

14 Intellectual property

What is intellectual property (IP)?

'Intellectual property' is the term used to describe rights over inventions or novel ideas (patents); over distinguishing marks that identify a particular brand of goods or service as coming from a particular manufacturer or supplier (trade marks); or over the form of things written, performed or designed, eg works of literature, art or music, films, sound recordings, broadcasts or computer programs (copyright).

Although detailed explanation is beyond the scope of this book, as the rights vary greatly and constitute a body of law in themselves, even in this brief form it is best to deal with each heading in turn. It should be noted that ECJ decisions have had a significant effect on the development of intellectual property rights in the EU.

What is the Community's attitude to intellectual property?

It is a balancing act between the need to encourage research and innovation with due protection, and the prevention of barriers to the free movement of goods in the EU. Because intellectual property rights can be used to divide a market, the aim is to have harmonized EU-wide protection for IP rights. However, there is also recognition that the current systems in the EU for patents, for example, are very expensive as compared with their US competitors' counterparts, and reducing costs is a priority. The information society has led to changing needs and this, together with the rapid development of world trade, has meant that IP protection has had to change, and provisions now tend to be internationally, rather than nationally, developed. There is mounting pressure for a global patent system.

Has anything been done to prevent territorial division by using intellectual property rights?

The ECJ, in a considerable body of case law, has distinguished between the rights themselves and their exercise (the so-called doctrine of exhaustion of rights).The basic principle is that once goods are lawfully marketed in one Member State, either by the owner of the intellectual property right or with his or her consent, then the goods can circulate freely in all Member States. Any limits on such circulation could be an infringement of Article 38 (ex 30) of the Treaty of Rome, which prohibits measures equivalent to quantitative restrictions on imports.

Patents

How can inventions be protected now in the EU?

EU patent protection can be gained either: by obtaining separate national patents in each country, using single or multiple patent applications (and work continues on harmonization of national patent legislation); or by a single European patent application at a national or regional (European) receiving office under the European Patent Convention (EPC), which is then processed through the European Patent Office to grant what is effectively a bundle of national patents.

What is the European Patent Convention, and how does it work?

It is the Munich Convention on the European Patent 1973, which came into force in 1978. All the Member States and some non-member European countries have acceded to it.

To obtain protection through the EPC, one application per patentable invention is filed either directly to the European Patent Office in Munich, or through a national patent office, designating which countries it is to cover. Any right granted may be made effective in the designated countries. Patent renewal fees are paid to the national patent offices. The EPC works well, but is expensive, and discussions continue on how to reduce costs.

What about the Community patent?

There is no such thing as a Community patent at present, because the Luxembourg Community Patent Convention of 1975, amended in 1989, has never entered into force. In concept a Community patent would differ from a patent granted under the EPC in that it would be truly 'unitary'. It would, for example, be enforced by a single court, and renewal fees would be paid to a single authority. It would not, at least initially, displace existing patent systems or the EPC.

Interest in the Community patent has recently been revived by the Commission, which in February 1989 heralded a new proposal for a regulation. However, any proposal would need to address the key problems of translations and judicial framework that have beset the original Luxembourg Convention.

What about the Patent Co-operation Treaty?

This Treaty, produced under the auspices of the World Intellectual Property Organization (WIPO), is adhered to by over 50 countries and permits patent applications to be filed in a single language in various places, nominating the countries the patent would seek to cover. After publication and a search report, and preliminary examination if requested, the application is sent to each of the countries nominated, and then treated as a national or a regional patent application. Over 65,000 filings, equivalent to 4.8 million national filings, were made in 1998.

Which is the best route to take – national, EPC or Patent Co-operation Treaty?

This is really a matter for specialist advice, but depends to some extent on which countries need to be covered, and translation costs.

What about biotechnological inventions?

The EC Directive 98/44EC on the legal protection of biotechnological inventions was adopted in July 1998. This Directive clarifies and harmonizes the legal protection available to biotechnological inventions in the Community. All Member States have an obligation to ensure that their national laws and practices conform to the Directive by 30 July 2000.

As to living substances, the Commission has taken the view that patenting is possible, although plant or animal varieties should remain unpatentable. A group of advisers to the Commission on ethical questions relating to biotechnological inventions has been set up. Plant breeders' rights are governed by a 1994 Regulation and by a 1961 International Convention on the Protection of New Varieties of Plants (as amended).

Genetically modified organisms (GMOs) and transgenic foods are subject to notification and safety assessment procedures under a system set up in 1991, with 1999 amendments, and sometimes to labelling under the Novel Food Regulation 1997. Up until June 1999, 18 licences for the production or sale of genetically modified products had been granted.

What about pharmaceuticals and medicines?

The European Agency for the Evaluation of Medicinal Products, usually known as the Medicines Agency, with a mixed system of registration and/or mutual recognition of national authorizations, provides a single central evaluation and subsequent market authorization valid throughout the EU for innovative medicinal products. National authorities may still grant national authorizations for products only intended for use in their national market. The Medicines Agency is sited in London, and should speed procedures, thereby enabling both veterinary and human use products to be marketed more quickly. The supplementary protection certificates regulations on extension of protection for pharmaceutical products and agrochemicals for up to a maximum of five years mirror the US and Japanese provisions.

What about software patents?

This is a difficult subject, partly because of the speed of development at this time. Software is frequently regarded as best protected by copyright. However, the possibility of a draft Directive on software patents has been raised.

Does the Community have any interest in other related patent matters?

Yes. As well as legal framework issues, the Commission has highlighted the provision of patent agent services across the Community as one of the areas in which it feels that a full Treaty-based approach needs to be adopted. An interpretative memorandum has been issued by the Commission.

What is a utility model?

This is a registered right, which grants exclusive protection for a technical invention that has less inventiveness or novelty value than one that is patentable; and no prior examination is required. It is not yet available in all Member States (eg the UK has no regime), but is a national right where it is available. The Commission has suggested that there should be Community protection through EU-wide recognition of national rights. The 1998 proposals for a draft Directive on Utility Models is a minimalist attempt to harmonize the key elements of national regimes, and remains under discussion.

What about industrial designs?

A proposed regulation on the establishment of a Community

design system for the legal protection of industrial designs remains under discussion, but there is a 1998 Directive to harmonize national legislation on the protection of designs. Implementation is subject to transitional provisions. Industrial design protection relates to the appearance of a product, eg it could relate to anything from a watch to a household appliance. In most EU countries the design has to be novel as well as have individual character to gain protection. Protection is for five-year periods renewable for up to 25 years. The provision is effective throughout the EEA.

WIPO is presently seeking to update the 1925 Hague Agreement on Industrial Designs, which currently has 29 members. This provides for a single application filing to protect industrial designs in all participating countries.

Trade marks

As with patents, the Community has recognized the value of trade marks, so considerable efforts have been made to achieve a clear system to meet the expectations of the parties selling goods throughout the Single Market.

Current harmonization, however, stops short of enforcement and penalty provisions, for which Member States have traditionally been competent. Publications such as the Green Paper on combating counterfeiting and piracy suggest that much can be done at EU level as well as national level, and that the Treaty of Amsterdam might form the basis of extended Community competence.

The whole question of parallel importing of trade-marked goods has recently been raised again, as the ECJ ruled in the Davidoff case that the selling of such goods in the EEA, imported from outside the EEA without the consent of the trade mark owner, was not allowed under the 1989/104 Directive on Trade Marks. The Council discussed a report on the situation in March 1999. It may be that there will be some amendment to the 1989 Directive that provided some protection to trade mark holders.

Are national trade mark provisions harmonized?

Yes. The 1989 Council Directive on Trade Marks (amended 1992) required the harmonization of Member States' legislation. Major differences included, for example, the test of what may be registered, and the extent of rights of a registered trade mark owner. This was required as there are different national systems of trade mark protection in the different Member States.

Is there a Community trade mark?

Yes. The Community Trade Mark Regulation 1994 set out the Community trade mark system and provided for implementation, with an office for registration of Community trade marks, called the Office for Harmonization of the Internal Market (Trade Marks and Designs), in Alicante, Spain.

A Community trade mark (CTM) is valid for 10 years, is renewable and can co-exist with national trade marks. The CTM, which is optional, covers all Member States with one application, and has been available since 1996. However, applications can only be examined for rejection on absolute grounds, eg of public order, or that it offends public standards, so a Community mark may be vulnerable to attack and possible cancellation by previously registered national marks. Applications may be made in the various Community languages, and Community marks may be held by anyone residing in the EU or in a third country acceding to the Paris Convention for the protection of intellectual property. The official languages are English, French, German, Italian and Spanish.

It should be noted that the Community trade mark is not intended to be mandatory, so if an applicant only wants to cover a mark in one or two Member States, he or she can still apply for a national trade mark.

Are any members of the European Union members of any other arrangements relating to trade marks?

Yes. Most members of the EU and EEA are among about 30 signatories of an agreement concerning the international registration of marks, which is administered by the World Intellectual Property Organization (WIPO). This enables nationals of, or established enterprises in, its signatory states to obtain from a single application in French or English in Geneva, registration of an international mark and protection for any or all of those countries (under the Madrid Agreement and Protocol on International Registration of Trade Marks 1989).

The Commission has proposed that the EU accedes to the Madrid Protocol and makes it and the CTM procedure complementary, with CTM holders able to request Madrid protection, and vice versa. It should be noted that under various Europe and co-operation agreements the Central and Eastern European states, and some others, have agreed to ratify the Madrid Protocol.

Copyright

What is the Commission's attitude to copyright?

Various Directives in the area of copyright have been adopted since 1991, which reflects the fact that copyright is assuming increasing importance, as the economic interests of authors, artists and other creators become more valuable, and warrant greater protection. With the improving speed of communications, the increasingly global nature of satellite broadcasting, the extending use of databases and computer programs, and the Internet, the whole field of copyright has broadened. This, together with the cost to industry and commerce of counterfeiting and piracy, has focused the attention of the Community on copyright, and the protection that should be available. A Commission communication in 1996 set out legislative requirements in respect of competition and barriers to trade in respect of (a) reproduction rights, (b) communication to the public, (c) distribution and (d) protection for anti-copying systems.

Is there any existing harmonization within the Community on copyright protection?

There is some harmonization at Community level, and the European Court of Justice has made some decisions that would affect all copyright holders within the EU.

A 1988 Green Paper, *Copyright and the Challenge of Technology*, pinpointed particular difficulties. These included the problems of piracy, the home copying of sound and audio-visual works, the question of distribution and rental rights for sound and video recordings, and the legal protection of computer programs and databases, together with the external aspects of copyright protection. That consultative document did not tackle some important subjects, namely industrial design copyright, the question of photocopying infringements, and copyright in cable or satellite TV performances. As a result, many consultative documents, action plans and proposals have followed on matters as varied as policy aims and proposed legislation on reproduction rights, new protection for on-demand transmissions from networks such as the Internet, and the 1999 draft Directive on Copyright and Resale Rights for Works of Art.

What sort of protection exists?

The situation is moving fast, and various provisions have been introduced or are under discussion to keep copyright protection in tune with changing needs. Examples include:

1. The 1991 Directive on Computer Software, which harmonized the position of Member States, requiring that they treat computer programs as literary works.
2. The 1992 Directive on Rental and Lending Rights and Neighbouring Rights.
3. The 1993 (Copyright Term) Directive, concerning the harmonization of the duration of copyright protection and certain related rights, defined copyright owners, setting the terms of protection at the life of the author plus 70 years, and giving 50 years for related rights. It introduced a new 25-year protection period for posthumously published works.
4. The 1996 Directive on the Legal Protection of Databases, which provides a two-tier system, with copyright aimed at the design of the system, the content of which is separately protected for 15 years. It should be noted that databases might also be affected by the Directive 1995/46 on the protection of individuals with regard to the processing of personal data and the free movement of such data.
5. Various provisions relating to topographies of semi-conductor products, satellite communications and broadcasting, television broadcasting standards, and telecommunications services generally.

What about encrypted services?

The 1997 draft Directive on Legal Protection for Encrypted Services would ensure that Member States would extend copyright protection to cover encrypted material that is digitally distributed. It would give rights to copyright owners to control distribution of works, enable copyright holders to develop and use electronic safeguards, and harmonize EU legislation on private copying. The Directive as drafted would extend to music, films and software. While this draft Directive is aimed at controlling illegal downloading and copying given the increased use of the Internet and satellite TV, it is recognized that policing it could be a problem.

What other provisions apply in the EU to copyright?

Some provisions relating to copyright differ between Member States, but they are all members of the Berne Convention for the protection of literary and artistic works, as well as the Universal Copyright Convention (UCC), so general principles are relatively harmonized, and provide a significant measure of protection.

What is the history of the Berne Convention?

It was first signed in 1886, and has been revised five times since then, the last major revision being by the Paris Act 1971.

It established the International Union for the Protection of Literary and Artistic Works (the Berne Union). Ninety-seven countries have acceded to the Convention, which provides that protection is extended (without formalities) to works by nationals of any country acceding to the Convention or if first publication takes place in a Berne Union country, ie a country that accedes to the Convention and complies with its general principles.

Most recently the WIPO Copyright Convention 1996, which is not yet in force or indeed ratified by many of the 30 countries required to bring it into force, effectively updates the Berne Convention as it requires adherence to it, but adds new provisions to strengthen some traditional rights and update protection available.

What is the Universal Copyright Convention (UCC)?

This is another international treaty, drafted in Geneva in 1952 under the auspices of UNESCO and coming into force in 1955. It was revised in Paris in 1971. Around 90 countries are members of one or other version of the UCC. Under it a member country undertakes to give the same protection to foreign works (provided they comply with Convention requirements) as it gives to its own domestic works. The work must have been written or produced by a Convention national, and first published in a Convention country. There are registration and manufacturing requirements, but in some cases exemptions apply. All copies have to bear the copyright notice '©', followed by the name of the copyright owner and the date of publication. This symbol has to be placed in a prominent position so as to serve as a proper notice of the claim.

Are there any other conventions concerning copyright?

Yes. There are various other conventions relating to particular problem areas, for example the Convention for the Protection of Producers of Phonograms Against Unauthorized Duplication of their Phonograms (Geneva 1971) has been signed by around 90 countries.

Piracy and counterfeiting

Are piracy and counterfeiting really important?

Piracy is a difficult, expensive and therefore important problem. It is defined for the purposes of copyright as the unauthorized reproduction for commercial purposes of works protected by copyright or similar rights, together with all subsequent commercial dealings in such reproductions. International Federation of the Phonographic Industry (IFPI) estimates indicate that, in 1998, 400 million pirated CDs were sold, valued at $4.5 billion, and making up 10 per cent of the global market in CDs. The estimated loss in the EU from illegal copying and piracy is significant. Not only CDs, but also videos, sound recordings and books, suffer from being illicitly copied and sold. While the UK and some other Member States belong to various conventions aimed at combating the problems relating to sound and television broadcasting, not all Member States have acceded to these conventions, and piracy problems in some Eastern European applicant countries are significant.

What is the difference between piracy and counterfeiting?

Piracy has been defined above. Counterfeiting occurs where there is a deliberate copying of a product or its packaging, label or trade mark. It has been defined by the Commission as 'the unauthorized use of a legitimate product's commercial presentation – in particular its trade mark or some other protected indication'.

What is the present position as regards protection in the Community?

A 1986 Regulation on the Free Circulation of Counterfeit Goods sought, on proper application by the trade mark holder, to limit the free circulation of counterfeit goods. This was extended by the 1994 Regulation on Counterfeit and Pirated Goods to enable swifter seizure by the authorities of goods that also infringed other IP rights. Recent amendments have extended provisions further to cover goods protected by patents and supplementary protection certificates.

The position for pirated goods is as follows:

- For books, the protection available seems to be satisfactory and effective, as all Member States belong to the Berne Convention.
- With regard to films and videos in the Community, copyright protection is inconsistent, with differing solutions to problems of ownership causing difficulty and confusion, but work continues on this.

- For sound recordings, the level of protection is not consistent throughout the Community.
- On broadcasts, and satellite and cable transmissions, the situation has been helped by the 1994 Directive on Copyright, Neighbouring Rights and Cable Transmissions, which enables broadcasters to obtain copyright for their entire trans-European transmissions in their home country. There is also a Council of Europe Convention on copyright in satellite and cross-border broadcasts.
- The Encrypted Services draft Directive should provide some protection in that area.

Useful information and advice may be obtained from the Commission, the IFPI or the Anti-Counterfeiting Group (see Appendix III).

What about the World Trade Organization and GATT agreements?

In view of the importance of protection of intellectual property rights generally, and the cost of counterfeiting (an estimated 5 per cent of world trade), the problem was discussed in the Uruguay round of GATT talks, whose texts were formally adopted in December 1994. These included agreements relating to Trade in Intellectual Property Rights (TRIPs). The problem of parallel importing is also likely to be discussed in this forum.

Licensing

What about the exploitation of IP rights?

This is complex. Enterprises that do not already do so should consider maximizing their return on patents, trade marks, designs and copyrights by licensing. However IP rights by definition create monopoly situations, and care must be taken concerning the competition rules. Expert advice is vital, and can avoid very costly mistakes (see also Chapter 10).

What is a licence agreement?

It is an agreement whereby one company or individual (the licensor) licenses or grants rights to another company or person (the licensee) to allow him or her to manufacture or assemble products, which may or may not be patented, or to use the registered name of a company or product, or its trade mark or brand name, in a particular way. Usually, the arrangements include payment of an annual fee, plus a commission or royalty, but licensing arrangements vary greatly. They are important because they enable firms to expand their operations with relatively little cost to themselves.

What kinds of licence are possible?

Licences that may be granted include rights under patents, trade marks, know-how, registered designs and copyright. There are various forms of licence:

- an *assignment*, whereby the licensor/assignor disposes of all his or her rights in the subject matter by assigning the rights to the assignee, who can then do what he or she likes with them;
- a *sole licence*, whereby the licensor retains his or her own rights, but agrees not to give any person other than the licensee rights within the scope of the licence agreement;
- an *exclusive licence*, whereby the licensor gives up his or her own rights in addition to agreeing not to give anyone else rights within the scope of the agreement;
- a *non-exclusive licence*, whereby the licensor is free to exploit the licence him or herself, and to give out other licences of the same subject matter in the same geographical area, but the licensee is also allowed to operate within the scope of the agreement.

Are there differences between licences for different purposes, for example registered designs or trade marks?

Yes. Licences relating to trade marks are generally referred to as registered users agreements, and require the monitoring by the licensor of the quality of the products licensed. The licensor usually has to pay the trade mark renewal fees. Licences of patents and know-how usually relate to the transfer of technology.

What is the attitude of the Commission to licences?

As has been seen in Chapter 10, the exploitation of intellectual property rights could appear to constitute a misuse of a monopoly. Because it is obviously necessary to ensure the proper level of protection for intellectual property rights so that investment in research and development continues, a system of block exemptions has been devised to give protection, in certain circumstances, from the competition or restrictive practices provisions for patent licences, know-how agreements, licences to perform and licences to use trade marks.

Which are the most important block exemptions?

Block exemptions for patents, know-how and franchising agreements come within the system set out in the 1996 Technology Transfer Block Exemption Regulation, which exempts various categories of technology transfer agreements from Article 81 (ex 85) of the Treaty. It provides also for joint agreements, so it may apply to mixed patent/know-how licences, but does not cover trade marks, copyright software or other agreements except where such rights are ancillary to the patents or know-how. The duration of the exemptions granted depends on the type of technology that is licensed. Market share is relevant, especially where it is felt that a company is seeking to prevent third-party access to a market. The regulation provides for notification procedures, to cover arrangements not specifically governed by the exemptions, to require notification to the Commission, which may then express opposition if appropriate within four to six months. It also includes useful guidelines.

What is the likely effect of the ongoing development of provisions relating to IP generally?

Intellectual property issues are becoming increasingly global and are under discussion in various fora, including the WTO, and WIPO, which is a branch of the United Nations Organization, based in Geneva, with an arbitration centre specializing in intellectual property disputes.

The importance of the protection of intellectual property to industry and commerce was reiterated in the Amsterdam Treaty. The Commission has expressed concern that too little is spent on R&D in the EU by comparison with its international competitors, and the proper support of intellectual property rights is seen as necessary to encourage private sector R&D spending. It is a field in which expert advice is needed.

Further information may be obtained from the European Commission, the Patent Office (an Executive Agency of the Department of Trade and Industry), the Chartered Institute of Patent Agents, the Trade Marks, Patents and Designs Federation, and the Institute of Trade Mark Agents (see Appendix III).

15 Enterprise and industrial policy and the information society

Enterprise policy

What is the Community's enterprise policy?

Enterprise policy covers a wide area and can be defined as the co-ordination of Community action to create a favourable economic and social environment for enterprises generally, in particular SMEs, and to increase and improve the services available to them. Much EU activity is geared to this, as the importance of supporting a climate in which enterprise, industry and innovation can flourish to the benefit of everyone has long been recognized. Various policy reviews have reflected the urgent need to reduce unemployment, and encourage research and development, because the EU is lagging behind its US and Japanese rivals in successful innovation. The milestone 1995 Commission Green Paper on Innovation was followed by the first Action Plan for Innovation in Europe: Innovation for Growth and Development 1996, which identified three main priorities:

1. to promote an innovation culture, both in society and in the economy;
2. to establish a good business environment in terms of legal, regulatory and financial provisions to promote innovation;
3. to promote more effective links between research and innovation and business.

The 1997 Action Plan for a Single Market had four strategic targets aimed at removing remaining obstacles to the Single Market. The first of these, on which immediate action could be taken, was to make existing rules for the Single Market more effective.

What was Agenda 2000?

Agenda 2000 was the Commission's detailed strategy with a single framework for the development of the EU after 2000 to enable the widening of the EU, presented in 1997. It encompassed not only the institutional and financial reforms and measures needed for widening the EU in the context of the applicant states, and the measures needed to prepare those applicant states, but also encompassed the strategy to strengthen growth, competitiveness and employment within the EU. This strategy reinforced the aims of the 1996 Action Plan, but went further, as in the Amsterdam Treaty the Member States had agreed to co-ordinate economic policies concentrating on fostering sustainable growth and job creation.

The main targets of Agenda 2000 in respect of developing internal policies for growth, employment and quality of life (as employment was seen as the key to better social conditions) were:

- creating the conditions for sustainable growth and employment;
- developing knowledge policies, by encouraging R&D, education and training;
- encouraging mobility, and an adaptable workforce, and promoting the information society;
- modernizing employment systems, eg by making social protection schemes more employment-friendly;
- improving living conditions, and the effectiveness of environmental and public health provisions;
- ensuring that environmental considerations are integrated into the design and implementation of all Community policies;
- enabling the progressive establishment of an area of freedom, security and justice.

Agenda 2000 also sought to maintain economic and social cohesion through the reform and more effective use of the Structural Funds. This means that regions where development is lagging behind and unemployment is high will get more support.

In Agenda 2000 the Commission suggested the further reform of the CAP, and set out a detailed analysis of the current position of applicant states from various aspects, ranging from ability to take on the *acquis communautaire*, to matters such as the independence of their central banks.

Has work continued in the context of encouraging growth and development in the EU?

Yes. For example, the December 1998 European Council Vienna Strategy supported action to help with employment, economic growth and stability; improving security and the quality of life; reforming policies and institutions; and promoting prosperity and stability. The 2000-05 strategic plan expands this in the context of enlargement.

The third multi-annual Programme for SMEs (1997–2000), which set out to assist SMEs, has been seen to be a success.

How is the innovation culture encouraged?

The Community aims through education and training to promote the understanding and use of technological advances, and the importance of creative abilities, and to increase mobility of researchers and students. Business managers are encouraged to achieve best practice in organizational methods, and a European benchmarking system is being developed, which will encourage better quality training and management in business and schools.

Public authorities are urged to encourage innovation, because of their huge public procurement programmes, and it has been suggested that they should be involved in monitoring, analysing and encouraging new systems development, with information channelled into a statistical Community database that could be used to compare results.

Intellectual property (patents, trade marks and copyright) protection systems are being looked at to encourage simplification and cost reductions.

How is the favourable environment for enterprises being achieved?

This is being achieved through encouraging the following.

(a) *Competitiveness.* This is looked at internally and in the context of the EU overall. An independent competitiveness advisory group (the Molitor Group) periodically produces reports and advises on priorities and policy. Its members, chosen for their individual expertise, include presidents and chairmen of multinationals, prominent trade unionists, academics and one representative of the Commission.

The Commission reports annually to the Council on European competitiveness in general *vis-à-vis* third countries, taking into account the effects on EU members of WTO and other international industrial partnerships, and co-operation agreements with third countries. Trade protection is seen as important, particularly to prevent discriminatory practices against EU members by third countries, so anti-dumping controls and negotiations on reciprocal access to third countries continue, eg via negotiations through the WTO.

Internally, attempts continue to ensure that EC competition rules are kept up to date, with proper exemptions from the competitive restrictions to protect innovation, and streamlined procedures (see Chapter 10).

(b) *The reduction of administrative burdens on enterprises.* This is an ongoing aim, focused particularly on SMEs, which suffer disproportionately from the costs of administrative and bureaucratic burdens. The Molitor Group suggested ways of easing these burdens, and much has already been done through the Simpler Legislation for the Internal Market (SLIM) initiative. A 1997 Commission Recommendation urged practical measures to reduce the bureaucratic burden on enterprises, and recommended single contact points – 'one-stop shops' – to advise business start-ups and to help new small business. It is in this context that it was suggested a push be made to agree the European Company Statute, the European Co-operative Society, the European Mutual Society and the European Association.

(c) *Common standards.* As it is impossible for EC standards authorities to keep up in legislative terms with the speed of new standards requirements, the Community is encouraging the adoption of common standards other than through legislation, ie by agreement (see Chapter 6).

(d) *Incentives through taxation and financing.* Taxation policies, although politically sensitive, can provide incentives and encourage investment. Reviews to establish areas where improvements are possible from a Community as opposed to a solely national perspective, such as taxation of cross-border payments, access to and encouragement of venture capital, and risk assessment, can be useful, but sometimes cause specific difficulties (eg the proposals for a withholding tax on investment income of non-residents and investment income earned abroad, particularly in international bond holdings, would cause enormous problems for the UK stock market, and drive significant business outside the EU).

(e) *Research and development and its exploitation.* The Commission's latest action plans focus on encouraging R&D and its exploitation through the fifth Framework Programme for R&D 1998–2002, at the same time providing particular safeguards for SMEs. The Structural Funds, Regional Development and other funds specifically include innovation encouragement as an important aim.

What about reducing barriers to trade?

In April 1999 the Commission approved a market access strategy to counter problems encountered by EU exporters. They have a database of over 1,000 such barriers and of these about a quarter are already being effectively dealt with, with negotiations being continued on many others.

How are SMEs defined?

Much confusion has arisen due to differing definitions of SMEs. In 1996 definitions were agreed (see Chapter 13). A recent report stated that the 18 million SMEs constituted 99.8 per cent of all companies in the EU, providing 66 per cent of total employment, and 55 per cent of business turnover. They are therefore seen as a significant engine of employment.

What particular action has been taken to help SMEs?

A Commission task force is responsible for developing and co-ordinating support facilities, grants and loans for SMEs, and successive action programmes have been useful, as they are aimed at supporting SMEs to enable them to assist economic growth and increase employment in the EU. Reports show that SMEs need help to improve their competitiveness, through better training, networking, encouragement to use of information highways, easier access to inexpensive finance, and effective information on market and production opportunities. The third multi-annual Programme for SMEs in the European Union 1997–2000 included useful initiatives, also supported in the context of the Amsterdam Treaty initiative and the Employment Confidence Pact.

How does the European Union stimulate SMEs?

The EU stimulates SMEs in a variety of ways:

1. *By the provision of seed and venture capital.* Many seed capital and venture capital funds have been set up, private sector participation encouraged, and an association to encourage mutual guarantee companies (MGCs) has been formed. CREA is a new pilot seed capital scheme. The European Investment Bank is active in larger-sum financing. New provisions to encourage risk capital growth to promote innovation facilitate equity holdings by investors in SMEs.
2. *By ensuring compliance cost assessments for new legislation.* The Commission ensures that compliance cost assessments are made at an early stage on any new proposals that might affect SMEs. The establishment of Business Test Panels in each Member State, to comment on proposals to make impact assessments for new legislation more effective, was agreed in 1998.
3. *By management and marketing training.* The impetus here is towards assisting in management training and marketing improvements to enable SMEs (particularly in industry) to compete in an increasingly competitive environment. The Euromanagement Network is useful.

4. *By simplifying VAT systems* generally, and particularly for SMEs, by raising the annual turnover threshold and seeking to establish a common system of VAT. In 1999 increases in limits were proposed: for small companies, to balance sheet totals of E(Euro)3.125 million and turnover of E5 million, and for medium enterprises to balance sheet totals of E12.5 million and turnover of E25 million.

5. *By facilitating the transfer of SMEs to different owners* where this is desirable or, for example, on the death of a partner or entrepreneur, or where there is a need to convert the partnership into a limited company.

6. *By state aid guidelines for assistance to SMEs.*

7. *By assisting with information and consultation*, eg through the Dialogue with Citizens and Business, launched in 1998.

What about financing of SMEs generally?

Besides the provision of seed capital funds, access to bank financing is seen as important, and the Round Table of Bankers and SMEs set up by the Commission established a list of recommended best practices as guidance to be implemented throughout the EU. It included guidance on risk assessment, treatment of high-risk customers, support for specific groups, encouragement of entrepreneurship and consultation, and increased transparency, with help for SMEs to improve managerial abilities. Many recommendations were reflected in the Innovation Action Plan 1997.

EASDAQ, the European Association of Securities Dealers Automatic Quotation is a new stock market for smaller companies to improve the availability of equity financing.

Has the European Investment Bank been useful to SMEs?

Yes. The EIB has stimulated growth through a number of mechanisms for medium and long-term funding, and supports projects relating to SMEs, regional development, transport and communications (eg TENs), energy, environmental protection, integration of industry and competitiveness. It may make loans directly for relatively large sums, or it may make loan facilities available through banks and other financial institutions for smaller amounts.

In considering projects, the EIB may look at the project to ensure eligibility, and takes into consideration the number of jobs likely to be created or maintained.

Further information is available from EIB (London Office), 68 Pall Mall, London SW1Y 5ES (tel: 020 7343 1200; fax: 020 7930 9939).

What else is the Commission doing?

The SME Community Initiative helps SMEs to adjust to the Single Market and internationally.

The continuing aims are to:

- develop further the Euro-Info Centre (EIC) network to facilitate access to community legislation and encourage the opening of new businesses;
- develop the confidential centres (BICS) and non-confidential partner search networks (BRE and BC-NET);
- step up activities to put business people in direct contact with one another, and promote cross-border subcontracting, eg through the Europartenariat and Interprise promotions;
- promote Community instruments for funding, and make it easier for SMEs to submit research projects.

A European SME Observatory was set up in 1992 to monitor the needs of SMEs and advise the Community, enabling structured proposals to be made.

The Commission third multi-annual Programme 1997–2000, in favour of SMEs, the craft sector and the liberal professions, drew together the existing actions and programmes to co-ordinate EU and national action. There is an insurance scheme backed by Commission funds to encourage risk investment in new technologies, and I-TEC (Innovation and Technology Equity Capital) aims to encourage appraisals and management of venture capital funds involved in the sector. New programmes and projects are being initiated or developed all the time.

What do the Europartenariat, Interprise and IBEX programmes do?

Europartenariat promotes regional development and encourages business expansion in the EU, its European neighbours and in the Mediterranean countries.

Interprise is aimed at co-operation between enterprises, public bodies and trade associations to strengthen the position of SMEs and encourage cross-border co-operation. There is encouragement for long-term co-operation agreements between large and small firms to promote quality control in subcontracting, and support to encourage SMEs to participate in EU research projects.

The IBEX (International Buyers Exhibitions) programme is also geared towards trade and networking across borders.

What form has the training initiative taken?

The Commission has put together a network of training organizations throughout the Member States with a training programme
module to help train advisers. There are sometimes funds available to finance organizations to train small local businesses, and
employment and training grants are available under the Structural
Funds and the European Social Fund.

What about language training and further education?

Language differences hinder SMEs co-operating with other firms
in other Member States, given the 11 different main languages in
the 15 Member States. The Lingua programme promotes language
training in schools and offices and is incorporated in the Socrates
education action programmes.

Various training programmes in further education aimed at
improving EU competitiveness have been useful. Emphasis is put
on co-operation between industry and universities, development
of trading partnerships (VITPs) within the framework of a
European network, and encouragement of international training
exchanges for students through the Leonardo da Vinci programmes. Many training, education and exchange programmes
are focused on the needs of SMEs, and the modern importance
for the EU of having a flexible mobile work-force.

What does the fifth Framework Programme for Research 1998–2002 cover?

The fifth Framework Programme (FP5) (which follows on from
the project-based FP4) is more purpose-based, focusing on:

- the resources of the living world;
- competitive and sustainable growth;
- the information society;
- international co-operation;
- the development of individual human potentials;
- innovation;
- the participation of SMEs, particularly aimed at countering
  unemployment.

In May 1999 the Council agreed to a resolution promoting the
participation of women in R&D programmes, and this is supported by the Women in Science initiative, which encourages consideration of women's needs in R&D.

It should be noted that this programme is open to 11 countries
that have applied to join the EU (the Central and Eastern
European countries and Cyprus).

Is it difficult for SMEs to participate in these programme projects?

Yes. It is easier for larger companies, rather than SMEs, to participate in EU R&D programmes, and in public procurement contracts generally. Attempts are being made to minimize these difficulties for SMEs, particularly through the encouragement of joint ventures, although their main problems remain. These are identified as:

- the maintenance of high quality;
- the ability to co-operate effectively with other firms;
- the bureaucratic requirements of the projects;
- the up-front investment requirements in applying for a contract – with no guarantee of success;
- lack of information about projects – in spite of the continuing efforts being made.

Have any of these problems been resolved?

Yes, although much depends on the SME itself. Besides favourable treatment in various schemes, the BRITE scheme (Basic Research in Industrial Technologies for Europe) was specifically amended to enable more SMEs to participate in R&D projects aimed at improving the competitiveness of European manufacturing industries, and even assisted some applicants to finance their applications. The CRAFT programme for co-operative research was introduced specifically for SMEs.

Industrial policy

Industrial policy is inseparable from enterprise and innovation policy in the EU, and is aimed at making the EU more competitive globally, particularly following a Commission communication in January 1999, which reported that European industry was not sufficiently exploiting globalization opportunities.

Successive communications and consultative papers since the 1990 communication that set out the EU industrial policy in detail have led to successive actions to fulfil the following aims:

- to promote intangible investments (eg intellectual property) by strengthening legislation and linking research more closely to needs;
- to develop industrial co-operation specifically by looking at national dominant positions and arrangements in a global context and facilitating co-operation and links with third countries in Europe and elsewhere;

- to ensure fair competition principally by controlling state aid and simplifying rules, by negotiating provisions within the WTO, and by monitoring reciprocal treatment in third countries;
- to improve the common customs tariff and to continue to remove distortions of competition inside and outside the EU;
- to modernize the role of public authorities and make their procedures faster, more transparent and more practical, to improve decision-making structures, and to overcome the difficulties encountered by businesses wishing to benefit from the Internal Market;
- to promote market access inside and outside the EU;
- to improve access to finance.

How is the Commission helping industry generally?

The Commission seeks to encourage greater investment in capital goods, urging Member States to stimulate this by:

- tax incentives and facilities for depreciation;
- the improvement of the business environment;
- promotion of industrial co-operation, especially with banks and other financial institutions;
- greater promotion of R&D;
- improvement in levels of technical harmonization;
- improvement of vocational training, and the availability of schemes to enable enterprises to re-employ skilled workers who have been laid off;
- ensuring structural regional aid does not benefit third-country enterprises at the expense of local industry;
- watching international markets to ensure reciprocal treatment;
- further support for SMEs.

The Community policy is that public authorities should not target and intervene to assist particular industrial sectors, flexibility being necessary where a particular industry is under threat, such as the shipping industry. It has urged that the modern approach to economic development should include considerations such as a reorientation of current technology from labour saving towards an emphasis on resource saving, with integration of environmental costs into the final price of goods and services. More thought is urged in respect of changes and their effects on the structure of urban and regional planning, and consequent social effects.

For example, the 1995 EU Industry Action Plan supported the development of the frontier-free Internal Market and the creation of the information society, and emphasized the need to take industry's needs in research policy into account, and to promote industrial co-operation. The use of benchmarking techniques to improve the competitiveness of EU industry was approved in 1996.

What about the steel industry?

The European Coal and Steel Community Treaty lapses in 2002, but these competences are being brought within those of the European Community. The planned restructuring of the steel industry has not been wholly successful, but financial support and controls on grants of national aid to ensure fairness continue. Difficulties arise particularly with regard to the perceived need to support Eastern European countries that export steel.

What about the aerospace industry?

EU aerospace industrialists regard the enormous US government subsidies enjoyed by their US competitors, together with their own limited access to US markets, as unfair. The Commission has set up a task force to co-ordinate EU effort to increase the competitiveness of, and reciprocal access for, the EU aerospace industry.

What about the commercial sector?

A 1996 Green Paper on commerce considered this sector in detail, defining commerce as the supply of goods and some services, and products such as tourism, whether as wholesalers, distributors or retailers, to the consumer. The 1999 White Paper on commerce, in the context of creating jobs and boosting competitiveness, aims to assist retailers and wholesalers by instituting a campaign to draw attention to the role of commerce (which employs about 17 per cent of the EU work-force), as well as identification of best practices. The White Paper suggests:

- better use of policy instruments to assist commerce;
- improvement of the regulatory and financial environment;
- strengthening competitiveness and promoting entrepreneurship;
- taking greater account of EU-wide and international developments;
- various specific EU programmes to help the commercial sector such as Commerce 2000, as well as more general programmes.

What sort of EC legislation applies to the commercial sector?

Many of the Directives on rights of establishment and freedom to provide services apply (eg the 1964 Directive in respect of wholesaling, commercial intermediaries and crafts; the 1986 Directive in respect of commercial agents; and the Broadcasting Directive 1989 for teleshopping), as do countless other provisions relating to consumer protection and standards. There are still barriers to cross-border retailing, not least the differing national provisions regulating commercial communications, and the sector is already being affected by the impact of new technologies and techniques such as telesales and the Internet. These new marketing possibilities also bring in regulation, eg on data use, to protect consumers.

Environmental considerations and provisions such as the need for resource saving in general impact on a wide area, for example urban planning, packaging and waste disposal legislation, and environmental protection regulations generally, such as on emissions. The environmental protection industry is one that is now growing in its own right, and work continues on improving the competitiveness of the recycling industry, with a Recycling Forum to advise the Commission. The LIFE programme supports schemes to assist environmental protection.

What about the tourism industry?

Two hundred million European citizens go on holiday every year, but it was only in 1992 that it was decided there should be a Community policy to support tourism in the EC. Tourism represents about 5.5 per cent of GDP, provides about 9 million jobs in the EU and involves about 2 million businesses. A 1995 Commission Green Paper urged improvements in competitiveness and consumer protection, regional development and protection and promotion of the national cultural heritage of Member States, and work continues.

Financial and practical support is provided. For example the PHILOXENIA programme 1997–2000 had four objectives: (a) improving information; (b) improving the legislative and financial environment; (c) removing obstacles to the development of tourism; and (d) promoting Europe as a tourist destination. Measures to facilitate travel in the EU for third-country tourists are encouraged (eg visa harmonization), and an expert group on tourism has been set up to make suggestions to promote job creation and stability in this sector.

What about the textile and clothing industry?

This has undergone restructuring, and the Retex programme was specifically geared to assisting. Protection mechanisms exist to prevent unfair dumping of textiles on the EU market, particularly from China and the Far East, although some EU countries feel these have not been sufficiently exercised. The Community imposes licences on imports from some third countries of clothing or textiles, which are subject to quantitative limits.

What about the trans-European networks?

These are being developed in the transport, energy and telecommunications fields. Intended to prevent isolation of peripheral regions, they increase business opportunities in these regions, and are being extended to the applicant countries of Eastern Europe. The Commission proposals for a Single Market for the provision of satellite communications services should also have a significant effect.

What about the energy sector?

The energy sector is included in the wide scope of industry policy, and its market is in the process of being liberalized. The availability of inexpensive energy is a vital component of the business environment needed to make industry competitive in the EU. There is concern among industrialists in particular as to the likely costs in terms of global competitiveness of proposed energy taxes intended to assist the environment (see Chapter 17).

The information society and electronic commerce

How are the information society (IS) and improved telecommunications perceived?

Although new technology traditionally leads to staff reductions, lower staff costs and more competitive prices in world market terms, yet electronic commerce is seen not only as an area of job creation, but also as a means to make EU industry and business more competitive in world markets. Trans-European networks (TENs) for information are vital if the periphery regions are not to be isolated, particularly in the context of extension of the EU towards the east. The cost of developing these is enormous, but likely to be funded largely by the private sector. However, an estimated 250 million people will have been connected to the Internet by 2000, and the Commission estimates that one in four new jobs will be derived from information society services.

How has Community policy relating to electronic commerce progressed?

The 1994 Action Plan set out the EU's perceived regulatory and other requirements for the Information Society, given the remarkable changes that are happening in the use of information networks and computer technology. It concentrated on: (a) improving the business environment; (b) investing through education; (c) improving the home quality of life; and (d) meeting the global challenge. A plan produced in February 2000 builds on this.

Electronic commerce includes the provision of services or trading using e-mail, the Internet, fax, databases, CD ROM, electronic directories and catalogues; or electronic transfer of funds, teleshopping and purchase of securities by electronic means. It can encompass providing educational material and services, and even digital TV commercials with viewer response mechanisms, besides trading documents such as bills of lading.

A 1997 Report set out a policy framework for EU action; for example, seeking to achieve standardization of access systems with a strong regulatory framework. A further 1997 report, 'Boosting Customers' Confidence in Electronic Means of Payment in the Single Market', sought achievement of secure electronic payment systems. A 1997 Commission Recommendation on transactions by electronic payment (for example, home banking, cash dispensers, etc) provided for safeguards regarding terms and conditions applicable, obligations and liabilities, with provision for a Directive if these measures were not effective. A 1998 Draft Directive on certain legal aspects of electronic commerce in the Internet Market (published in 1999) concerned free movement and freedom of establishment with regard to financial services, proposed harmonized rules where necessary and for dispute settlement and national regulatory procedures (Political Agreement 1999).

The Electronic Signatures Directive 1999 enables origin and authenticity of data received electonically to be checked, and gives legal recognition to electronic signatures in contracts. It also provides for home country control of e-commerce, and applies the principles of free movement to services in this field which is fast moving, so wide-ranging communications and projects have been produced, even a proposed pilot project to establish the usefulness of the Information Society for developing countries. Information Technology is a priority and a significant part of the 5th Framework Programme for Research and Technological Development 1998–2002 ('Investing in the Future') includes IT in many other projects, eg to encourage teleworking, which will reduce physical travel requirements.

A four-year action plan targets promotion of the safer use of the Internet, combating illegal and harmful content.

A comprehensive review of the regulatory framework for electronic communications was started in November 1999 and intended to search out and reduce barriers to cross-border trade.

This will cover licensing, infrastructures and access, and should lead to considerable simplification and greater competition. The need to take action to improve the digital market and proposals relating to the radio spectrum were also agreed.

The Information Society Project Office information Web site is on: http://www.ispo.cec.be/.

What about the global dimension?

There is a significant international IS dimension, particularly in view of WTO and transatlantic agreements. The Community is therefore involved in various international negotiations relating to trade barriers in this field, eg in the introduction of a regulatory framework for the new generation of Universal Mobile Telecommunications Systems (UMTS), which will have more sophisticated global coverage; and the 1999 World Radio Conference concerning agreements on radio frequencies for mobile telecommunications systems. Internet governance is a matter where international co-operation and discussion are necessary, particularly because the problems of 'cyber crime' have grown swiftly, and the global harmonization of provisions and co-operation between countries are recognized necessities to control, for example, cyber-pornography, hacking, money laundering, illegal gambling, fraud and copyright infringement. A 1998 proposal would make fraud in electronic commerce and counterfeit of non-cash payment means a criminal offence in all EU states, with provision for effective penalties.

How does the EU keep abreast of changing needs?

There are two independent advisory bodies. The Information Society Forum, with representatives of many different groups ranging from network operators and industrialists to academics, makes proposals for priority projects, and produces an annual report. The High Level Group of Experts researches and reports on the social and sociological effects of likely changes. It prepares reports on various matters such as the impact of new technologies on work patterns, improvement of management systems, education, health care, and developing human resources.

There are now Directives or proposals on such matters as online IS services, access, supervision, freedom of establishment, home country compliance, encrypted services, electronic signatures, unsolicited e-mail and automatic tagging of Internet messages. It should be noted that EU consumer protection provisions do apply to electronic commerce.

What about postal services?

The 1992 Commission Green Paper, *The Development of the Single Market for Postal Services*, analysed their importance and set out objectives and the means to achieve them. These included harmonization wherever possible, and partial liberalization of postal services, with some services reserved to ensure a universal inexpensive service. In December 1996 the Council decided that the target date for liberalization of postal services, direct and cross-border mail, should be 2003, with a timetable for decisions before 1 January 2000. It emphasized the need to ensure universal affordable services throughout the EU with harmonized criteria for service providers, and weight and price limits for domestic post. Postal service quality currently varies greatly in the EU; and this area has to be considered against the changing background of the information society. Postal needs remain important despite electronic communications, such as fax and e-mail.

What about telecommunications?

Liberalization of telecommunications has been effective since January 1998, and this has driven down prices, particularly since Commission investigations of discriminatory pricing in some Member States. Good telecommunications are a vital element in the strategy to make Europe competitive in world markets, so the Users Advisory Council, set up in 1994, advises the Commission on its information technology and telecommunications policy.

Harmonization of technical standards and effective liberalization of the sector to encourage fair competition are the main elements of EU policy originally set out in the 1987 Green Paper, *The Development of the Common Market for Telecommunications Services and Equipment*, aimed at improving the market environment. Since then there have been many proposals and Directives on the liberalization and use of telecommunications networks and infrastructure, the provisions of services, the supply of equipment and the application of competition rules to the sector, many of which are beyond the scope of this book.

Is the liberalization of telecommunications and voice telephony networks effective?

The 1995 Resolution defined the principles to be respected in establishing a framework for liberalization of telecommunication services and infrastructures. It stated that universal service obligations and the financing of non-profitable areas must be considered, as must the interoperability of networks, not only within the

EU but with third-country compatible access. Liberalization has proceeded more swiftly than envisaged in many countries in the EU, and the European Committee for Telecommunications Regulatory Affairs (ECTRA) has sought to harmonize national licensing conditions, and to apply a one-stop-shop system for applicants. However, proposals relating to full liberalization of all postal services in the EU remain under discussion.

What about global telecommunication developments?

The liberalization of global telecommunication markets, ie telephone, satellite, fax, mobile telephone, paging and private leased circuit services, is the subject of a wide-ranging deal under the WTO 1997 accord, signed by 68 countries, whereby the EU, US and Japanese markets agreed to be completely open to domestic and foreign competition from 1998.

The Commission continues to encourage R&D programmes, and to negotiate access to markets in third countries. Its work must be seen in the context of the agreement between the biggest worldwide operators and suppliers of wireless equipment on a single global strategy based on an Internet protocol, which takes into account the development of the next generation of hand-held telephones, which will be able to use data and multimedia services.

What about data use and protection?

Policies and action in various areas are linked to telecommunications and science and technology, and seek to encourage the interconnection of networks and services to increase competition, and so lower user costs. It should be noted that the transmission of personal data is controlled differently in different Member States, despite various Community initiatives, and users should be careful despite the 1995/46 EC Directive on protection of individuals with regard to the processing of personal data and the free movement of such data.

What about the Integrated Services Digital Network (ISDN)?

This network, providing a broad range of voice data and image transmission services to be added to existing telephone networks, remains under discussion.

What about television and audio-visual policy generally?

The audio-visual sector is important, as about 350 million people in the EU watch TV for an average of two hours every day. A 1994 action plan, *Towards an Information Society in Europe*, set out to reduce the enormous US share in the European audio-visual market – over 50 per cent of TV programmes, and 80 per cent of cinematographic distribution, except in France – by ambitious initiatives and support for European productions.

The Television without Frontiers Directive 1989 sought to create a European audio-visual area with monitoring systems, and minimum legal rules to enable free movement of televised programmes, with provisions to protect minors, and restrictions on advertising time. This was amended to ensure reservation of a proportion of broadcasting time and budgets for European productions, and the strengthening of rules concerning advertising time, home shopping (ie direct offers to the viewing public) and the protection of minors.

The 1997 Directive revising the 1989 Television without Frontiers Directive set out the new legal framework for TV broadcasting in the Single Market. It covered such matters as licensing of major events to ensure that a large proportion of the public should not be deprived of free access to broadcasts of important events such as the football World Cup, and listed the criteria to be taken into account in establishing what is 'of major importance to society'. It tried to curb mergers and acquisitions in the broadcasting media so as to safeguard pluralism and competition, and provided for a contact committee to be set up to monitor the implementation of the Directive.

The Audio-visual Observatory was set up in 1993.

Because the Commission looked to the audio-visual sector to create 2 million new jobs by 2000, the Media II programme for 1996–2000 concentrated on three areas: training of audio-visual professionals; project development; and distribution, broadcasting and post-production activities.

Do WTO proposals and provisions impact on telecommunications generally?

Yes. For example, under the WTO communication on the implementation of the International Trade Agreement, about 40 countries agreed to remove customs duties on various IT products by 2000 in four stages. It covered computers, software, monitors, semi-conductors, telecommunications equipment and fibre optics. More recently, the QUAD Group (the EU, the US, Japan and Canada) is negotiating agreement on the inclusion of wider liberalization relating to telecommunications in the next round of WTO talks on liberalization of trade in services, to include electronic commerce and transport services.

What about satellite communications?

The 1997 action plan to promote the EU as a global player in satellite communications was proposed in the context of the world satellite market being worth some ECU 300 billion by 2005, and has been followed by various provisions and proposals. There are two kinds of satellite communications: satellite personal communications systems, which provide world-wide mobile communications, and very broad band and digital communications, which provide Internet-type multimedia services. In 1991 agreement on high definition TV (HDTV) was reached with a Directive to encourage its development and broadcast by satellite.

What about satellite navigation systems?

The huge cost of developing such systems has led to the Galileo project, which seeks to safeguard EU interests in the development of global satellite navigation.

Does the EU get involved in space technology?

Yes, the European Space Agency (ESA) works closely with the Commission. The ESA supplies the hardware (launchers, satellites, etc) and the Commission helps to exploit them (see Appendix 1).

What about science generally?

In 1994 the European Assembly of Science and Technologies was created to assist the Commission to develop and implement Community science and technology and R&D policy. Many different scientific disciplines are involved in the FP5.

What are the overall effects of changing and developing standards?

Harmonization of standards and swifter communications widen the market. New information highways, the Internet and changing technology are revolutionizing the way in which business is carried out. Those who may be affected by changing technical standards, whether as users, traders or manufacturers, should co-operate closely with their national standards bodies, which can negotiate with their needs in mind only if they know of them. Changes are made swiftly. Benchmarking of best practice initiatives was launched in 1997. It is vital that companies ensure their work-forces are trained to take advantage of the new technologies, and here various programmes may help (see Chapter 16).

Is it difficult to get information about available help?

No, but it is time-consuming. Enterprise and industrial policy assists business people, whether managers, customers or clients. If enterprises do their homework properly they may well find a great deal of help available to them and, particularly with the FP5 programmes, new vistas could open. The key is the time that needs to be set aside consistently to find out what help is available, what is being proposed and where and whether there are European counterparts that want to form trading or other business links. In other words, business people have to keep on trying, as the right opportunity may take some time to materialize (see also Chapter 20).

Further information may be obtained from the European Commission, European Information Centres and Web sites, the relevant government departments and relevant trade associations. The Commission has published a useful guide to the EU's Structural Funds covering 2000–06.

16　Social policy

Social and employment policies

What is the background to the Community's social policy?

The work-force in the EU is over 150 million, with an estimated 8 million people self-employed and many people doing temporary work. Small and medium-sized firms (SMEs), including micro-enterprises (0–9 employees), account for about 70 per cent of employment.

The Commission's attitude to the harmonization of social measures is best summed up by ex-President Delors' statement that there can be no social progress without economic progress, and no economic progress without social cohesion. Social measures are the vital counterpart of the construction of a single economic market.

The free movement of workers, improvement in living and working conditions and equality of opportunities are stated aims of the Treaty of Rome, and the subject of various provisions.

Does Community social policy support these aims?

Yes. The Community has long been working towards the improvement and harmonization of workers' rights, which are important in the context of free movement of workers. Various provisions protect the health and safety of workers generally, and in specific sectors, such as coal, steel, nuclear energy, road haulage and fishing vessels. Successive action programmes have led to many proposals and reports, and work in this area continues.

What is the basis of social policy?

Intensified dialogue and consultation on social issues in a Community context between social partners, ie employers, employees, trade unions and public enterprises, became known as the 'Social Dialogue'; and there have been many reports on social policy issues.

The 1988 Degimbe Report dealt with the social dimension of the Internal Market, and in 1989 the Commission, seeking a mandate to introduce an action programme, produced the Social Charter of Fundamental Social Rights, usually called the 'Social Charter' (see below). The 1989 Action Programme itself set out over 40 proposals, including 17 Directives. Since then many reports have been produced, for example on family policy (considering the effects of the reduction in the number of marriages and the fall in the birth-rate), annually on the employment situation, and on low pay.

Successive papers and proposals have dealt with the importance of making the EU more competitive *vis-à-vis* third countries, encouraging more co-ordination at national and Community level, and have urged growth to combat unemployment, seen as causing other problems, such as rising crime, poverty and urban decay. Successive documents have outlined strategies aimed at encouraging solidarity, fighting social exclusion of disadvantaged groups, supporting the fight against poverty, encouraging better training and better focusing the EU social action programmes. These have encouraged measures to tackle unemployment, flexible working, working time proposals, reduction in non-wage labour costs and taxes, and the search for growth areas in terms of jobs.

A 1996 communication on the future of the Social Dialogue at European level was intended to promote social dialogue, as this is seen as the way forward for many social issues, particularly where EU legislation would be difficult to achieve. It is now seen as an important part not only in developing relevant policy, but also in carrying it forward. The Employment, Labour and Market Policy Committee started in 1997 to monitor trends and policies in the EU, and assists the Social Affairs Council in employment matters. The Committee consists of two relevant ministers from each Member State, and two Commission members.

The European Foundation for the Improvement of Living and Working Conditions supports social initiatives with research, and is situated in Dublin.

What are the most recent trends in social policy?

Employment creation has been singled out as a priority, and the latest Broad Economic Policy Guidelines and the European Employment Pact in 1999 support this.

In July 1999 the Commission issued a communication outlining EU strategy for modernizing social protection in the context of changing work patterns and social structures. It concerned: making work pay and provide secure income; making pensions safe and sustainable; promoting social inclusion; and securing high quality health protection. Following this, in September 1999 the Commission adopted an employment package to strengthen employment policy, growth and jobs in the EU, to be discussed by the Council in December 1999. The Joint Employment Report for 1999 considered actions already taken by EU members. The Commission has now suggested that the Council makes recommendations on the separate social policies of Member States based on comparisons with EU Employment Guidelines. The recommendations proposed concern: youth and long-term unemployment, reforming tax and benefit systems, lifelong learning, promoting service sector jobs, reducing fiscal pressure on labour, gender issues, improving statistics and modernizing work organization. The Employment Guidelines for 2000 refer to four areas: the need to encourage employability; adaptability; equal opportunities; and entrepreneurship. They emphasize the need to encourage information society skills and to help older workers and 'returners'.

Have there been problems implementing social policies?

Yes. Some Member States (most notably the UK) have disliked the level of interference with national social measures in policies proposed, and have in the past blocked various provisions on social or employee rights. Frequently the most relevant difficulty is the economic impact on countries required to revise upwards their social and wage standards. At a global level, the EU urges that priority should be given in granting aid to countries with social development strategies.

Did the Single European Act and the Treaty on European Union impact significantly on social policy?

Yes. Before the SEA came into effect in 1987, voting had to be unanimous, so legislation was difficult to achieve. The SEA allowed agreement on some proposals by majority voting on matters relating to, for example, recognition of professional qualifications and the alignment of national standards (including proposals for minimum standards relating to the working environment, and occupational health and safety), and for laws about the establishment and functioning of the Single Market. Under the TEU protocol (the UK abstaining), the other Member States agreed that various extra social issues should be decided by majority vote. Majority voting was extended again in respect of social issues under the Amsterdam Treaty.

How did the Treaty of Amsterdam affect social policy?

The Treaty of Amsterdam 1997 included a chapter on employ-ment, which gave Member States the task of promoting flexible labour markets, education and skills in the context of job creation; and the Community's area of competence now encompasses citi-zens' rights, to include combating discrimination on the grounds of sex, race, religion or disability (previously this was a matter for individual Member States, all of which had signed the Council of Europe's Convention for the Protection of Human Rights and Fundamental Freedoms). Emphasis was placed on better co-ordi-nation between Member States aimed at job creation and fighting unemployment throughout the EU.

The Amsterdam Treaty gave effect to the UK's decision to join the Social Protocol and sign up to the Social Chapter, so the UK now fully participates in discussions and enforcement of relevant provisions, such as the Works Councils and Working Time Directives. Majority voting in respect of social matters has been extended to include Employment Guidelines, incentive measures and rights of establishment.

What was the Social Charter?

The Charter of Fundamental Social Rights for Workers was an agreement without legal effect concerning the proper aims of social policy, signed by all Member States (except the UK) in 1989, and included the following headings:

1. The improvement of living and working conditions (includ-ing those of seasonal and part-time workers), and proposals relating to, for example, collective redundancy procedures.
2. The right to freedom of movement. Under the Charter this implied entitlement to equal treatment, including social and tax advantages, and that conditions of residence should be harmonized.
3. The right to exercise any trade or occupation on the same terms as those applied to nationals of the host state, and social protection as for nationals of the host state for Community citizens in gainful employment.
4. The right to fair remuneration for all employment and, to this end, that a fair wage should be established.
5. The right to social protection, together with a minimum income for those unable to find employment or no longer entitled to unemployment benefit.
6. The right to freedom of association and collective bargain-ing, ie the right of people to belong to the trade union of

their choice (and also the right not to belong to a trade union), bargaining rights and the institution of conciliation and arbitration procedures.

7. The right to vocational training. Every worker should have the right to continue vocational training all through his or her working life.

8. The right of men and women to equal treatment.

9. The right to information, consultation and worker participation. This is aimed particularly at companies or groups having operations in more than one Member State.

10. The right to health, protection and safety at the work-place.

11. The protection of children and adolescents. The minimum working age should be 16, and there should be special vocational training for these groups (see below).

12. Provisions for elderly people. Every citizen in retirement or early retirement should have an income that guarantees him or her a reasonable standard of living, with a specified minimum income, even if he or she has no entitlement to a pension.

13. Provisions for disabled people. There should be measures aimed at achieving the best possible integration into working life for this group, together with various related measures on mobility and so on.

Has the Social Charter made a difference?

Yes, even though most of the areas it covered came within the social dimension of the Rome Treaty, and action had already been taken or was under consideration on many topics. The Charter was an attempt to make a cohesive whole of the rather fragmented social policy.

Should the Social Charter be distinguished from the Social Chapter?

Yes. The Social Chapter was the agreement on social policy made between the Member States excluding the UK, which was appended to the TEU in a protocol (sometimes called the Social Protocol) signed by all the Member States including the UK that enabled the other Member States to proceed to legislate with qualified majority voting on social affairs matters without the UK, but using the Community institutions. As stated above, the UK has now agreed to participate, and this was made effective in the Amsterdam Treaty.

Are there any other social policy statements similar to the Social Charter?

Yes. Some inter-governmental organizations have produced statements such as the International Labour Organization Convention
and the Council of Europe Social Charter.

Have Community policies had an impact on unemployment?

In July 1999 average unemployment in the EU was 9.3 per cent,
so this is seen as a major issue.

It is difficult to assess the impact of the completed Internal
Market and of Community legislation in this area. Some argue
that extra employee rights lead to extra wage costs, and so lower
employment. Others argue that a floor of rights is important in a
civilized society so as to prevent exploitation of employees and
excessive hardship.

Various Community action plans have encouraged job creation
policies and schemes.

The European Confidence Pact for Employment launched in
1996 was aimed at encouraging co-ordination of policies in the
EU to encourage complementary strategies. Following this and the
Jobs Summit in 1997, it was agreed that the Member States
should draw up National Employment Plans (NAPs), which are
then reviewed by the Commission. These are based on the
Employment Guidelines to cover (a) developing employment, (b)
improving employability, (c) encouraging adaptability of employees and employers and encouraging equal opportunities. The
Commission Report may be followed, if appropriate, by recommendations made to specific countries.

The Broad Economic Policy Guidelines 1999 emphasized that
sound economic policies with good public financing encourage
job creation when linked to low inflation and wages.

New employment initiatives are encouraged through the
employment Structural Funds, the European Investment Bank, the
European Investment Fund, the European Social Fund (ESF), the
European Regional Development Fund (ERDF) and the European
Agricultural Guidance and Guarantee Fund (EAGGF).

There are various programmes to help to reduce unemployment, particularly where Community policies themselves lead to
unemployment (eg a cut in fishing quotas) (see also the discussion
of European Structural Funds in Chapter 5). The special support
programme (SPEC) for employment creation is set against high
unemployment in the EU.

As illegal employment in the EU is significant, a Council recommendation in 1996 suggested measures to prevent the illegal employment of third-country nationals, to include criminal and civil sanctions for those who employ or facilitate the employment of illegal workers.

Past jobs initiatives have included substantial extra funding through the Edinburgh Facility supporting infrastructure projects, funding through the EIB to create jobs in SMEs, support for TENs and most recently an enhanced role for the EIB in promoting job creation.

A 1999 draft Directive is aimed at lowering the VAT rate for labour-intensive jobs such as in the care services, and building and vehicle repairs sectors, in cases where the services are supplied direct to the consumer and no significant competitive distortions would result.

What is the Commission's attitude towards trade unions and employers' organizations?

The Commission consults closely with trade unions through the ETUC (European Trade Union Confederation), with employers' organizations through the Association of European Chambers of Commerce and Industry (Eurochambers) and the Union of Industrial and Employers' Confederations of Europe (UNICE) and with the social partners generally through the Social Dialogue. The Social Charter refers to the right to belong, or not belong, to a trade union, and following Amsterdam this is now specifically referred to in the Rome Treaty (Article 136).

What about employee participation?

Care should be taken not to confuse the participation of employees in the equity of the enterprise for which they work (such as share participation schemes) with their participation in decision-making. The Commission has long tried to strengthen all employee participation and consultation procedures, mainly in the context of company law harmonization (see Chapter 13), and new partnership and participation-based forms of work organization were urged in a 1997 Commission Green Paper.

What about employee consultation?

There are various provisions promoting consultation procedures with workers: (a) generally, and (b) in the event of redundancies in companies operating across borders, ie in European-scale undertakings or groups of undertakings. The Collective Redundancies Directive 1975 introduced general minimum rights of consultation in certain cases, and the 1992 Directive on Collective Dismissals in Multinationals extended provisions relating to procedures and information for workers in different Member States.

What does the European Works Council Directive require?

Briefly, the 1994 European Works Council (EWC) Directive 1994 requires undertakings with 1,000 or more staff overall in the EU, and at least 150 in at least two Member States, to set up works councils to consult employees. Its provisions relate to minimum information requirements and consultation. There are proposals to extend it. The UK, originally not party to this Directive, now applies it.

Following the failure of the social partners to agree provisions, the Commission produced a 1998 draft Directive intended to complement the EWC, which would require all enterprises with 50 or more employees to set up employee information and consultation committees to be consulted on strategic changes, eg the redundancy or sale of subsidiary companies, without any cross-border requirement included in the draft. This remains under discussion.

What is the Community's attitude to women employees?

The Commission has long promoted equality as the Rome Treaty set out the principle that there should be equal pay for equal work for men and women employees; but women in the EU earn an average of about 20 per cent less than their equivalent male colleagues.

The principle of equality was again underlined in the Amsterdam Treaty, and is now set out in Article 141 of the consolidated Treaty of Rome, which specifically indicates that the article is not intended to prevent positive discrimination where this would make it easier for the under-represented sex to avoid a disadvantage. It should be noted that equality legislation applies equally to men.

There are various supporting provisions:

- The Equal Pay Directive (1975) extended the principle of equal pay for equal work to provide for equal pay for work of equal value. In fact, the direct enforcement of this Directive provides an example of the power of the European Court of Justice, whose judgement in a case (*Macarthys Ltd* v *Wendy Smith*) in 1980 forced a change in UK legislation to bring the equal pay laws in the UK into line with the Directive.

- The Equal Treatment Directive (1976) extended equality to employment, training, promotion and dismissal, and dealt with both direct and indirect discrimination based on sex, marital status or family status.
- The Social Security Directive (1978) provides for equal treatment in state social security schemes, including contributory and non-contributory benefits.
- The Occupational Social Security Directive (1986), amended by a Council and EP Directive 1997, bans discrimination on the basis of sex, or marital or family status, and covers equal treatment in occupational, pension and other benefit schemes for employees and self-employed people.
- A 1986 Directive concerns equal treatment for self-employed men and women.
- There is a Directive on the burden of proof in legal actions in cases of sex discrimination.
- A voluntary code of practice to ensure men and women are paid equally for work of equal value, adopted in 1996, gives useful practical advice on the application of the principle, and a 1996 case supports the view that in actions brought under Article 141 (previously 119) even immediate successors can be used as comparators.

What about pregnant women?

The 1992 Directive in respect of the protection at work of pregnant women, or women who have recently given birth (the 'Pregnant Workers' Directive 1992, brought in under the 1989 Health and Safety 'Framework' Directive), required employers to carry out risk assessments and protective action to ensure such workers would not be exposed to harmful substances or agents, and could include granting paid leave. The provisions extend to women who are breast-feeding who, for example, may not be obliged to carry out work that might expose them to lead or its derivatives. The Directive also gives a woman, after one year's continuous employment, a right to 14 weeks' maternity leave and statutory sick pay.

The 1996 Directive on Parental Leave (maternal and paternal) provides for extra leave with some costs borne by government. The Directive gave effect to the parental leave agreement between the social partners in December 1995 (in accordance with the social agreement annexed to the Union Treaty) whereby workers, male or female, would be guaranteed three months' unpaid parental leave before a child is eight.

In 1995 the Commission proposed a study to consider the reconciliation between working life and family life, and set up the

Families At Work Network to analyse and spread experiences between enterprises on the best ways of balancing family and professional life, including, for example, childcare arrangements. Work on this continues.

Are there any specialist bodies promoting equality?

Yes. There are specialist bodies within the EU that promote equality. Examples include:

- the Childcare Network, which looks at children in the EU with particular reference to their effect on the employment of women and equality of opportunity;
- the Office of Equal Opportunities, which is part of DG V (the Directorate General for employment and social affairs);
- the Advisory Committee on Equal Opportunities, which represents the statutory bodies promoting equality in Member States;
- the Women's Information Service, which produces a multilingual bi-monthly newsletter entitled *Women in Europe* to disseminate information about employment policies in the Community;
- the Committee on Women's Rights set up by the EP to encourage progress in the whole field of equality of opportunities.

Further information about equal rights and opportunities can be obtained through the Citizens First initiative from the Commission, from a freephone (in the UK: 0800 581 591) or on the Internet at http://citizens.eu.int.

What about sexual harassment?

This issue relates to both sexes, but tends to impact more on women.

The 1991 Council recommendation and code of practice on dignity at work included practical guidance for social partners aimed at preventing sexual harassment, defined as unwanted conduct of a sexual nature or other conduct affecting the dignity of women or men at work. It includes verbal and non-verbal conduct as well as physical action. The recommendation and code of practice have been followed by consultation with the social partners with a view to drawing up a policy on sexual harassment in the work-place that could be negotiated as a collective agreement.

What about other assistance for women?

There are programmes that assist women. The NOW (New Opportunities for Women) Programme was launched in 1991 and still continues. Networking and informational initiatives continue.

The Daphne Programme for 2000–04 is to support projects combating violence against women, young people and children in the EU, and is set against a background of 67 per cent support in a poll for EU action to combat domestic violence against women, and (91 per cent) against children.

Sex tourism is a growing problem, and a Commission communication in 1999 outlines future plans to combat it.

What about part-time workers and fixed-term contract employees?

Provisions relating to part-time work impact chiefly on women, but numbers of part-time workers have been increasing in the EU. A 1994 discussion paper was followed by a 1997 agreement signed by the social partners to give part-time workers, male or female, certain legal rights to equal treatment with their full-time colleagues. The agreement was followed by the 1997 Directive, which requires that part-time, temporary and fixed-term employees should be given the statutory rights and occupational benefits enjoyed by full-time employees on a pro rata basis. These include occupational pension schemes and access to vocational training, pay for shift work, sick-leave schemes and paid holiday leave. It enables part-timers to get share options and staff discounts, for example.

In March 1999 a voluntary agreement was signed by the social partners, now encapsulated in a draft Directive, to ensure that there is no discrimination against fixed-term employees *vis-à-vis* permanent employees, and providing for an EU framework to control abuses.

What about health and safety protection?

A 1991 Atypical Workers Directive ensured that fixed-term, part-time, seasonal and temporary workers would have the same rights to health and safety protection as other employees.

Are there any provisions for disabled workers?

There have been various programmes, as about 37 million EU nationals suffer from some form of lasting or serious mental, sensory, psychological or physical disability. About half of these people are of working age.

The HELIOS programme targeted four areas: functional readjustment; educational integration; economic and social integration; and self-reliance. Other action concerns the vocational rehabilitation of handicapped people, education, training, employment, social security, mobility, housing, and the promotion of useful appliances for the elderly and the disabled.

The Commission is encouraging a Community-wide system of exchange of information to help co-ordinate action on disability problems. Following a communication from the Commission on equality of opportunity for people with disabilities, which looked at various areas such as education, work, mobility, welfare systems and equality of opportunity, a Council resolution in December 1996 called for the Community and Member States to mainstream the disability perspective into all relevant sections of policy formulation, and to assist disabled people to integrate fully into society. In May 1999 there was a resolution on equal opportunities for persons with disabilities. A draft Directive on the safe transport to work of employees with reduced mobility remains under discussion. The Commission has published a useful 1997 handbook, *Making Europe Accessible for Tourists with Disabilities*.

The European Disability Forum (EDF) is a consultative body with 150 representatives to promote the rights of disabled people. Funded through the Commission, it is a useful source of information. The Handy Net Database System includes information for disabled people, and a multilingual periodical entitled *Interact News* may be ordered from its offices in Brussels (see Appendix III). Other publications include *Helioscope*, and *Helioflash*.

What about the elderly?

About 15 per cent of the Community population are over 65, and over 60 million people in the EU are over 60, so the establishment of a European model of proper assistance to older people and various initiatives and pilot projects are in hand. The whole question of pensions remains under discussion and was explored in a 1997 Green Paper in relation to their provision, the transferability of benefits between Member States, and improvements and guarantees in respect of their management. A 1997 Commission report on the demographic situation in the EU noted the impact of an increasingly ageing population.

What about the protection of children in the work environment?

The protection of children and adolescents was included in the Social Charter.

The Council Directive 1994 on the Protection of Young People at Work set minimum health and safety provisions for young persons at work. Employment of children under 15 is prohibited (except, for example, children of at least 14 performing light work, or taking part in cultural, artistic, sports or advertising activities, or children involved in work or training schemes). The Directive is set against a background of at least 1.5 million school-children over 15 working in the EU outside school hours. Statistically they are more likely to suffer accidents or ill health caused by their work environment. Thus children and adolescents up to 18 in full-time education are limited to 12 hours employ-ment per week, and two hours of light work on a school day. There are also provisions relating to insurance, rest periods, night work, etc. Some EU members have been given extra time to implement this Directive (eg the UK).

What about the protection of children generally?

Child pornography and sexual exploitation of children seem to be growing problems. Joint action to combat child pornography was agreed in December 1998, and measures against sex tourism both within and outside the EU are being supported by the Commission.

An EP Committee of Enquiry has been set up to study the prob-lem of the sexual exploitation of children (there are an estimated 28,000 under-age prostitutes in Germany alone). A 1996 Commission Green Paper relates to action to protect children from pornography and other illegal material in audio-visual media and also in electronic media, eg on the Internet. A European Charter of Children's Rights has been proposed, and the 1996 draft Convention of The Hague on the Protection of Minors remains under discussion.

There is a Council of Europe Convention on the exercise of children's rights; and the International Labour Organization Convention aimed at abolishing child labour was passed some 26 years ago, and has been signed and ratified by 72 countries (not including the UK and the US). ILO currently estimates that there are around 250 million children aged between 5 and 14 at work just in the developing countries.

Has the EU done anything about poverty?

In 1996 the Commission estimated there were about 52 million people in the EU living below the defined poverty line, so this is an important issue in terms of social costs, crime and quality of life. Co-ordinated economic and employment policies are seen as assisting in preventing social exclusion and alleviating poverty, and these are important elements in Community policies. A 1998 report concerns the economic and social implications of industrial change, and work on this problem continues.

Are there any provisions on other employment issues?

Yes. There are many Directives, draft Directives and resolutions. These include:

- A 1991 Directive on a written statement of terms and conditions (proof of the employment relationship). Work of less than an average of eight hours a week is not covered by this Directive, but is dealt with in the 1996 Directive (see below).
- The 1996 Council and EP Directive on cross-border subcontracting and the posting of workers. The 'Posted Workers' Directive gives minimum rights to workers posted from other Member States on temporary secondment, so as to provide for protection in relation to health, holidays, safety, maternity leave, etc similar to that of comparable workers in the country of secondment. Minimum wage provisions also have to be respected if the secondment is for longer than a stipulated time.
- The EC Business Transfer (acquired rights of employees in transfers and mergers) Directive 1977 protects acquired rights so that a transferee automatically takes on the rights and duties under the contracts of employment or collective agreements existing at the time of the transfer until such time as changes are agreed. This does not generally apply in insolvency situations, but where there is a new owner of a firm.
- A 1997 Directive amends the 1977 Directive, and defines more closely the scope of the safeguards and liabilities, in particular including a clause banning discrimination on the basis of race, sex, age handicap, sexual orientation, skin colour, religion or nationality. As the legislation is complicated, the Commission have produced an explanatory memorandum.
- The Protection of Employees in the Event of their Employers' Insolvency Directive 1980 set up independent guarantee institutions and minimum levels of protection.

What about health and safety in the work environment?

About 10 million employees are victims of accidents or occupational disease each year. About 8,000 die. Inevitably, employees benefit from increased health and safety standards and environmental provisions generally (see Chapter 17).

The European Agency for Health and Safety at Work, sited in Bilbao, collects and disseminates data, and maintains a library and register of hazards. The protection of workers against hazards at work is encouraged by successive Safety, Hygiene and Health at Work Action Programmes, and employees have a duty to assist their employers in these aims.

Are there many Directives, satellite Directives, regulations or proposals in this area?

Yes. The 1989 Framework Directive, and the 1989 Directive on the Minimum Health and Safety Requirements in the Work-place aimed at the introduction of measures to improve the health and safety of workers at work, and set out the basic responsibilities and duties of employers and employees: risk assessment, preventative measures, the taking of health and safety advice, first aid, hazard and fire safety, electrical fittings, etc, together with the maintenance of accident and disease records, hygiene, first aid requirements, employee consultation and information, proper safety training, and other relevant matters. The Temporary Workers Directive 1991 extended the provisions to temporary workers.

The Framework Directive led to a series of satellite and other Directives covering many aspects of health and safety in the work-place. Examples include provisions relating to:

- machinery and work equipment, including minimum health and safety requirements for new and second-hand machinery;
- personal protective equipment, which requires the provision and use of such equipment where necessary and a framework for harmonized standards for the equipment itself;
- the manual handling of heavy loads, providing for avoidance of such handling wherever possible, and the proper training of employees;
- VDUs, now called 'DSEs' (display screen equipment), providing for eye examinations, the training of employees, and minimum health and safety requirements;
- the use of electrical equipment in explosive atmospheres, to ensure conformity with standards;
- the security and safety of workers in the open skies or in underground mining industries;
- minimum requirements and improved training and health surveillance for employees exposed to noise or electromagnetic fields or waves (although sea and air transport are excluded);
- the extension of major hazard controls;
- the protection of employees from biological agents, dangerous substances and carcinogens and asbestos;
- temporary and mobile sites (in a 1992 Directive);
- safety signals and signs;
- action to combat resistance to antibiotics;
- the integration of health protection into other policy areas.

What about the Working Time Directive 1993?

The Working Time Directive 1993 set out minimum daily and weekly rest periods, and minimum provisions for annual leave. The Directive is complicated, and fairly detailed as to possible allowable derogations. Proposals to extend its main provisions to some presently excluded employees, eg non-mobile transport workers, have been agreed (1999), but with a lengthy year lead-in period. The Directive is set against the background of tiredness being a significant cause of accidents and errors. There is some concern about abuses as individual employees may contract out of the provisions.

What about obtaining health and safety information?

To ensure access for workers to information concerning health and safety in the work-place, the Commission publishes a free quarterly magazine called *Janus*. Further information may be obtained from the European Commission, the British Standards Institute (BSI) or the Health and Safety Executive Web site: http://www.open.gov.uk/hse/hsehome.htm.

What about the general health of workers and others?

Cancer causes about 840,000 deaths annually in the EU with up to 1.3 million new cases diagnosed each year. Under the TEU the Community has a role in respect of general health. The continuing aims of the Commission are to keep data, spread information, improve care and promote more screening and research.

The fourth General Community Health Programme covered:

- an action plan to prevent cancer;
- health promotion, information and training support;
- prevention of drug dependence;
- the prevention of Aids and other communicable diseases such as TB (a Health Monitoring Programme for 1997–2000 concentrates on communicable diseases);
- an action plan to speed up research into BSE, Creutzfeldt-Jakob and related diseases.

There is research into neurological illness, and analysis of health trends EU-wide.

Tobacco consumption causes 500,000 deaths in the EU each year, but some 200,000 families in the EU rely on tobacco for a living. Action in other related areas includes labelling of tobacco products (1989), the directive to ban tobacco advertising, and production. A 1999 draft directive will require further reductions in tar levels, greater warnings on packets, and more details of additives.

The 1999–2003 Community Action Programme focuses on pollution-related illness, and rare diseases, and is geared towards encouraging co-operation between Member States.

What about other health issues outside the work-place?

An action plan for 1999–2003 targets accidents involving children and elderly people, and the reduction of suicides. Twenty million people have accidents at home or in their leisure time each year, of which 3 million are admitted to hospital, and 100,000 die (including some 10,000 children). The numbers of suicides have been increasing. About 43,000 commit suicide, and 700,000 attempt to do so every year in the EU.

Free movement

Can any citizen of any EU country work anywhere in the Community?

The Treaty of Rome provides for the free movement of persons in the EU. Originally freedom of movement within the Member States was restricted to workers in paid employment, but since 1993 the right has been general.

Citizenship of the European Union means that every person holding the nationality of a Member State is a citizen also of the EU. Every EU citizen has the right to live and work anywhere in the EEA (ie the EU, plus Iceland and Norway), albeit there are public policy controls, which are only restrictively applicable, if there is a serious threat. Thus citizens can move freely in the Community, and work, provided they comply with the local requirements, although they may not be able to undertake some public sector jobs, eg in national defence areas.

The most important Directives are:

- the 1964 Directive on co-ordination of special measures concerning the restriction of movement and residence of foreign nationals justified on grounds of public policy, public security and health;
- the 1968 Directive on abolition of restrictions of movement and residence in the Community of workers of Member States and their families;
- the 1972 Directive extending to workers and their families the right to remain in the territory of a Member State after having been employed in that state. Special measures on the basis of public policy, public security and public health have also been co-ordinated.

There is an EU provision on the publication of details about work vacancies in the EU, and the European Employment Services network (EURES) gives details of jobs available throughout the EU. It helped over 1 million employees to work outside their home country in the EU in 1996–97, and holds details of around 100,000 jobs in the EU. Nationals of one EU country may reside in another EU country for a defined period to look for work. Problems remain, largely due to delays in implementing EU provisions, but also in relation to pension and social security benefits in other Member States, and to apprentice status, for example.

What about the posting of workers?

The Council and EP Directive 1996 on the posting of workers gave minimum rights to workers posted from other Member States on temporary secondment, so as to provide protection in relation to various basic rights, eg to holidays, health and safety, maternity leave, etc, similar to that given to comparable indigenous workers.

Do EU citizens have to prove their status?

Yes. A valid passport or national identity card is required. In fact, EU passports have been available since 1985, and EU citizens can even vote in local and EP elections when they are resident in a Member State outside their home state.

What about third-country workers?

The Community has signed some bilateral accords with third countries guaranteeing non-discrimination for non-EU citizens in respect of terms and access, conditions of work and social security benefits. There are Council resolutions on such matters as admission of third-country nationals for educational purposes, and limited provision for when they are entering to carry on a professional activity. There are provisions on the issue of standard visas, and expulsion of third-country nationals (see Chapter 4).

Do the social security, unemployment and pension provisions differ from state to state?

Yes. The Commission has published practical guidance, as the situation is complicated, and covered by various regulations. Work continues on provisions to enable individuals to preserve or add to entitlements if they move to work in different states. A 1999 Regulation is intended to supplement the provisions, which already relate to employed and self-employed persons, to extend to students who are insured under a general or special social security scheme and studying in a Member State other than their own. A draft directive to facilitate pan-European pension funds is expected in 2000.

What about the migrant employee's family?

If an EU citizen takes up employment in another country, then that person and his or her family should be treated in the same way as nationals of the country in relation to pay, working conditions, tax, trade union rights, social security and education. Housing in particular still causes problems, so the Commission has set up Citizens Advice Services to advise on citizens' rights under Community law. The Euro Citizen Action Service (ECAS) can also assist.

What about recognition of job skills, training and vocational qualifications?

It rather depends on host-state recognition. There are areas of difficulty for non-regulated professions, but the European Centre for the Development of Vocational Training (CEDEFOP) is promoting recognition, and various Directives are in force requiring Member States to recognize 'certificates of experience', which relate to particular qualifications and experience obtained in another Member State.

'Euro qualifications' in various subjects including languages and business administration skills (recognized Community-wide) are now being offered successfully at many training centres (see Appendix VI).

Jobs covered by recognition provisions include:

- managerial and self-employed work in the wholesale trade;
- self-employed work in the manufacturing, processing, repair and construction industries, including architects;
- self-employed work in the retail trade, or in providing food, drink and accommodation;
- self-employed work directly, or as an intermediary, in the wholesale coal trade;
- work in various services, including transport, post-recreational and personal services, as well as itinerant traders, insurance agents and brokers, and self-employed work in services related to transport, travel agencies, hairdressing, storage and warehousing.

The above is not an exhaustive list and further detailed information should be obtained from CEDEFOP, the Internal European

Policy Division of the Department of Trade and Industry, the European Commission (DG V) or the European Foundation for the Improvement of Living and Working Conditions (see Appendix III).

What is the situation for the recognized professions?

Professionals encounter specific difficulties, even though the principle that employed and self-employed professionals should be able to practise throughout the EU has been confirmed several times by the European Court.

What about medical practitioners, lawyers, trademark and patent agents, accountants, engineers and other professionals?

If they comply with the various conditions set out in Directives in force, and with local requirements such as residency permits, doctors, nurses responsible for general care, midwives, dentists, vets, architects and pharmacists can have their professional qualifications recognized, and can work throughout the Community.

Sectoral Directives such as the 1977 Directive on freedom to provide cross-border legal services were followed by the general Directive 1988 on mutual recognition of professional qualifications, which applies to a very wide range of professions, where they are regulated by the state or by a chartered professional association, and which require at least three years' education and training or university (or equivalent) qualifications. A Commission study on recognition of diplomas and professional qualifications ended in 1994; and the 1997 Directive on rights of establishment of lawyers qualified in one Member State to practise fully in other Member States has been agreed.

What is the general effect of these provisions?

Their effect is that if the education and training leading to a professional qualification are broadly equivalent to those in another Member State, then the qualification will be accepted as equivalent and the professional will be able to become a member of that profession without having to re-qualify. If the education and training differ substantially as to time or content, then the host country can require an aptitude test, or a period of supervised practice of not more than three years, but re-qualification as such will not be necessary. There is a complementary Directive 1992 on training and education relating to qualifications of less than three years.

The position on the recognition of diplomas and other qualifications is one that is constantly changing. Any person requiring further information should consult the professional body in the country concerned and/or the European Centre for the Development of Vocational Training (CEDEFOP), or the European Commission (see Appendix III).

Are there any Community initiatives in the field of education and training?

Yes. There are many. The TEU included a new chapter on education, vocational training and youth, and there is a continuing recognition of the need for, and series of initiatives to encourage development of, the mobile, well-trained and flexible work-force that will be needed to keep the EU competitive in the 21st century.

Eighty per cent of the EU educational and vocational training budget is handled through the Socrates Programme, which supports cross-border co-operation in schools and higher education establishments in the EU through various programmes, many of which encourage language training. Particular arrangements are made for disadvantaged young people. Socrates II runs from 1 January 2000 to 31 December 2004, as does the Leonardo da Vinci Programme for vocational training. This promotes cross-border co-operation, trainee trans-border exchanges and continuing vocational training, encouraging the development of language skills in all the official EU languages and Icelandic, Irish, Luxembourgish and Norwegian. It is developing a large network between employers and training organizations to improve continuous training, and to combat social exclusion.

What about programmes for students and young people?

There are over 114 million people under 25 years of age in the EU, so it is important to encourage student mobility. Besides the Socrates and related programmes, the Youth for Europe Framework Programmes include useful initiatives, and about 70,000 young people should benefit from them by working in other countries. Open University and distance learning are also encouraged. The European Training Foundation is sited in Turin, and oversees the training programmes. Some programmes are geared to EFTA and East European countries. Some are particularly aimed at assisting open education and distance learning.

Are young people affected by other policies?

Yes. For example, in the context of regional policy, the Commission has proposed programmes in the following areas:

- integration of basic network systems;
- strengthening of human resources, in particular in areas of training, female employment and employment of disabled people;
- the strengthening and integration of rural areas.

Computing and IT skills in education are encouraged, and the pilot scheme for the European Voluntary Service for the Young is enabling thousands of young people to participate in environmental or social action in other Member States.

What about education and training to meet the perceived needs of successful enterprises?

The emphasis on encouraging a mobile, well-trained, up-to-date and globally competitive work-force at all ages has gathered momentum, and there have been various programmes to encourage this since the 1995 Green Paper, *Teaching and Learning – Towards a Learning Society*, identified six aims:

1. to encourage lifelong learning;
2. to bring schools and business closer;
3. to encourage staff mobility;
4. to introduce second-chance schemes for those threatened with exclusion;
5. to promote proficiency in three EU languages in a network of participating schools for Europe;
6. to encourage a re-examination of the tax treatment of investment in training.

These aims have been endorsed since, eg in the Amsterdam Treaty and Agenda 2000, and promoted in various action plans. CONNECT is part of the Europe of Knowledge initiative, and is a study of knowledge acquisition in the EU.

What is the effect of staff and professional mobility?

Business people have a larger pool from which to draw their employees, and may recruit staff well trained in other EU countries who may have various languages to offer. The projected mobility is having a broadening and competitive effect on professionals and others, and it may even cause a migration of trained professionals to better-paid areas. Equally, it often improves the standards of the schools, institutes and other places where training is carried out.

Can any conclusions be drawn from the development of social policy?

Employment costs are seen as significant in the context of keeping the EU competitive in world markets, so policies are becoming more market-sensitive. Unemployment can result from unacceptably high costs, and this in turn is costly not only in financial, but also in human and social terms. For these reasons the Member States in the Amsterdam Treaty agreed to align their employment policies in a way consistent with the Community's economic policy, and to promote a skilled and adaptable work-force, as well as labour markets that respond quickly to economic change. These and the issues of better co-ordination of health and emergency care, and medical insurance regimes, are constantly under revision to seek improvements.

Globally, the EU supports iniatives to improve social conditions in developing countries and elsewhere. It particularly supports the EU applicant countries, which have to comply with existing EU provisions in the context of the *acquis communautaire*.

17 The environment, energy, agriculture and fisheries

Environmental policy

How wide is EU environmental policy?

Environmental policy covers the protection and improvement of air, land, sea, fauna and flora, forestry, inland waters and coastal protection, and global issues are included. There are conservation and protection provisions for wild birds, and habitat and biotype protection provisions, with increasing emphasis on sustainable development in accordance with Earth Summit agreements.

What is environmental policy?

The principles were first defined in 1972, and stated that:

- pollution should be prevented at source;
- environmental policy must be compatible with economic and social development;
- all planning processes must take environmental considerations into account;
- the polluter must pay.

Joint activities concerning environmental policies have been undertaken by the Commission for some years, and five successive Community action programmes have resulted in many legislative measures with significant environmental effects. The Community monitors and introduces standards, and other appropriate legislation, and environmental studies are encouraged.

How did the Single European Act and later treaties affect environmental policy?

The SEA of 1986 formally introduced the environmental dimension into EC policy. The TEU expanded this and specifically required that environmental considerations be taken into account in any new policies or provisions. The Treaty emphasized the need for a precautionary approach, to avoid rather than to have to rectify problems, and enabled qualified majority voting in some areas relating to the environment. The Amsterdam Treaty 1997 expanded and strengthened Treaty provisions on the environment.

Urged on by the EP and public opinion, the Commission is active in the environmental field (there are around 350 Directives, regulations and decisions in force) and is authorized to negotiate agreements on various environmental pollutants and problems, not only within the EU but world-wide, as environmental protection is increasingly seen as a global problem.

What sort of international conventions exist?

There are about 180 international environmental conventions on various matters from trade in endangered species to atmospheric pollution and waste disposal. Examples include the Geneva Convention on long-distance cross-border atmospheric pollution, the Vienna Convention on the protection of the ozone layer, and the 1987 Montreal Protocol on the progressive elimination of harmful gases and new harmful ozone-depleting substances. The GLOBE organization brings together legislators in different countries with the intention of encouraging a balanced world environment. A world fund for the environment to assist developing countries to take action to protect the environment and the ozone layer is administered by the World Bank with the co-operation of United Nations organizations.

The UN Convention on cross-border environmental impact assessments was signed by the Community in 1991, and the EU has provided considerable assistance to improve nuclear safety in Central and Eastern Europe.

What did the fifth EU Environmental Action Plan target?

The fifth Environmental Action Programme, 'Towards Sustainability 1992–2000', focused on the environment with medium and long-term objectives set in five specific areas: industry, agriculture, energy, transport and tourism, with five priorities:

1. To integrate environmental considerations into other policies.
2. To support public transport initiatives, clean technology and local and regional issues.
3. To use different areas, eg education, to promote environmental protection.
4. To consider ecological issues.
5. To strengthen the EU's role in international initiatives.

The comprehensive action plan to achieve sustainable development followed the UN Conference on the Environment and Development in Rio de Janeiro in 1992 (often called 'the Earth Summit').

What is sustainable development?

'Sustainable development', specifically referred to in the Amsterdam Treaty as a matter to be taken into account in promoting economic and social progress in the EU, has been variously defined, but the concept is that economic development and activities should be accompanied by measures to protect the environment from further degradation, or even to enhance it. The UN Commission on Sustainable Development was set up to monitor the progress of Earth Summit agreements, and the EC is closely involved. The European Council in 1997 urged a strong response to the risks of climatic change, and closer co-ordination between social and environmental policies, and further acceleration towards sustainable development in accordance with the Earth Summit agreements. For example, in 1998 there were proposals for policy changes to make agriculture more sustainable.

Following the Earth Summit in Rio, the Commission adopted a report in February 1998 on EC biodiversity strategy aimed at preventing or lessening significant reductions or loss of biodiversity. It targets conservation, education, exchange of information, sharing the use of genetic resources, and the sustainable use of biological diversity.

Various studies and proposals include Agenda 2000, which specifically referred to improving implementation and enforcement of environmental regulations, and the integration of environmental considerations into the design and implementation of all Community policies.

What is the European Consultative Forum on the Environment and Sustainable Development?

This consists of members from EEA countries. It produces recommendations and reports to assist policy-making, and there is now considerable emphasis on sustainability in all areas.

What about responsibility for environmental damage?

The 1993 Commission Green Paper considered civil liability for environmental damage, together with recovery of costs for restoring the environment. It was based on damage prevention and the 'polluter pays' principle, which is referred to in the Packaging Directive 1994. The principles set out are increasingly visible.

Have there been problems in establishing a common EU environmental policy?

Yes. There have been problems because of costs, varying problems in Member States, intensive lobbying by industry, and frequent difficulties in proving the link between damage caused and the various processes. However, the Chernobyl nuclear disaster brought a dramatic realization of the cross-border effects of accidents involving dangerous substances, and increasing realization that nature has to be protected, as the point can be reached where regeneration becomes impossible.

What sorts of provision have been passed?

For example, the 1985 Directive on the Assessment of the Effects of Certain Public and Private Projects on the Environment has a continuing impact, and its scope has been widened. In 1986, agreement was reached on a whole range of areas, including transfrontier shipment of dangerous waste, dumping dangerous substances and curbing pollution of the sea from land-based sources. There are provisions or drafts on toxic and other waste, standards of quality of drinking water and water for other purposes, surface and underground water protection controls for agricultural practices, air quality, the promotion of a new approach to nuclear safety, and the storage of radioactive materials and waste. The emission of nitrogen oxide from aircraft is also included.

What about financial support?

There is a European Environment Fund, 'LIFE'; and financial support is available through various programmes for private projects and research into new technologies that can reduce or prevent pollution or help the environment, for example through the STEP programme. Programmes have provided funding for a range of studies from earthquakes to the urban environment.

What is the European Environment Agency?

The independent European Environment Agency, established in 1990, collects data for the scientific evaluation of ecological problems throughout the EU, and produces assessment reports on the state of the environment. It is sited in Copenhagen and has close links with other international bodies, eg the UN, WHO, OECD and UNICE. It co-ordinates work in the EU and EEA and provides objective independent advice and information on environmental matters. It includes on its board representatives of the EP, the Commission and the Member States.

What about global warming?

In 1995 the Council presented a strategy and supporting procedures to enable it to reach CO_2 emission targets, which were to stabilize emissions at 1990 levels by 2000 in EU countries, in the context of the UN Framework Convention on Climatic Change. The strategy included greater encouragement of energy efficiency and taxation of CO_2 emissions (see also 'Energy' below). Work continues on harmonization of air quality standards to improve and update existing provisions, and air pollution data may be exchanged and made publicly available under the 1996 Framework Directive on the Assessment and Management of Ambient Air Quality. Following the Global Warming Treaty in Kyoto in December 1997, guidelines and a strategy on climatic change, aimed at reducing greenhouse gas emissions and thereby effecting greater ozone layer protection, have been produced. Unfortunately the Kyoto Protocol on climatic change has yet to be formally ratified by the US and EU countries, so negotiations continue.

Increased control of car and small utility vehicle exhaust emissions is part of the Community's plan to inhibit global warming. Vehicle emissions are targeted as high pollutants, so emissions have improved, and efforts are being made to reduce traffic volumes in cities. Under the ALTER (Alternative traffic in towns) initiative some EU cities (Athens, Barcelona, Florence, Lisbon, Oxford and Stockholm) are to allow entry only to vehicles with low emissions from 2001.

Proposals to cut air pollution further by 2010 were proposed by the Commission in June 1999.

There are proposals to reduce emissions for large combustion plants and gas turbines from 1 January 2000, combined with encouragement to use biomass.

What does the 1996 Framework Directive on Integrated Pollution Prevention and Control (IPPC) provide?

This Directive requires consideration of the impact of various types of pollution on the environment as a whole (eg air quality should not be considered on its own while ignoring water pollution). It also requires certain enterprises or installations to use best available techniques to prevent or minimize emissions, and a detailed approval and permit procedure to be followed before operating start-ups, with a different procedure for installations already operating. The Directive enables public scrutiny of national control levels.

The activities covered by the Directive include:

- the energy industry;
- the production or processing of metals;
- the manufacture of mineral and non-metallic products;
- the chemical industry;
- various other industries using, for example, dyes, ink or paper;
- waste management enterprises.

What about noise levels?

Various regulations, Directives, studies and consultative documents relate to the permissible noise levels of, for example, new aircraft, tractors, grass-cutting machinery, domestic appliances and machines in factories and workshops. Simplification of existing legislation to curb outdoor noise continues.

What about chemicals, biochemicals, micro-organisms and other potentially or actually dangerous goods or substances?

There are many measures controlling the marketing and use of dangerous chemicals, and the classification, packaging and labelling of dangerous substances and preparations. There are requirements seeking to limit major accident hazards, and control the export and import of certain products, such as fertilizers and sewage sludge. There are two Directives that control the contained use and deliberate release to the environment of genetically manipulated micro-organisms, and require their labelling. There is a 1994 Directive on the approximation of the legislation of Member States on the transport of dangerous goods.

What about genetically modified organisms (GMOs)?

A 1990 Directive on the deliberate release of GMOs into the environment provided for controls, notification systems for research, accident procedures and waste disposal, and a further Directive will strengthen this. There are labelling provisions for GM foods.

What about water protection?

The 1976 Framework Directive on the discharge of dangerous substances into the aquatic environment with its associated Directives set discharge limits for certain substances and set quality standards. A further Framework Directive on water to strengthen provisions is close to agreement. It is intended to replace the six current water protection Directives, and set policy guidelines, aiming to achieve good quality of all waters (fresh water, surface water, drinking water, bathing water and groundwater) by 2010. This covers river basin management plans and designation of protected areas with special requirements and particularly covers over-abstraction and sustainability. The 1998 Directive on the quality of water for human consumption is aimed at improving standards. Efforts have been made in all areas and, for example, about 95 per cent of EU beaches meet the minimum standards required (88 per cent in the UK) for bathing water.

What about waste?

The Community produces more than 2 billion tons of waste each year, 30 million tons of which is dangerous, and there are funds available for research into recycling systems. There are many studies, strategies, proposals and provisions on various different kinds of waste. Examples are: the 1975 (amended 1991) Waste Framework Directive; the Hazardous Waste Directive 1991; and the 1992 Waste Transfer Directive, which enabled the Community to accede to the Basle Convention on the Transboundary Shipments of Hazardous Waste. This included a prohibition on shipment to non-OECD countries of hazardous waste for disposal; and a 1998 Regulation bans certain hazardous waste exports.

There is a draft Directive to amend the 1994 and 1996 Directives on the transport of dangerous goods by road and rail, which could also affect waste.

The 1996 strategy for waste management emphasized the need for waste prevention, with manufacturer/producer liability through a product's life cycle from production to eventual disposal as a key element, and a provision requiring recycling of cars is close to agreement.

The Directive on Landfill Sites 1999 concentrates on reducing and preventing waste production, provides for the use of landfill for biodegradable waste, and bans the disposal of old tyres.

The proposed Directive on civil liability for waste, which would impose strict liability (ie liability irrespective of fault) on any producer of waste causing damage to the environment, or damage or injury to persons or property, has been widened but remains under discussion.

What about nuclear waste?

The management, storage and transport of radioactive and nuclear waste are the subject of special provisions. The EU produces about

50,000 cubic metres of radioactive waste per year, and the aim is that the EU should be self-sufficient in nuclear waste disposal.

What about packaging waste?

About 50 million tons of packaging waste are produced annually in the EU. The 1994 Directive on packaging and packaging waste aims to ensure that by June 2001 between 50 and 65 per cent of packaging waste by weight will be recovered, and between 35 and 45 per cent by weight will be recycled or used to create energy. It is a detailed provision with objectives for packaging standards and marking, and provisions on the disposal of heavy metals into the environment. It does not affect the imposition of national requirements that go further, but does include the 'polluter pays' principle.

What about the eco-label?

The eco-label award scheme enables a special logo to be awarded to appropriate products meeting specific criteria: they must be safe, have a reduced environmental impact in their whole life, and remain efficient for their purpose. The award is made by a designated competent national body, and may be for EU or non-EU products. Under a 1993 Council Regulation, companies in industry may participate in a voluntary Community Eco-management and Audit Scheme leading to an EMAS certification.

Can an individual make a complaint?

Individuals can make complaints to the Commission concerning the environment, and in appropriate cases the Commission will take governments to the European Court of Justice, at no cost to the original complainant. The difficulty with regard to obtaining information has been addressed by the 1990 Directive on the Freedom of Access to Information on the Environment, which aims to enable anyone, without having to prove an interest, to obtain information relating to the environment from public authorities or bodies with public responsibilities for the environment and under the control of public bodies.

What about the urban environment?

The 1990 Commission Green Paper on the urban environment identified two priority areas: the physical structure of cities including such matters as planning, transport and the enhancement of natural areas; and reducing the impact on the environment of suburban activities such as industry, energy management, urban waste and the management of water; and various provisions have resulted. Since then, and following in particular the 1997 Agenda 2000 strategy, the concept of sustainability has focused on poverty and its impact on the environment, with efforts to co-ordinate urban planning to protect and enhance the environment as far as possible, to the benefit of EU citizens.

What about the marine environment?

Recent disasters prompted the Council to define guidelines for the transport of dangerous substances, such as oil and chemicals, by sea. It was suggested that a system of severe penalties for polluting the environment be introduced in co-operation with the IMO (International Maritime Organization). It has been urged that mandatory routes be used to avoid sensitive or valuable environments, with reinforced stricter tanker inspections, increased use of pilots, scrapping of old tankers, and the development of a common 'language of the sea' for mixed crews. There are papers on a common maritime safety policy. In 1993 all Member States undertook to ratify existing international conventions for marine safety (see also Chapter 9).

What about the rural environment?

Agriculture is a very significant source of environmental pollution, and many studies and provisions seek to address this, eg those concerned with the release of nitrates into the environment. There is encouragement for set-aside to provide natural habitats, and encouragement for organic farming, besides research into the use of biomass and other by-products of farming.

Is forestry important in the EU?

Before the accession of Austria, Finland and Sweden, the Community's export deficit in rough timber was second only to its deficit in petroleum products. Since the accession of the Nordic countries and the growth in other Member States of the forestry industry, the position has changed, but there is now considerable concern at the adverse impact of acid rain, which because of trans-border pollution affects a significant proportion of all trees in the EU. In 1997 a Commission communication set out a strategy to reduce acid rain in the EU. There is support for planting extra trees, and for developing the forestry business, while encouraging national habitats for indigenous species. The Commission's forest strategy was aimed at expanding forestry by 12 million hectares by 2000.

Are there any regulations concerning forestry policy?

Yes. For example, because about 45,000 forest fires start in the EU every year, the Community finances research into satellite monitoring (the FUEGO project) to enable swift responses. Community regulations relate to the protection of forests against fire and atmospheric pollution, and various working groups exist to assess damage and possible solutions. The FOREST (Forestry Sectoral Research and Technology) programme concentrates on forestry resources, wood technology, and helping SMEs in this area, in particular with regard to the question of recycling.

It should be noted that aid is given to tropical forests in third countries. Further information is available from the Commission (see Appendix III).

What about flora and fauna?

The Commission is responsible for co-ordinating conservation measures by Member States. There are protective orders for many species of birds, and various controls on hunting. Ivory from African elephants, and products made from baby seals, whales and other cetaceans are banned. Revised lists for the protection of endangered flora and fauna are produced periodically, and a 1996 Regulation tightened restrictions concerning trade in endangered species.

What is the approach to the cultural environment: archaeological, cultural, architectural or historic treasures and visual arts?

All Member States currently have national restrictions on works of art, aimed at protecting national treasures. A Directive protects national treasures by way of a system for the return of cultural assets that have left a Member State, and establishes authorization procedures; and funding is available to preserve and enhance awareness of the EU's cultural and architectural heritage. Proposals on percentage payments to artists on resale of their works remain under discussion.

In respect of visual arts, the TEU provided that the Community should encourage co-operation in respect of culture, so subsequent action plans and programmes have been designed to preserve the cultural heritage of the EU and promote awareness in third countries. These include programmes to encourage theatre, dance, book translations, audio-visual works and other cultural activities.

What is the effect of environmental policy generally?

Environmental protection has a high political profile, so the likely environmental impact of any new developments or processes must be considered at the planning stage. Penalties include requirements to make expensive changes, or even to cease the activity, following an environmental assessment under the 1989 Environmental Assessment Directive.

Equally, enterprises involving environmentally harmful processes or substances would do well to fund research into alternatives, or plan modifications now.

It should be noted that some of the measures on the health and safety of employees have links with environmental policy, as indeed have many other provisions and policies, such as the imposition of exhaust emission standards for motor vehicles. It is worth remembering that there are funds available under various action plans and programmes (such as the ENVIREG and MEDSPA programmes through the EIB and the European Regional Development Fund), which have environmental elements.

Further information may be obtained from the European Commission, the DETR and the Royal Commission on Environmental Pollution (see Appendix III).

Energy

Is the Commission's energy policy linked to its policy for the environment?

Yes. Its broad objectives, areas for action, special programmes and provisions encourage environmentally friendly energy efficiency and environmental protection in the EU and world-wide. The 1995 Green Paper on the future of energy policy covered various aspects including environmental impact assessments, and higher yields. The subsequent 1995 White Paper set out a five-year programme with the objectives of meeting global competitiveness and including the liberalization of internal gas and electricity markets, ensuring supply availability, and protection of the environment. The 1996 Green Paper concentrated on renewable energy sources. The Community also supports the reduction of carbon dioxide emissions to reduce the greenhouse effect both in the EU and elsewhere.

Work continues to achieve energy supply security, with improved competitiveness linked to a service obligation of uninterrupted supply, and the creation of energy exchange networks, information retrieval and analysis. A master plan for the development of trans-European energy networks was published in 1997, the intention being to widen access to grids, because some 40 per cent of the Community's current energy needs are supplied from third countries (Norway, Russia and Algeria) and this is likely to rise to 60 per cent within 10 years. Public procurement procedures in the energy field are being developed.

What is the European Energy Charter?

The Energy Charter relating to the exploitation of energy resources is a 1991 political declaration aimed at international co-operation to improve security of supply in Europe. Signed by 51 countries including many OECD members, it set up the European Energy Centre to consider supply and environmental aspects, and to resolve international tensions.

An international convention, known as the Basic Agreement or Treaty of the Charter, set out the legal framework for international co-operation in the field of energy to turn the Charter aims into a binding legal instrument, covering trade in energy linked to the provisions of the WTO, protection of investments, national treatment of foreign operators, dispute settlement procedures, transit and environmental protection. This was signed by most participating states in 1994 (although not by Canada and the US), and has not yet been ratified by all signatories. There is also a protocol concerning energy efficiency.

Is the Community doing anything else in the field of energy supply?

Yes. The Commission is looking at ways to simplify Community legislation relating to energy. Its policy is to subject energy supply in the EU to open competition with two constraints: the need to maintain security of supply, and a service obligation of uninterrupted provision. There is strong emphasis on sustainability.

What about liberalization of the markets in energy supply?

The move towards completion of the Internal Market in energy supply urged by the Council in 1986 has progressed.

As to *electricity*: in 1994 the Council agreed the four principles necessary for the liberalization of the electricity market. They are reflected in the Electricity Directive 1996, which liberalizes the Internal Market in electricity in stages. The principles are:

• Electricity generation will be opened to competition, but Member States can use authorization procedures, and/or call for tenders for new production plant.

- Energy companies must keep separate accounts for production, distribution and transport activities to ensure transparency.
- Network provisions must not be bureaucratic.
- Public service obligations, where imposed, should be transparent and easily monitored to ensure fairness and compliance.

As to *gas*: the whole question of the liberalization of gas supply remains difficult, because the markets vary significantly from state to state. The 1998 Natural Gas Directive reflects the principles of the Electricity Directive, but phases in changes over 10 years and defines the customers eligible to choose gas suppliers.

As to *hydrofuels*: a 1994 Directive concerns licences to explore for and produce hydrofuels. A competitive framework is to be created for the grant of licences in the oil sector.

As to *renewable energy sources*: a 1997 White Paper indicated that the aim was to achieve renewable energy sources supplying 12 per cent of EU energy needs by 2010, so there is funding for research and assistance for development in this area, with an EU framework for access to the internal energy market for electricity from renewable sources. This was followed in April 1999 by a working paper on the creation of a liberalized Internal Market for electricity from renewable resources including wind, hydroelectric, solar, biomass and photovoltaic energy.

What about nuclear power?

There are various controls and collaborative R&D programmes in Europe. The Commission produced a safety-oriented nuclear programme in 1996, but public concerns remain, and public opinion has encouraged Member States to phase out nuclear power. In 1999, the Commission proposed a programme for decommissioning old nuclear power stations and managing the resulting radioactive waste.

What about the coal mining industry?

For some time national subsidies for this labour-intensive industry have been closely scrutinized by the Commission. The emphasis on the reduced use of carbon fuels has led to a drastic reduction in the coal mining industry in the EU, as has the availability of cheap imports. In 1998 about 58 per cent of coal used was imported into the EU. The RECHAR programme is aimed at assisting coal-mining areas in restructuring.

What about the promotion of energy efficiency?

The Community strategy is to continue to reduce CO_2 emissions by 2000, in the context of the UN Framework Convention on Climatic Change, and even more thereafter; to encourage use of the SAVE programme of energy efficiency; and to study the possibilities for even lower vehicle emission standards, together with the use of national CO_2 emission taxes. New norms have been set for energy efficiency, supported by quality labels for the most efficient equipment. A 1997 Commission communication targeted reduction of greenhouse gas emissions by 15 per cent as compared with 1990 levels, by savings through better management, and by promotion of renewable energy sources. Council conclusions in 1999 are aimed at a reduction in the energy wasted by consumers, eg by leaving equipment on stand-by.

What is the general thrust of EU energy policy?

Energy efficiency and use of sustainable energy sources, preferably those that help with waste problems, are encouraged. Ever-increasing energy taxes to promote energy saving are likely, providing incentives to ensure that any new plant and equipment is reviewed for energy efficiency, and that existing equipment is frequently checked to ensure compliance with norms. Increased liberalization of the energy market is bringing down prices in some areas, more particularly for the larger consumers. The increased use of biofuels will bring a significant change to industrial energy use, and those involved in research in this area would do well to consider applying for funds under the various programmes.

Agricultural policy

What is the CAP and when did it start?

The Common Agricultural Policy (CAP) was set out in Articles 32–38 (ex 38–46) of the Treaty of Rome in 1957.

The aims of the CAP are:

- to increase agricultural productivity by promoting technical progress, ensuring national development of agricultural production and optimum utilization of labour;
- to ensure a proper standard of living for the agricultural community, by increasing earnings;
- to stabilize agricultural markets;
- to ensure the maintenance of reasonable consumer prices for agricultural products;
- to ensure availability of supplies.

How have agricultural trends changed since the start of the CAP?

The CAP is set against a changing agricultural background. In 1960 one person in five in the European Community worked on the land, but now the situation has changed, although the percentage of agricultural workers still varies from state to state. The integration of East Germany into the CAP in 1990 made a difference, as did the accession of Austria, Finland and Sweden. Farm employment remains the main source of income for well over 10 million people in the EU, and a subsidiary source for many others, but represents under 3 per cent of GDP; and CAP accounts for a significant proportion of the EC budget, which has to be agreed by the EP.

What has the CAP done?

The CAP attempted to control production and prices in the agricultural sector by intervention buying and monetary compensation amounts (MCAs, abolished on 1 January 1993), import levies and the subsidized export of surpluses plus export restitutions (ie subsidies to exporters when the Community price is above the world price) where necessary. Problems of butter mountains, wine lakes and milk over-production resulted. These in turn led to very high costs to the Community, including those for storage and disposal of surpluses, and eventually to a radical reform of the policy.

The CAP has always caused discontent among Member States, partly because there are really only three contributing countries. Its problems have been aggravated by the administrative burdens encountered by Member States in carrying out the policies and, perhaps surprisingly, by fraud, misuse and improper administration of funds. The Commission is now recovering funds from countries that paid out Community funds without having made sufficient checks.

How does the CAP work now?

The CAP essentially offers financial support, which varies from product to product.

Every year, target prices for some commodities are set on Commission advice by the Council of Ministers. These establish the sum that a producer might reasonably expect to receive for products. Intervention prices are set for some products (eg beef, butter and skimmed milk). These are usually well below target prices and are the prices at which the national intervention boards or support agencies become obliged, under certain conditions, to buy in produce offered to them. The stocks bought may be held in case of future shortages, sold, converted into other goods (eg wine into alcohol), or otherwise disposed of.

Exporters of relevant products may receive subsidies if world prices are below target prices. Financial support is given to producers of certain products (eg flax and silkworms).

Import levies can be introduced under the CAP system, to raise prices of products from third countries to the price levels of equivalent Community products, and import quotas to the EC from third countries are controlled in respect of various agricultural goods, but reviews have to be undertaken to ensure that the provisions relating to a particular sector reflect changing needs, and international trade (eg WTO) agreements.

How are the financial operations of the CAP administered?

They are administered through the European Agricultural Guidance and Guarantee Fund (EAGGF), often referred to as FEOGA, from the French initials. The fund is divided, with a part allocated to improving agriculture infrastructures, and the remainder to fund the intervention policy. The aim of the agrimonetary regime introduced in 1995 was to reduce CAP costs, and to avoid dramatic price changes due to currency fluctuations in the different Member States. A 'green money' rate is used for agricultural products, with a fixed exchange rate closely aligned to the actual currency rate, and protective taxes and subsidies where the gap widens unacceptably. To keep prices stable, producers are increasingly to receive direct subsidies, and intervention prices are being progressively lowered.

Changes to CAP with support price cuts were agreed in March 1999 based on Agenda 2000 proposals with the aim of preparing CAP for enlargement and the inclusion of new applicant countries into CAP.

What are the major problems with the CAP?

Surpluses and exchange rate fluctuations cause problems, but the latter may be improved somewhat by the introduction of the Euro. CAP is costly, so a tougher policy philosophy, more budget control with sanctions for improper application of the rules, and more environmentally friendly methods of production are being encouraged.

What of the future of the CAP?

At the time of writing there is dissatisfaction about the difficulties agriculture is facing in the EU, and concern that rules are being unfairly flouted or imposed, eg with regard to the beef (BSE difficulties) and sheep markets, and there is concern at the cost implications of the integration into CAP of the applicant countries to the EU, which could double the numbers of agricultural workers, and add 50 per cent to land in agricultural use. The Eastern European countries are already enjoying increased market access, and there is concern among EU agricultural producers as to the effects of this.

There are other aspects of agricultural policy besides funding and surpluses. Improved environmental use of set-aside is being encouraged. There is a harmonized commodity coding system, and a harmonized system of animal health inspection. More common standards are being introduced for intra-EU trade in live animals and animal products, and provisions on the transport in the EU of live animals. There are common policies to combat animal diseases, and provisions that relate to abattoirs, where standards have not yet been rigorously enforced in all Member States.

For agricultural machinery, implementation of common safety standards is resulting in the removal of technical barriers to facilitate exports by smaller manufacturers.

Attempts continue to be made to persuade farmers to grow crops in which the Community is not self-sufficient and so reduce the need to import. The Commission is successfully supporting frameworks for rural development aid in over 40 regions.

What about organic farming?

More environmentally friendly methods of production are being encouraged, and organic production is governed by a regulation providing for production, labelling and inspection of organic foods, whether plant-based or livestock. An EU seal of approval will be available, with about 180 conditions, including an agreement not to use antibiotics or GM products in animal feed.

What about veterinary provisions?

There are many veterinary and phytosanitary provisions, many of which are geared to consumer safety. The EU Food and Veterinary Office (FVO) in Ireland, established in April 1997, monitors the observance of food hygiene, and veterinary and plant health provisions, and carries out inspections. This took over from the Office for Veterinary and Phytosanitary Inspection and Control, and consists of representatives from Member States and the Commission, and independent experts. Further information is available from its Internet site (http://europe.eu.int/comm/dg24/). A 1997 programme provides funding for the eradication of targeted animal diseases including rabies, with a 100-kilometre vaccination barrier zone in countries on the EU's eastern border.

Because of concerns about the resistance in humans to antibiotics, about 20 antibiotics are banned in animal husbandry, and more have been recommended. Equally there are provisions to phase out growth-promoting drugs, with four already prohibited.

There are various provisions relating to animal welfare, on the transport of animals and, recently, agreement on increasing the size of cages for battery hens, with their phased abolition by 2012. Animal welfare standards are included in WTO agricultural trade liberalization negotiations.

What about access to EU markets for third countries?

Many agreements exist, and negotiations continue between the Commission and third (non-EC) countries concerning access to markets. Agreement has been reached on tropical produce through Lomé, for the African, Caribbean and Pacific states, and through GATT and WTO negotiations. Sometimes difficulties arise with regard to specific arrangements, eg in respect of bananas, where there are conflicts of interest.

What is the effect of agricultural policy generally?

The agricultural and agricultural machinery markets are more open, so trade has increased, but so has competition from third countries. There has been a significant effect on costs of agricultural machinery and products, and food. It is important that those involved in agriculture and related goods and services, or who may have grants and assistance available, keep a close watch on the operation of the CAP, to ensure that their interests are kept in mind in continuing negotiations on long-term strategies. The BSE crisis in the UK has shown up limitations, and the strength of the agricultural lobby, and the responsibility for food products in the context of consumer health and safety has been transferred out of the Directorate dealing with agricultural matters.

The agricultural sector causes significant environmental pollution, so environmental provisions should be watched as controls increasingly affect farming methods.

Further information may be obtained from the European Commission, the Ministry of Agriculture, Fisheries and Food, and the Food and Veterinary Office.

Fisheries

Does the Commission have a common fisheries policy (CFP)?

The first fisheries policy was established in 1970, and there have been revisions since. A review is currently under way intended to lead to a report of the CFP in 2001.

In 1986 two important measures were agreed: a 10-year structural policy, and a package of technical measures to safeguard fish stocks. Despite the 1992 tough revision of fisheries policy, set out in a regulation that included significant fishing fleet reduction provisions, a crisis situation has continued, and serious concern about fish stocks remains. Simplification of the regulatory framework has included the reduction of total allowable catches (TACs), monitoring of catches, some import controls and the monitoring of third-country catches and landings. Enforcement has proved a problem for on-shore centres, and a satellite monitoring system came into effect in 1998 to monitor fishing vessels over 20 metres long.

A fisheries ban on drift nets, agreed in 1998, is scheduled to come into effect on1 January 2002, with assistance for fishermen affected.

What are the aims of the CFP?

They relate to the sensible management and conservation of fish stocks by way of the grant of fishing quotas agreed annually by the Council of Ministers. They are backed by financial assistance for the industry, and enforced by a group of EU inspectors. They cover the structure of the fishing industry, modernization of fleets (including structural measures to encourage the demolition of small vessels), and improvement of loading, processing and marketing conditions.

The TACs regulation set up a system of Community fishing licences for EU and foreign vessels operating in EU waters, based on the state of fish stocks. Successive Fisheries Programmes have incorporated measures for fisheries into the Structural Funds, finalized commercial rules for the Common Market Organization (CMO), and sought to create a Mediterranean fisheries policy and to negotiate fisheries agreements with third countries.

The fourth Multi-annual Guidance Programme (MAG IV), which runs from 1 January 1997 to 31 December 2002, takes a more global approach, and introduces catch reductions of 20 per cent for over-fished areas, and 30 per cent reductions for areas with depleted stocks. (It should be noted that the Commission asked for higher reductions, but was overruled by the Council of Ministers.) There are regulations on the use of net sizes in certain areas to protect dolphins caught in tuna nets, and a marine aquaculture research programme is proving successful.

What about the fishermen?

A common marketing organization provides for protection of fishermen, and an information exchange network is being supported. There is a drive towards fleet reduction, and PESCA is an initiative to help job creation schemes for resigning fishermen. There is financial assistance to assist early retirements in this context; and there is assistance for small-scale coastal fishing and fishing communities.

A 1992 Directive concerns minimum health and safety requirements for fishing vessels.

What about the movement of fish products?

There remain difficulties in this area. Regulations that came into force on 1 January 1993 included guideline prices for various fish products, and responsibility of producers for fishing and aquaculture products, and the Financial Instrument for Fisheries Guidance assists promotional campaigns for fish and fish products. A 1994 Regulation related to the direct landing of third-country fishing vessels in EU ports, and there has been agreement on the problem of quotas so as to ensure that there is less incentive for 'quota hopping', whereby the fishing boats of one Member State register in another so as to use the quota of that country.

Are there any international agreements?

EU fishermen fishing in third-country waters account for about 25 per cent of EU fish products.

Access to Community waters still causes difficulties, and various international agreements with third countries have been concluded (eg with the US, Canada and Morocco). The WTO agreements and UN conventions must also be taken into account.

Further information is obtainable from the European Commission (DG XI) and the Ministry of Agriculture, Fisheries and Food (see Appendix III).

18 The EU and international affairs

What is the constitutional basis of the European Community?

It is an independent entity with all the powers of a sovereign state within its areas of competence.

What about the sovereignty of the Member States?

They have formally transferred many of their sovereign powers to the Community, which can then negotiate on their behalf, as, for example, in the World Trade Organization negotiations. In areas of foreign policy the situation is complicated. The TEU gave the EU responsibilities in foreign and security policy under the second pillar, but national sovereignty is retained, and joint positions are established through European Political Co-operation (EPC) (see Chapter 2). The Amsterdam Treaty set up common strategic frameworks in this area, whereby decisions by Council should normally be unanimous; but if a Member State abstains, then the decision may be made, and the abstaining state may decide whether or not to participate in the action. In relevant cases a Member State may declare that its national interests are at stake.

Has the Community signed any agreements?

Yes. It has agreements with more than 120 countries, and many multilateral agreements. Around 130 countries have diplomatic relations with the EU itself, as distinct from the Member States. Because the Community is such a large trading bloc, trade agreements and foreign policies necessarily go hand in hand.

What about security policy?

Increasingly, foreign policy and security policy are being linked, and the Western European Union is being brought closer to the EU. Through the EPC procedure, the WEU and the Commission work closely in the context of economic and political union. Also, the development of a common foreign and security policy seems to be leading to a common defence policy, although there are sometimes difficulties as not all EU members belong to NATO, and those that do have certain obligations to NATO. Equally some Member States are not members of the WEU (Denmark, Austria, Finland, Ireland and Sweden), but all agreed to the Amsterdam Treaty writing in peacekeeping missions and humanitarian operations, which may involve some or all Member States as appropriate.

What about the European Parliament's influence?

The EP influences foreign policy, as its views have to be taken into consideration by foreign ministers in their political co-operation meetings. The EP has the right to veto the accession of any state to the EU, or international trade and economic association agreements with other states, organizations or groupings.

What do these international agreements cover?

As the Member States harmonize their attitudes and policies, so the Commission's role in negotiating trade agreements (which are then approved by the EP and the Council of Ministers) expands.
   Agreements cover such matters as:

- industry and customs tariffs;
- relations with Third World countries;
- agricultural matters and produce;
- fisheries, eg the fish catch;
- industrial sectors in difficulty (eg, to moderate growth and price maintenance in the steel and textile industries);
- research and science (there are co-operation agreements with about 100 countries on various matters including nuclear fusion and energy);
- the environment (for exchange of information with other countries);
- transport, in particular with those countries adjacent to the Community;
- assistance and co-operation agreements in respect of trade and development.

What about protectionist measures taken by third countries?

These do occur, and an advantage of the EU and its 375 million market population is the increased political clout that can be brought to bear on countries with protectionist tendencies, eg Japan and the US.

What is the European Economic Area (EEA)?

It is an agreement signed by all governments concerned to extend the Single Market to EFTA countries (presently Iceland, Liechtenstein, Norway and Switzerland) and to make a trading bloc of 19 countries. The EEA proceeded without Switzerland (which has observer status) and Liechtenstein, which subsequently joined in May 1995. It came into effect on 1 January 1994, and the EEA bloc accounts for over 35 per cent of world trade. A free trade pact with Switzerland is being developed.

What has been the intended effect of the EEA?

It was intended as a stepping stone for countries in EFTA wishing to join the EU, and indeed three of the members of the EEA (Austria, Finland and Sweden), who were members of EFTA when the EEA agreement was signed, joined the EU on 1 January 1995. Under the agreement, the EFTA countries excluding Switzerland became part of the EU's free movement of goods, services, capital and people, and other Single Market provisions apply, as does the abolition of non-tariff barriers. The EEA is a free trade area and not a customs union so, for example, non-EU members do not have to levy VAT. The EC public procurement Directives for works, supplies and utilities are extended to them, and competitive tendering provisions apply. There is wider access in respect of fishing rights. The extended trading area has obvious advantages in the lifting of non-tariff barriers.

It should be noted that the Community has bilateral agreements with Switzerland concerning free movement of EU/Swiss citizens, transport policies, access to markets, public procurement, research and development and many other areas.

Do EEA countries have to apply EC legislation?

Yes. Although under the EEA non-EU countries have only a limited role in formulating EU legislation, the EFTA countries joining the EEA undertook to adopt EC Single Market legislation, and much of the agreement mirrors the Treaty of Rome. There are various complementary measures. For example, the Lugano Convention 1988 on Jurisdiction and Enforcement of Civil and Commercial Judgements is similar to the Brussels Convention and has been entered into by all EFTA and EU countries. However, the EFTA countries in the EEA are not bound by the TEU, the plans for EMU or common foreign and security policy.

What about the competition provisions?

These apply in the EEA, and are controlled in EFTA countries through the EFTA Surveillance Authority, based in Geneva, together with an EFTA court, and in the EU through the Commission and the ECJ, the bodies working closely together. There are rules to determine how cases are allotted.

Were any other new institutions formed?

Yes. Two other new institutions were formed: the EEA Council with EU and EFTA ministers and representatives of the Commission; and the EEA Joint Committee with EU and EFTA officials. This administers and ensures compliance with the agreement, decides on new initiatives and ensures unity of approach.

What is the Nordic Council?

This is a body for inter-parliamentary co-operation of the Nordic countries: Denmark, Finland, Sweden, Norway and Iceland. It holds two sessions each year to discuss policy and co-operation. Nordic MEPs may be joining in discussions in the future.

What about the Faeroe Islands?

The EU/Denmark/Faeroe Islands Trade Agreement 1996 was based on free trade with some exclusions.

Does the EU have an important role to play in the development of Eastern Europe?

The union of East and West Germany and the political developments in Central and Eastern Europe created renewed impetus towards strengthening Community assistance to those countries. Much has been done by the Commission, which has a co-ordinating role, to boost reform and co-ordinate aid initiatives in co-operation with the Group of 24 OECD and EU countries under various programmes such as PHARE. A financial framework was also set up through the European Bank for Reconstruction and Development.

There are now various association, partnership, trade, and scientific and technical co-operation agreements including some Europe Agreements with these states, many of which have applied for membership of the EU.

What is the effect of a Europe Agreement?

A Europe Agreement gives Associate EU Member status and free access to the EU market for most goods, and sets out the framework for future relations. Europe Agreements have been negotiated with Bulgaria, Hungary, Poland, the Czech and Slovak Republics, Romania and Slovenia, who have all requested membership of the EU, and with the Baltic states, Estonia, Latvia and Lithuania.

In some countries, eg Bulgaria, additional social aid has had to be given, as worsening economic conditions have led to great hardship, including hunger (see also Chapter 1).

What is the current situation with regard to the countries of the old Soviet Union?

The situation since the break-up of the Soviet Union has been confused, not least because of the different groupings. It is useful to understand these:

- The CEECs are the Central and Eastern European countries: Bulgaria, Hungary, Poland, Romania, the Czech and Slovak Republics and former Yugoslavia.
- The Visegrad countries are another grouping for Hungary, Poland and the Czech and Slovak Republics, which have formed themselves into the Central European Free Trade Association with Slovenia. Some other CEECs may join it.
- The CIS or Commonwealth of Independent States is the former Soviet Union minus the Baltic states, ie: Armenia, Azerbaijan, Belarus, Georgia, Kazakhstan, Kyrgyzstan, Moldova, Russia, Tajikistan, Turkmenistan, Ukraine and Uzbekistan.
- The Baltic states are: Estonia, Latvia and Lithuania.

It is interesting to note that a Baltic Commission has been set up by 32 coastal regions in the Baltic states and Denmark, Finland, Germany and Sweden, to promote peace and regional co-operation.

What about Russia?

Russia is a most important trading partner, and a partnership and co-operation agreement is now in effect. Political and economic relations are developing. Various grants are given, for instance to support around 15,000 weapons scientists to redirect their skills towards, for example, nuclear waste disposal, medical research and energy production through the International Science and Technology Centre. The Founding Act on Mutual Relations, Co-operation and Security between NATO and the Russian Federation, signed in 1997, has been welcomed by the EU. The situation in Russia itself remains uncertain, as the economy is under stress, and at the time of writing it is suffering from terrorist activity.

What are the aims of the EU with regard to development of Central and Eastern Europe?

The EU aims to help the new republics to build stable market economies by improving the industrial development framework, encouraging privatization, restructuring and modernization, and promoting investment.

The PHARE (Poland and Hungary Assistance Reconstruction Economic) programme and system, tailored to the needs of the countries being aided, now covers a wider area of support than the TACIS revised programme now in force, as it has been fully extended to other Eastern European states, such as the Czech and Slovak Republics, Romania, Bulgaria, Slovenia, Albania and the Baltic states. Under PHARE, significant economic assistance from G24 is co-ordinated by the Commission.

Partnership and co-operation agreements provide a framework for applicant countries to develop political dialogue and close relations, to establish a pluralist parliamentary democracy with an established rule of law and respect for human rights, and to introduce a market economy.

There are partnership and co-operation agreements with the Ukraine (the EU's second most important trade partner in the former USSR after Russia), Armenia, Azerbaijan, Georgia, Kazakhstan and Kyrgyzstan and Uzbekistan, and partnership and co-operation agreements are being negotiated and signed with other states such as Moldova. Reconstruction funding is being provided for Bosnia and Herzegovina. A free trade provision for industrial goods incorporated in a Europe Agreement with Slovenia will come into effect on 1 January 2001, so Slovenia will be able to participate in some EU programmes.

What does the TACIS programme do?

TACIS is the equivalent of PHARE, albeit not so far reaching, for the CIS countries and Mongolia. It is a well-supported programme of technical assistance to provide advice, know-how and practical experience. Successive TACIS programmes have focused on energy, food distribution, transport, financial services, human resources and nuclear safety, and other specific areas such as vocational training, SMEs, equal opportunities, human rights and environmental needs.

Is there a strategy to assist countries of Central and Eastern Europe to join the EU?

Yes. The Copenhagen European Council in 1993 set out the prerequisites for a country to join the EU (see Chapter 1), and the pre-accession strategy to enable CEECs to accede to the EU was defined by the European Council in 1994. There was a 1995 White Paper on the approximation of legislation of associate countries in Central and Eastern Europe, and another paper on the effect on the CAP. Following the 1996/97 Inter-Governmental Conference (IGC), the Commission put forward *Agenda 2000: For a Stronger and Wider Europe*, setting out its detailed strategy for strengthening and widening the EU. This has been endorsed by the Council. Various initiatives have followed and preparations for enlargement stepped up. Action includes increased dialogue, preparations to enable applicant countries to undertake the pressure of competition of the Internal Market, adjustment of association agreements, promotion of investment, co-operation in various fields, integration through the trans-European networks, and in culture, education and training. Various EU programmes are open to applicant countries.

Which Central and Eastern European states have applied to join the EU?

The Central and Eastern European states that have applied to join the EU are: Hungary (1994), Poland (1994), Latvia, Slovakia, Estonia, Bulgaria and Lithuania (1995), and the Czech Republic and Slovenia (1996). Armenia and Georgia have indicated their long-term aim of joining the EU. Accession negotiations have already opened with the Czech Republic, Estonia, Hungary, Poland and Slovenia, and will open with Bulgaria, Latvia, Lithuania, Malta, Romania and Slovakia in February 2000.

The Commission has suggested that Albania, Bosnia, Croatia, Macedonia (FYROM) and possibly Serbia should be urged as a group to build up good relations with mutual co-operation before they seek to apply for accession. Stabilization and association agreements (SAAs) were agreed in June 1999, encompassing economic and trade relations, political dialogue, co-operation in justice and home affairs and financial assistance, and would integrate applicant countries into EU structures.

What about the Mediterranean and the Maghreb countries?

The Euro-Mediterranean Partnership was formed in 1995 with the establishment of a free trade area by 2010 as its aim, and brings together the 15 EU members and 12 Mediterranean states: Algeria, Cyprus, Egypt, Israel, Jordan, Lebanon, Malta, Morocco, Palestinian Authorities, Syria, Tunisia and Turkey. Its objectives are a common area of peace and stability, a shared zone of prosperity with the establishment of a free trade area and (substantial) support from the EU, for example through the MEDA II programme, the development of human resources, and the promotion of understanding of the different cultures in society. Free trade is gradually being established through bilateral agreements (Euro-Mediterranean association agreements).

Turkey applied in 1987 to join the EU, but its accession has been blocked by Greece and there are concerns about its human rights record. However Greece's stance has recently softened, and Turkey may be given pre-accession negotiation status. There is already a Customs Union Agreement with Turkey, whereby Turkey has adopted the Common Customs Tariff, so qualitative restrictions and customs charges and duties having equivalent effect between the EU and Turkey have already been abolished.

Agreements are in place and constantly being developed with Algeria, Egypt, Jordan, Lebanon, Morocco, Syria, Israel and Tunisia. The agreements with the Mashraq countries (Egypt, Jordan, Lebanon and Syria) concern free access to the EU for industrial products, giving some customs preferences for various agricultural products, and financial aid through the EIB.

The Euro Arab Dialogue was established in 1973 as a forum for discussions with the Arab countries. There is also a wide-ranging agreement with the Gulf Co-operation Council (GCC), which comprises Bahrain, Kuwait, Oman, Qatar, Saudi Arabia and the United Arab Emirates (UAE).

Trade links with Israel are well developed, and there are various EU/Israel trade and co-operation agreements. A technical and scientific co-operation agreement was signed in 1996 and two mutual access to public procurement agreements were signed in 1997.

Finally, a Black Sea Economic Co-operation Regional Organization of 11 countries has been set up, with a secretariat in Istanbul.

What agreements exist with Asia?

Various trade and co-operation agreements have been concluded by the EU with India, Bangladesh, Pakistan and Sri Lanka. Some of these countries also have bilateral agreements on textiles under the WTO (GATT) multi-fibre arrangements. Humanitarian and emergency aid has been made available to various countries. The more recent co-operation agreements, eg with Mongolia and India, include human rights provisions and are designed to promote co-operation more generally than before.

The partnership agreement with India not only promotes political dialogue, but also supports consideration of matters of mutual agreement such as drug trafficking, disarmament and money laundering. Around 25 per cent of India's exports are to the EU, and approximately 33 per cent of its imports are from the EU.

There is an EU co-operation agreement with Nepal, and aid is given for development projects in various areas, eg Bangladesh.

What about the Association of South East Asian (ASEAN) countries?

This includes Brunei, Cambodia, Laos, Malaysia, the Philippines, Singapore, Thailand and Vietnam. There are close contacts between the EU and these countries, which will collectively have a population of 500 million in the near future. An EU/ASEAN joint declaration in 1997 reaffirms the intention to develop mutual relations. In 1993 ASEAN/EU trade was higher than between the EU and North America.

There are 21 countries participating in the Asia-Pacific Economic Co-operation (APEC) with tariff reduction and elimination agreements.

What about China?

Trade links are developing between the EU and China, particularly with regard to energy, and humanitarian and emergency aid has been made available when needed. The return of Hong Kong to China on 1 July 1997 is making a difference, as Hong Kong is the EU's 10th largest trading partner. It is hoped that China will shortly join the WTO, and negotiations continue.

What about the Far East and Pacific Rim countries generally?

Trade has increased dramatically with this area.

The ASEM group of 25 foreign ministers from ASEAN, China, South Korea, Japan and the EU are planning a co-operation network for the future. ASEM may be widened to include Australia and India in the future. Aid is still given to some countries, eg Vietnam, where it facilitated the reintegration of about 61,000 nationals.

What about relations with Japan?

There is a significant Community trade deficit with Japan. Although Japanese protectionist trade practices continue, and the Commission even brought Japan before the WTO for contravening the WTO Government Procurement Agreement in 1997, exports to Japan continue to rise. The Commission has a programme of assistance (EXPROM) for EU firms wishing to enter the Japanese market, part of which is the Executive Training Programme (ETP) in Japan, which sponsors young executives through language and in-house training. A Gateway to Japan 1997–2000 trade promotion campaign, supported by the Commission, has helped 10 trade sectors to enter the Japanese market.

What about Australia?

EU/Australia scientific and technical co-operation agreements and a joint declaration are benefiting joint research programmes, as is a framework trade and co-operation agreement.

Are there any trade agreements with the USA?

Many agreements exist between the EU and the USA on the peaceful use of atomic energy, environmental matters, fisheries, Mediterranean preferences, citrus fruit, pasta, and the export of steel products. The Transatlantic Policy Network was launched in 1992 to strengthen EU/US co-operation, and since then the 1996 New EU/US Transatlantic Relations Agenda and Action Plan to increase business and cultural links has been followed by the Transatlantic Economic Action Plan (TEP) and the New Transatlantic Marketplace Plan (proposed in 1998), which aim to deal with remaining regulatory and other barriers between the EU and US in goods, services, public procurement and IT. A joint EU/US committee is being set up to police mergers in respect of competition provisions.

What about Canada?

There is a framework agreement between the EU and Canada on economic co-operation and trade promotion, and an agreement on fishing rights. A 1996 Action Plan included foreign and security policy and the fight against terrorism and drugs. A 1997 EU/Canada Customs Co-operation Agreement assists in facilitating trade and combating customs fraud. A 1996 Political Declaration and EU/Canada Action Plan is similar to the 1996 Transatlantic Relations Agreement with the USA.

What about Central America?

The EU currently takes nearly 20 per cent of Central American exports, and provides about 19 per cent of its imports. It became the first financial aid donor to Central American countries to encourage a move away from illicit drug production, to promote their economic growth and revive inter-regional trade. The General System of Trade Preferences (GSP) has been extended to some Central American products. There are various co-operation and aid agreements with the six Central American countries (Costa Rica, El Salvador, Guatemala, Honduras, Nicaragua and Panama). A joint EU/Central American Declaration in February 1995 stressed the need for further co-operation and sustainable economic development, and there is increased co-operation to assist reforms.

Are there any agreements with Latin American countries?

Yes. There are action plans, trade agreements and guidelines for financial and technical co-operation with Latin American countries, which benefit from development aid, general preferences and help with their exports. The Commission is continuing to negotiate further agreements. There are various trade and co-operation agreements with Uruguay, Mexico, Brazil and Chile; and with the Andean Community countries of Bolivia, Colombia, Ecuador, Peru and Venezuela, and extensions of some of these are under discussion. There are aid programmes for some Latin American countries, the EU providing well over half of overseas development aid in Latin America.

What about the Mercosur countries?

These are Brazil, Argentina, Uruguay and Paraguay, and they are aiming to create an EC-style Common Market. There are EU/Mercosur co-operation conventions and programmes, with EU financial, technical and administrative support, and association and trade liberalization agreements being negotiated. The establishment of an EU/Mercosur inter-regional association with a long-term strategy is likely.

What about agreements and relations between the African, Caribbean and Pacific states (ACP countries) and the Community?

There are extensive agreements with these countries relating to aid and trade, and the form for renewing Lomé is under discussion. In 1991 the Community set the principle that development aid should be linked to respect for human rights.

What was the historical basis of these agreements?

In 1957 an implementing convention covering trade and aid was added to the Treaty of Rome, which provided for negotiation by the Community (as opposed to individual Member States) with overseas countries and territories (OCTs) of the Member States. A European Development Fund (EDF) was set up, to be applied as grants (mainly for infrastructure projects), principally in Francophone Africa.

What was the Yaoundé Convention?

Many former colonies of Community Member States became independent in the 1960s, and by 1963 the 18 countries of the Associated African States and Madagascar had negotiated a separate five-year convention with the European Community, with a second EDF including loans as well as grants. The Yaoundé Convention provided for preferential trade agreements, and the establishment of joint institutions at ministerial and parliamentary level.

What did the Lomé Conventions do?

By 1975, with the accession of the UK to the European Community, 20 Commonwealth countries and other independent states – 46 in all – signed the first Lomé Convention (after Lomé, capital city of Togo) to run for five years. This replaced the Yaoundé Convention and set out the objectives and principles of co-ordination and co-operation between 'the Community and the ACP states, and aimed to promote the economic, cultural and social development of the ACP states and consolidate and diversify their relations in a spirit of solidarity and mutual interest'.

The Lomé Convention set up preferential trade agreements, provided for aid and gave some protection to commodity producers. The second Lomé Convention introduced assistance for the mining sector in ACP countries.

In 1984 the third Lomé Convention, signed by an even larger group (66 ACP countries and 10 EC Member States), emphasized the protection of the environment, human rights, and the expansion of fishing and shipping.

Lomé IV, signed in 1989 for 10 years ending in 2000, emphasized the promotion of democracy. The package for Lomé 2000-05 is likely to be ECU 13.5 billion. The emphasis was changed radically from the classical project-oriented 'aid' approach, to a specific programme assistance approach. There is close co-operation with other aid donors as regards the co-ordination of policy, and the IMF and World Bank are the main partners. The new financial dimension of the Convention targets structural development of ACP economies, with the approaches being tailor-made for the countries concerned. Private sector development is being encouraged, with funds from the EIB made available for revenue-earning and infrastructure projects.

What is the present geographical spread of Lomé?

The geographical spread of Lomé now encompasses the EU, the 71 countries of Africa, the Caribbean, and the Pacific, with South Africa holding partial membership, and various countries of the southern and eastern Mediterranean signing co-operation agreements. In 1976, it extended co-operation to most of the developing countries of Latin America and Asia, and now covers well over half the countries of the world. Cuba has applied for observer status.

What are the joint institutions?

The joint ACP-EC Council of Ministers takes decisions. The Joint Assembly of Parliamentarians is advisory. The Centre for the Development of Industry and the Technical Centre for Agricultural Co-operation are executive. Help is given to countries to try to improve their production systems, and marketing techniques and structures.

What is happening now?

Continuing research, consultative documents and negotiations consider the effectiveness of, and difficulties encountered with regard to, the development of relations, co-operation and aid to ACP countries in the context of WTO developments and the enormous difficulties being encountered by many of these countries in servicing their debts.

How do the debts of developing countries affect Lomé countries?

Debts cause insuperable problems for many Lomé countries. The EU has launched various initiatives, such as guidelines on debt relief, and is now looking at the possibility of giving some balance-of-payments support to enable a new start for some countries. The private sector is encouraged to help by facilitating foreign and European investment, but in some ACP countries the economic future still appears bleak.

How do politics affect the Convention programmes?

There is strong emphasis on keeping politics out of programmes and grant aid, while still ensuring that informed assistance and advice are readily available. Structural development to enable countries to achieve self-sufficiency is strongly encouraged. Technical and financial assistance is given and preferential trade provisions apply. With very few exceptions (marginal ACP agricultural products), all products (including textiles) are allowed duty-free and quota-free access to EU countries *without reciprocity*. The fisheries and sugar protocols are important, and indicate an attempt to link rural incomes in Europe to those in the Lomé countries. There is also co-operation on regional development, cultural exchange and training, and a Community human rights policy seeks to minimize flagrant violations of basic human rights in Lomé countries.

What sorts of projects, programmes and contracts are financed by the Community?

There are three main areas: agriculture, transport infrastructure, and the energy-mining industry. The policy is weighted in the Mediterranean countries towards industrial schemes, and in Asia and Latin America towards agricultural development and food security. Three kinds of contract are financed:

1. *Works contracts* – for the construction of roads, railways, airports, ports, irrigation and drainage projects, schools, medical health buildings, and telecommunications networks (these constitute 52 per cent of the contracts placed).
2. *Supply contracts* – for the provision of agricultural equipment, vehicles, pesticides and fertilizers (30 per cent of the contracts).
3. *Service contracts* – including training programmes, feasibility and technical studies, and works supervision.

Invitations to tender for contracts are issued according to an agreed procedure and ACP firms do get a percentage preference. Further information can be obtained from the European Commission.

What about South Africa?

Trade with South Africa is increasing. A generalized Preference Agreement came into effect in 1994, but a trade development and co-operation accord agreed in 1999, providing for a free trade area with the EU and increased development aid, may be delayed. Since April 1997 South Africa has had partial membership of the Lomé Convention.

What about French Overseas Departments (DOMs)?

The French DOMs (Réunion, Guadeloupe, Guiana and Martinique) form part of the EC and have the status of regions of France, but only certain provisions of the Treaty of Rome apply.

The multi-annual POSEDOM programme is designed to assist Community territories geographically distant from the rest of the EU. It assists with, for example, improvement of air transport and also encourages regional co-operation with ACP countries nearby.

Which are the other autonomous or semi-autonomous regions with special relations with a Member State?

The Canary Islands are autonomous regions of Spain, and the Azores and Madeira are autonomous regions of Portugal. The Channel Islands and the Isle of Man do not belong to, but have a special relationship with, the UK.

Are there any independent countries within the EU borders with special provisions?

Yes. There are special provisions for such countries. Andorra is not a part of the EU or its treaties, so there is an EC/Andorra trade agreement. Monaco is not part of the EU but, by agreement, is part of the EC customs territory, so free movement of goods applies. San Marino is not part of the EU, but has extended customs and residence agreements with the EU. The Vatican is regarded as a foreign or third country, but no agreements have been made with it.

What about humanitarian aid?

A very large amount of aid is distributed every year, over 80 per cent being used to relieve the consequences of drought and civil strife, and the rest helping those affected by natural disasters. Sometimes the aid is centrally administered, and sometimes through the individual Member States and co-ordinated by the Commission.

The European Community Humanitarian Aid Office (ECHO) supports over 150 humanitarian aid organizations. The aim is now moving towards the prevention of natural disasters. ECHO difficulties often concern misappropriation of relief by racketeers. The latest guidelines on future policy on aid to the Third World accentuate the need to alleviate poverty, but other projects are supported. For example, in 1997 ECU 1.5 million was given to assist mine clearance and health assistance in Cambodia, and in 1999 large sums were provided to assist humanitarian aid agencies in Kosovo.

What conclusions can be drawn?

Although anti-dumping measures have been used where necessary, eg on China, Thailand and India, the European Council has specifically stated that the 'Internal Market should not close in on itself'. As has been seen, the Community is very active in negotiating trade agreements world-wide. When it is realized that, as a trading bloc, the Community's share of world trade is more than that of the US, it is clear that international trade forms an influential basis for the Community's world-wide international relations policy. Sheer size frequently enables the EU effectively to encourage reciprocity for EU goods and services in other countries. Japan and the US are obvious examples of reciprocity having to be carefully monitored.

The WTO agreements are having a significant impact on world trade and international relations.

Further information may be obtained from the European Commission, the Commission's Information Offices, the Developing Countries Trade Agency, the London Chamber of Commerce, the Centre for Development of Industry, and the World Trade Organization (see Appendix III).

19 Commercial strategies

Free movement of goods, services and workers, and freedom of establishment (ie the freedom to set up a business anywhere in the Member States), are all rights established under the Treaty of Rome. Many business people have come to accept the completion of the Internal Market, and now the establishment of the Eurozone, with the consequent broadening of the 'home' market to include the whole EU and the EEA countries. Many have not, and prefer to 'think local'. It depends on their aspirations. This enormous market-place brings benefits, burdens, opportunities and competition for all those in business within its area. Now with the impact of the Internet and global trade, competition and new markets are increasing.

So what should enterprises do?

These are some of the things they should do, consider or ask:

- They should first assess or reassess their position in their own national market and, if appropriate, in other markets in which they operate.
- They should then set their optimum targets by looking at their market share, and that of their competitors.
- They must talk to their customers to establish the customers' continuing needs, and possible changes in fashion.
- They must look to their own firm to assess whether (and if so what) changes are needed.
- Do they have the necessary staff expertise? Is extra training necessary?
- Do they have the sort of Information Technology (IT) systems to deal with Internet orders, the Euro, electronic trading and the swift response capacity that 21st-century traders and consumers will want? Have they got a Web site?
- Do their premises meet their likely needs? Could space be used more effectively by staff 'hotbedding' desks, and working more at home?

- Enterprises should try to think ahead to assess the likelihood of foreign competitors entering their national market, and watch the situation closely to see how it develops. Forewarned is, to some extent, forearmed.
- Are they sure that their professional advisers are up to date and effective?
- Are they able to quote for, or seek quotes for, their goods or services in the Euro, and is their sales literature up to date?
- Would they be eligible for any EU grants? Free information is available through the Commission and the Euro Info Centres (EICs), and on their Web sites.

In short, now could be a good time to have a comprehensive look at the business.

Should enterprises watch EU legislation?

Yes. They should consider current provisions, not forgetting ECJ decisions, and wider international developments; and keep under consideration any proposed changes that might affect their own particular business, or indeed the businesses of their competitors, suppliers and even clients, taking into account the shift away from national parliaments of the legislative initiative. They should watch EU negotiations within the WTO and with other markets, eg the US. The new round of WTO trade talks started in Seattle in November 1999 but, although expected to last for three years, they ran into severe difficulties with opponents of global liberalisation in the ascendant and a perceived lack of an agreed agenda.

Further information may be obtained from the WTO, the European Commission, or the Department of Trade and Industry.

What about non-national markets in the EU?

Once an enterprise has properly assessed its home base, and secured or planned to secure its position, then it is probably in a better position to look at the likelihood of success if it moves into other European markets. It should, for example, look at the possibility of making database searches for buyers and opportunities, or seeking the assistance of a market and information research company.

Are there any unexpected hazards?

Yes, those manufacturing and selling goods and services may still come across differing health and safety standards, different national specifications and standards, and possibly even different measurements and quality control, or professional requirements, in different Member States. Varying rates of VAT can lead to quite considerable variations in prices and affect marketing strategy in different countries. There are transport costs and differing controls for advertising, besides, for example, different attitudes to paying on time, and debt-collecting difficulties. Quoting in Euro will make price differentials between Member States more transparent, so they may have to be presented in a different way.

The Commission has a Market Access Strategy for Exporters Database with free access to businesses, which includes useful information about customs and internal taxes in various export markets, and details reported EU barriers to trade.

Do consumers differ from country to country?

Yes. Recent studies show considerable differences from place to place. For example, in some countries and even regions, people are more likely to be ready to try new products and brand names than in others. This affects marketing strategy, as the customer and his or her differing needs and expectations must be considered.

Are some of these differences and requirements illegal?

Sometimes restrictions may be illegal because they constitute restrictive barriers to trade, so it is worth making sure your lawyer has a keen eye and a good working knowledge of Community legislation and competition policy (see Chapter 10).

Generally, what is legally on sale in one EU country may be legally sold in another EU country unless a 'public interest' ban is found to be appropriate (or if the goods are the subject of a special relationship and imported from a third country). Cross-border business is helped by a number of factors, and the Commission is taking a stricter line on enforcement of Community legislation.

The Cassis de Dijon Ruling 1987 by the European Court of Justice confirmed the principle that goods lawfully circulated in one state in the Community can be sold in another, and that one Member State can only block such an import from another if it deems it essential to the protection of health and defence of consumer interests. There have been many other judgements since, the thrust of which has been to provide that Member States must treat national goods and those coming from other EU countries in the same way.

The Commission has produced a guide to redress and enforcement called the Dialogue with Citizens and Business Service. Its freephone number is 0800 581 591. Its Internet site is: http://citizens.eu.int/originchoice.htm.

What about the effect of the Euro?

Within the Eurozone, cross-border trading will be made much easier by the existence of a single currency. It is vital that all enterprises wishing to trade in the EU, whether in or outside the Eurozone, are prepared for the impact of the Euro. The year 2002, when Euro notes and coins will be in circulation, is not far away, and even simple details, eg as to whether printing fonts include the Euro, and whether software can deal with currency calculations, need to be checked. In general, contracts are covered by a Regulation (1103/97), but it is worth asking a legal adviser anyway.

Banking arrangements should also be reconsidered. Considerable advice has been made available by national government departments, and by the Commission.

Is the achievement of Community transport policy · objectives making a difference?

Yes. The lifting of internal borders, the liberalization of freight, maritime and air transport, and the development of the trans-European networks make it cheaper, faster and easier to send goods further or to obtain supplies from further afield. However these changes also make it easier for cross-border competitors in Europe to supply new markets.

How does the EU help EU enterprises wishing to export to third countries?

The EU as a significant trading bloc is better able to negotiate useful trading agreements with other countries, and to enforce reciprocal treatment than the individual Member States. For example, the Information Technology Agreement 1997, together with a deal liberalizing telecommunications services, which was agreed between the US and the EU under the aegis of the WTO, will phase out most tariffs for IT products by 2000, and will have an enormous impact on this sector. The EU's Market Access Database on the Internet with useful information is at: mkaccdb.eu.int.

Are the changes in public procurement policy making a difference?

Yes. It is vital to monitor the enforcement of the EU's public procurement policy because public sector markets have been opened up to stronger competition, and there is help available for smaller companies who wish to participate (see Chapter 10). It is also important to understand the extension of the public procurement market achieved through the WTO agreements.

Does the trend towards mergers, acquisitions and the purchase of subsidiaries in other Member States affect the market-place?

Yes. The continuing trend towards increased collaboration between companies, and more cross-border acquisition activity, make a difference. As companies sell over a wider area, so they buy over a wider area. Some companies may benefit from this, just as some may find it more difficult to protect themselves from hostile take-overs and increased competition.

Is industry moving its manufacturing and other bases around more?

Yes. Powerful incentives, such as lower employment costs, local tax incentives and government aid in areas of special development, or centres of excellence in particular fields, encourage some companies to move their bases from existing or traditional areas more often in the search for lower production costs, sometimes with devastating effects on the area left. Smaller companies should keep a watch on the likely moves by their suppliers and clients to ensure they are not heavily committed in one area only to find that their biggest client has moved to another.

Is it possible to list factors a company should watch as part of its commercial strategy?

Much depends on the sector concerned, but it should look in detail and periodically review its own overall position as well as that of other firms having an effect on its business, including consideration of the following points:

- those supplying its raw materials, and possible alternative suppliers;
- those supplying its components, and possible alternative suppliers;
- the suppliers or manufacturers of its finished goods;
- the channels of distribution of these firms and the company itself;
- its own current customers and its potential for securing new customers;
- the possibility of new entrants and new factors in the market;

- the possibility of legislation or regulations in any of the above areas that could affect the company in question.

What kind of questions should be asked?

Again, these depend largely on the business itself and what factors might affect it, but, for example, the bargaining power of suppliers or buyers could change to reduce or increase costs or prices. It is important to consider general matters such as the following:

- Exchange rate fluctuations and their likely effects; and the impact of the Euro.
- Credit costs. These, and the normal credit period offered to buyers, vary, ie buyer expectation is different in different countries. Late payment is a significant problem in some countries, and extra costs should be built into the contract, which should be carefully drafted to reflect the reasons for any differing prices.
- Interest rates. They differ in Member States, and sometimes it is worth shopping around for the best rates available. Banking services' costs should be scrutinized.
- The possible impact of government grants or their withdrawal on the enterprise, its competitors, or others in the chain of supply and demand.
- Any restructuring of the industry or services supplied.
- The possible effects of parallel trade, ie buying products where they can be obtained most cheaply and selling them where they can command the highest price. This may well affect marketing strategy, so trends must be carefully watched. It should be noted that swingeing fines can be imposed on companies trying to enforce export bans within the EU, so parallel importing has increased.
- The effect of counterfeiting – if any – on the business. It is important to understand how to use protective provisions so they can be activated quickly.
- Packaging requirements, which should not be intended to partition markets.
- The general trend in the economy of the country or regions concerned.

What about the business environment?

This must be taken into consideration, and depends on the following points:

- The political strategy of the governments of the 'home' countries and the countries in which a firm operates, and the Commission's European political strategies.

- The stage of market development in the industry or sector. If this is booming – excellent, but there will be more competitors. If it is declining, enterprises should be looking towards the possibility of going into new products with new development strategies.
- Third-country competition. It is important to consider this. By reason of its position, professional infrastructure, financial markets and simple company law, the UK is often regarded as a useful base from which to move into other European and Commonwealth markets, and so encounters particularly significant incursions by third-country companies. A different argument is that it is better to site head offices in mainland Europe in a country already within the Eurozone.
- The possible uses, value and coverage of patents, know-how, trade marks and relevant copyrights and design copyrights.
- The developments in electronic trading, such as the effect of electronic signatures and local provisions.
- The impact on the business of sustainability and environmental requirements.
- Infrastructure, transport and communications availability in the area under discussion.

Is market research part of assessing the business environment?

Market research is not necessarily part of assessing the business environment, but it is important. A firm wishing to establish its position would be wise to carry out market research programmes periodically, and should get professional help if it has no experience in this field.

What questions should be asked?

As much information as possible should be gathered and evaluated, including, for example:

- the extent of the current market and any changes necessitating new action by the company to improve market exploitation;
- changes in the expectation or attitudes of customers necessitating different marketing strategies;
- the marketing strategies of competitors, and whether there is anything to be learnt from these;
- advertising, packaging and public relations, and any changes to relevant legal requirements;
- political and public attitudes to, for example, environmental issues and their effects on the company, and sustainability in terms of processes;

- technological changes;
- any relevant changes to the company's own position (eg to its assets, resources, cash flow, etc), including its vulnerability to third-country companies, and also any taxation changes;
- relevant European and international standards and likely changes to them. Mutual recognition in respect of standards rather than harmonization means that these are less likely to cause problems, and the Community's own institutions, CEN and CENELEC, combine with various national equivalent bodies to produce European standards. These help considerably, particularly with regard to public procurement contracts, but the move towards global standards should be taken into account (see Chapter 6).

Where can information be found?

If professional help is not obtained, then it may be useful to consider the following sources of information: Chambers of Commerce, business links, trade associations, local reference libraries, European Commission information offices, relevant government departments, business information centres, the embassies of the countries concerned, and the Internet. The Commission has produced a useful list of databases of interest to SMEs, available from its information offices, and its CORDIS database is particularly useful as regards EU research and development information.

What about the company's own strategy?

It is important to consider in detail the answers to the following questions:

- What are the aims or objectives of the company for the next five to ten years?
- Should it expand into new areas or concentrate more on existing operations, or possibly on fewer but larger areas? Could it meet the needs of new customers?
- Should it embark on collaboration with other companies in other markets to expand or protect its own interests?
- Are the staff adequate? A personnel audit should be carried out (ie a careful consideration of the capability and performance of existing management and staff). Any need to bring in expertise and future company policy needs should be considered – a company's best asset is its staff. Language needs and special skills should be looked at, and the possibility of in-house training of staff considered. The importance of first telephone contacts with an enterprise should be remembered, as should the impact of a Web site, for example.

The above questions refer mainly to the enterprise and its markets: should the product itself be looked at?

Yes. It is particularly important to look systematically at such matters as:

- product design;
- production processes;
- strict quality control (particularly with strict liability for defective products in mind) and the insurance position for product liability claims, not forgetting directors' liability;
- distribution and terms of agreements, which should reflect liabilities of importers and manufacturers;
- customer service, maintenance and marketing;
- future product development, taking into account the need to comply with applicable standards in the intended market;
- the provisions relating to consumer protection and liability for the product or service;
- price and the possibility of currency pricing, including credit terms;
- insurance for export credit, credit or currency fluctuations;
- product or service liability insurance;
- demographic trends and their likely impact on the market;
- sustainability and packaging – given the increasing trend towards looking at the environmental impact of a product, inclusive of packaging, from manufacture to disposal. The eco-label scheme enables less environmentally damaging products to be identified, and is a useful marketing tool (see Regulation 880/92). Information may be obtained from the UK Ecolabelling Board.

What about new product or service development?

This can give a company a competitive edge on its rivals. Usually the best way to discover the right product is to have a brainstorming session with the staff as they are often a good source of ideas for new or improved products, and it is good management practice to consult them periodically.

What about research and development (R&D)?

Depending on the size of the company and its area of operation, R&D can be vital to the long-term future of the company, or irrelevant and a drain on much-needed resources. Consideration should be given to co-operating with another company to cut costs. There are programmes to encourage SMEs (see Chapter 15) and an EU R&D Framework Programme. The Commission's telephone helpline is 010 32 22 36 51 51.

Can the government or Commission help with grants?

All national governments and the EU assist or fund some research and indeed other projects, particularly as there is now a drive to encourage employment; and there are grants specially geared to help SMEs. Structural Funds or Regional Enterprise Grants may provide help, and indeed for larger projects there may be the possibility of loans through the European Investment Bank (EIB). The Commission spends half its research budget on commercial application research programmes, and has produced useful guidance for applicants, but many companies find the conditions on which grants are given too restrictive, and prefer instead to collaborate with other enterprises. The Commission is also encouraging the promotion of R&D through national tax incentives. Funding sources include the EIB, EIF, Eurotech and equity capital. There are projects to encourage funding, eg seed capital provision (see Chapter 15). Further information can be obtained from the Euro-Info Centres.

What about export credit insurance?

Provision for this varies in the different Member States (see Chapter 12).

Are general attitudes important?

Yes. The development of the EU means that companies already regard a much larger area as their 'home' market, and are becoming far more international – even global – in their thinking. This has been the case for many years for the multinationals, but now many professional advisers such as accountancy and legal firms are networking more, and widening the territorial spread of their advice capability, either through their own capabilities, or through strategic link-ups.

What about getting commercial agents in other Member States?

This is one way of encouraging distribution of products or services. Agents are defined differently and have varying rights and duties in different Member States, although the provisions have been harmonized considerably by the 1986 EC Directive on the co-ordination of the laws of Member States relating to self-employed commercial agents, which set out the basic rules regulating the main provisions of commercial agency contracts on the rights and obligations of principals and agents.

A commercial agent is defined in the Directive as any self-employed intermediary (which includes individuals and companies) who has continuing authority to negotiate the sale or purchase of goods (note: not services) on behalf of another person (the principal) or to negotiate or to conclude such transactions on behalf of, or in the name of, that principal. Some agents are not covered by the Directive, for example unpaid commercial agents, receivers or insolvency practitioners, officers of a company empowered to enter into a commitment binding on that company, partners who are lawfully authorized to make commitments binding on their other partners, and commodity dealers and various others such as distributors acting on their own account. Member States may provide that the Directive shall not apply to persons whose commercial agency activities are considered secondary by the law of that Member State.

What was the aim of the Commercial Agents Directive?

It attempted to achieve a common expectation of rights and duties for enterprises wishing to act as agents or principals in other parts of the Community. Some rights were new to the UK, such as the right to payment after termination of an agency agreement for transactions mainly attributable to the agent's efforts during the agency, but concluded after the agency ended. The Directive also provided for payments to agents following termination of the contract in some circumstances, even if the agency ends because the agent dies, and may require payment of damages for losses or loss of commission. In 1996 the Commission published a bulletin on compensation and indemnity provisions in the EU.

Has the Directive made a difference to businesses involved in agency agreements?

It has made a difference in some countries, including the UK, and commercial agents and their principals should read it. The relevant implementing legislation varies in the Member States, and therefore must be taken into account for matters such as the requirement to have agency contracts in writing in order to be valid, and for some restraint of trade clauses. Further information may be obtained from the European Commission, national government departments and trade associations.

What about setting up a company, a branch or a subsidiary in another Member State?

All these routes are possible, and should be carefully and expertly considered by professional advisers, taking the specific needs of the enterprise into consideration, and the different liabilities that directors can incur in different Member States. Many factors are relevant, such as the present and projected scale of operations, the target market, tax provisions and staff costs. Frequently it is best to use the local form of company, and registration provisions vary from state to state. EEIGs may be useful for developing research projects, for example, but may not themselves make a profit. The European Company Statute may be one option in the future (see Chapter 13).

What about packaging?

It is vital to get this right. Besides being attractive to customers, it may have to carry certain information required by law, and be easily disposable, so it is better to ensure compliance with the legislation in all the intended market countries from the beginning. It also makes international advertising easier.

The Packaging and Waste Directive 1994 applies to all packaging sold in the EU. It requires Member States to set up systems seeking to ensure that by July 2001 (except for Greece, Ireland and Portugal, which have until 2005) between 50 and 65 per cent of waste packaging is recovered; and between 25 and 45 per cent of each material is recycled, ie that up to 50 per cent of the waste will be reused, recycled, composted or used to create energy. Since 1998, packaging can only be sold if it complies with the Directive in terms of recoverability and recyclability.

This is a detailed provision, which sets objectives for packaging standardization and marking, and provisions on the disposal of heavy metals into the environment. It includes the 'polluter pays' principle. It does not affect national provisions that go further. This means that enterprises must take into account not only the Directive but also national provisions, and realize that enforcement will become more rigid as the target dates draw nearer.

What about advertising?

Well-targeted advertising is vital, and the scale and type of advertising undertaken will depend on the product or service, and the budget available. There are controls on advertising, as to the product (eg credit services) and as to what can be said (eg comparative advertising). Tobacco advertising is to be banned from

October 2006, although it will still be allowed in specialist maga-
zines and at the point of sale. This means that sponsorship of
events will be phased out. Remember that one sympathetic article
about a firm or product in a business magazine may be worth a
great deal of advertising space. Many public relations and advertising agencies have international coverage and can give invaluable
advice (see also Chapter 7).

What about liability for defective products or services?

The 1985 Directive on liability for defective products provided
for strict liability of manufacturers and suppliers, and even
importers in some circumstances. It has now been extended in a
1999 Directive to primary agricultural products and game. The
complainant has to prove the damage, the defect, and the relationship between the two for the producer to be made liable.

Although there is currently some liability for defective services,
it can be difficult for the injured party to prove the fault or negligence of the service provider. A 1990 draft Directive on liability
for services involving a lack of safety was withdrawn, but guidelines with texts governing specific areas and complementary codes
of conduct are under discussion and should be kept in mind.
Enterprises should consider their position carefully, including the
possibility of product and service liability insurance (see also
Chapter 7).

Should there be a pricing strategy from the outset?

Yes. It should be remembered though that EU policy is to reduce
the differences between prices charged for the same goods in various Member States, so in practice wide differences in prices can
make parallel importing worth while. This can be both difficult to
stop and very costly for the manufacturer. Some variations will be
caused by VAT, government price controls, insurance, distribution
costs and the costs of servicing effective guarantees further from
the manufacturing base.

What is dumping?

This is pricing goods at below the economic price. It is usually
outlawed because of its adverse affect on local companies, as it
can be used to squeeze them out of business, giving a stronger
hold on the market to the predator company. An extra (anti-
dumping) duty may in some cases be imposed on importation of
such goods by the EU.

What if the price is kept artificially high?

If the price is kept artificially high, EC restrictive trade practices and competition provisions may come into play (see Chapter 10).

What about finance and financial movements?

All the major clearing banks offer useful advice to companies wishing to expand into new markets, and make considerable expertise available to their clients.

What about unfair contract terms?

The 1993 Directive on Unfair or Abusive Terms is aimed at protecting consumers and others by harmonizing provisions that varied greatly in the EU. It covers standard term contracts, and contracts not individually negotiated, or contracts where there is unfairness as between the parties, and makes offending clauses unenforceable. Care must be taken, as provisions applicable are slightly different in the various Member States.

What law will apply to contracts made in two or more Member States?

It is advisable to make a specific choice of law in your contract as lack of clarity could cause difficulty. There are various accepted rules, and the question is addressed in the 1980 Rome Convention on the law applicable to contractual obligations, covering products and some services. This provides detailed rules to determine which law would apply if the parties do not choose an applicable law, and (usually) the law of the country with which the contract has the closest connection would be applied. The Convention has been ratified by most but not all Member States.

What about data protection?

There is a package of six Directives on the protection of personal data, but the most significant for most people is the 1995 Directive on the protection of individuals in relation to the processing of personal data. It aims to 'protect the fundamental rights and freedoms of natural persons, and in particular their right to privacy with respect to the processing of personal data'. It includes general principles of good practice, and the requirement of security, and extends to manually held as well as electronically held data.

The Directive was set against the background of the increasing value of personal data for subject targeting, and the growth in cross-border consumer transactions, but lack of harmonized rules even at a minimum level in the EU. Although all Member States had signed the Council of Europe Convention on the subject (which is less specific than the Directive), they had not all implemented it.

Further information is available from the Consumers in the European Community Group (BEUC), the Commission, or relevant trade associations.

What about late payment of invoices?

This is a problem throughout the EU, and various attempts are being made to tackle it. The Community average is over 60 days, going up to about 120 days in Italy and Greece. SMEs suffer particularly, as it is more difficult and expensive for them to obtain credit than their larger counterparts, who are also better able to fund recovery proceedings. The Commission issued a recommendation in 1994 that:

- contracts should include precise payment terms;
- in the event of late payment there should be compensation payable to the creditor, based on the real market rates of interest (ie it should not be cheaper to pay late than to borrow the money);
- procedures for recovering credits should be fast, simple and cheap (and should not necessarily entail engaging a legal adviser);
- VAT should not be payable until invoices are paid;
- for public procurement contracts, maximum payment deadlines should be 60 days.

Following this recommendation, the situation worsened, so a 1997 Commission report suggested a statutory right to interest on commercial debts, with public bodies required to pay interest automatically if they do not settle invoices within 60 days. Political agreement was achieved in July 1999 on the draft Late Payment Directive, which gives a statutory right to interest of 6 per cent above the ECB lending rate following 30 days in default of agreement.

What about litigation?

Litigation is costly and time-consuming, but the firm, whether large or small, that is prepared for litigation will do much better than its less well-briefed counterpart. The golden rule if an enterprise is pursuing payment is to ensure, before litigating, that funds exist to reimburse it. Reputable credit reference agencies are worth consulting, and it is often easiest to seek help from a reputable debt collection agency, rather than embark on costly litigation. However, some enterprises prefer to take proceedings themselves, or enlist the help of their legal advisers.

The Strasbourg Agreement 1977 on the transmission of applications for legal aid has been ratified by all EU and EFTA states except Germany, The Netherlands, Iceland, Liechtenstein and Switzerland. Thought should be given to providing for alternative dispute procedures such as conciliation, mediation and arbitration, albeit to be effective both parties must have an equal interest in resolving the relevant dispute. However, it is important that the appropriate rules be chosen at the negotiating stage, as deciding on precise rules later can be expensive. The 1997 Convention on the cross-border service of documents in civil and commercial proceedings is now the subject of a draft Directive.

What about the enforcement of judgements in the EU?

The Brussels Convention on the Jurisdiction and Enforcement of Judgements on Civil and Commercial Matters 1968, usually referred to as either the 'Brussels Convention' or the 'Judgements Convention', impedes forum shopping (ie bringing a case in the most advantageous place for the plaintiff) and aims to ensure only one court has jurisdiction and is competent to hear a claim, eg concerning a bad debt, by way of (usually) a registration procedure in other national courts. It also provides that a relevant judgement must be recognized and enforced in other Member States; but it does not cover all matters. The Convention was extended by the Brussels II Convention 1998 to some areas, such as matrimonial matters and joint parental responsibilities for children, and these form the basis of a regulation proposed in 1999, which is likely to be amended.

Not all EU states have acceded to the Brussels Convention: some are signatories to the parallel Lugano Convention 1988, similar to the Brussels Convention, which has been ratified by all the EFTA states and most EU member signatories to the Brussels Convention.

What about lotteries?

The position on lotteries is set out in the European Court of Justice Schindler decision, which states that the importation of tickets and advertising for a lottery organized in a Member State is an act related to a service activity; that national legislation banning lotteries nationally is contrary to the movement of services; but that a lottery may be banned in a Member State on public policy grounds.

Are there any conclusions to be drawn from all this advice on business strategy?

Yes. It is vital that:

- the management structure is carefully thought out before any action is taken;
- responsibilities and expertise are carefully and clearly matched;
- staff communications structures ensure that everyone knows what is happening, and that they comply with consultation requirements.
- those negotiating with representatives of firms from other countries must try to achieve an understanding of their normal negotiating stance and expectations;
- there must be great care that misunderstandings due to language difficulties are avoided, since they can cause insuperable problems;
- it is ensured that there is an understanding of any administrative differences that need to be ironed out, to avoid later difficulties or even mistakes leading to fines;
- the plan of action is carefully drafted, but not inflexible;
- there is firm credit control to minimize late payment of debts, with buyers and sellers, including agents, understanding the enterprise's requirements and procedures.

Are there any final conclusions to be drawn as to the effect on commercial strategies of the developing EU?

Yes. In a changing environment every efficient business – whether small or large, and whatever its field of operations – will need to keep its commercial strategy continually under review. It is hoped that this book has explained why. There is plenty of help and advice and even some financing available, but finding it can be time-consuming. Of particular impact on business will be the development of e-commerce, and the availability of less expensive labour in the 'new' countries negotiating to join the EU.

20 Common European defence, foreign and security policy, and civil defence

What is the present position with regard to a common European defence and security policy?

This comes under the second pillar of the Treaty on European Union (TEU) under inter-governmental arrangements, which stated that common foreign and security policy (CFSP) includes all questions relating to the security of the EU. Under the Western European Union (WEU) Declaration, it was agreed that the role of the WEU should be strengthened so as to form the European pillar of NATO, looking forward towards a common defence policy and, in time, to common defence in the EU. In May 1999 the ministers of the WEU backed a proposal to merge the WEU into the EU to form its defence arm. The details of an EU common security and defence policy have been agreed, which would give the EU military capacity to deal with regional difficulties and carry out peacekeeping and humanitarian missions without NATO agreement. In July 1999 the UK and Italian governments launched an initiative aimed at encouraging the formation of a pan-European defence force as the EU component of the NATO forces, supported by an EU defence equipment audit, and separate from the Eurocorps (see below).

The senior post of EU High Representative for Foreign and Security Policy has been created, and Javier Solana Madariaga was appointed in 1999. He is also General Secretary of the WEU.

It is felt that these initiatives will lead to the eventual integration of the WEU into the EU, with concerns being expressed by some countries such as Turkey, which may oppose these changes.

Up until now the military, as opposed to the political, alliances in Europe have come under the WEU and NATO treaties. All Member States are members of WEU, except Denmark and the neutral countries of Austria, Finland, Ireland and Sweden. Not all Member States are members of NATO.

The whole question of the development of the three areas of CFSP and defence has been the subject of considerable study and discussion.

The Amsterdam Treaty provided for peacekeeping and peace-making missions and humanitarian operations, which would be carried out by the WEU together with some or all of the Member States, depending on the situation. It also provided for agreement by consensus for common strategies in the EU on defence, with the Council normally deciding by unanimity, but enabling a Member State to abstain, which would not prevent a decision being made; and the abstaining state would be able to choose whether to participate in the action decided on. However, in very important cases a Member State is able to declare that its national interests are at stake.

What is the Eurocorps?

This is best described as the embryo European army. It consists of about 50,000 men from Belgium, France, Germany, Luxembourg and Spain, and is operational for humanitarian and peacekeeping operations. It should be distinguished from the Euroforce, which is a joint French, Italian and Spanish project for an air, sea and land unit intended to be the Mediterranean counterpart of Eurocorps.

The main organizations concerned with security and defence

In order to understand the development of European security and defence policy, it is important to be able to distinguish the main organizations concerned on a global scale. It should be noted that these are not European Union but international organizations.

The Western European Union (WEU)

First started in 1948 as the Brussels Treaty Organization by Belgium, France, Luxembourg, The Netherlands and the UK, it was extended in 1954 to include Germany and Italy. It now has four kinds of members: 1) full members, ie all EU members except Denmark, Ireland, Austria, Sweden and Finland, which belong to the next group; 2) members with observer status; 3) associate members, such as Turkey, Norway and Iceland; and 4) associate partners, such as Bulgaria, Estonia, Hungary, Latvia, Lithuania, Poland, Romania, the Czech and Slovak Republics and the Ukraine. The associate partners are generally those countries that have concluded Europe Agreements with the EU, so as to bring them gradually into this area of EU policy-making.

As stated above, the WEU is likely to be integrated into the security and defence arm of the EU.

What is the role of the WEU?

The WEU co-ordinates defence policy and equipment, and collaborates closely with NATO and the EPC (European Political Co-operation). Its role is to make Europe and the US partners within the renewed Atlantic Alliance; and to contribute to the establishment of a European security policy. There is an agency to monitor disarmament agreements; and dialogue on the structure of a future European Collective Security System continues with the Balkans and Eastern and Central Europe despite difficulties. The WEU Institute of Security Studies was established in 1990 to encourage co-operation and the establishment of a European identity, and will be developed into a European Security and Defence Academy.

In 1996 WEU members agreed that it should begin humanitarian operations with NATO logistical support within two years. Its role as 'the defence component of the EU and as a means to strengthen the European pillar of the Alliance' was then confirmed. Following the Amsterdam Treaty, a new policy planning and early warning unit to monitor international developments and their possible implications for the EU is being set up, which consists of specialists from the Member States, the Council and Commission of the EU and from the WEU itself to assist European Council policy decisions.

At the end of 1999 it was decided that the EU should be able to access the WEU's expertise and information and be capable of operating without the support of NATO and the US if appropriate. Plans were drawn up to the effect that, by 2003, there would be an EU military force with up to 60,000 troops available within 60 days. This force will handle crises and perform peacekeeping and humanitarian operations for up to one year. It is intended that it should work within the principles of the UN Charter.

The North Atlantic Treaty Organization (NATO)

The North Atlantic Treaty was signed in 1949. Its associates include Belgium, Canada, Denmark, France, Germany, Greece, Iceland, Italy, Luxembourg, The Netherlands, Norway, Spain, Portugal, Turkey, the UK and the USA. The Russian Federation has signed a Founding Act on Mutual Relations, Co-operation and Security with NATO. More countries wish to join, including Romania, Slovenia, Georgia and some Baltic states.

NATO's aims are to safeguard the freedom, common heritage, and civilization of its peoples, founded on the principles of democracy, individual liberty and the rule of law. The Organization is intended to be an insurance for peace. Defence has priority, but the NATO agreement also encompasses various political, economic, scientific and environmental co-operation arrangements. In NATO agreements are reached by a unanimous vote of the governments that comprise the North Atlantic Council. The conference parliamentarians from NATO countries, known as the North Atlantic Assembly, meet annually. Its secretariat headquarters is in Brussels.

The Organization for Security and Co-operation in Europe (OSCE), previously called the Conference on Security and Co-operation in Europe (CSCE)

The OSCE, set up in 1975, is a process for negotiations, now with over 50 members, with the aim of providing a discussion forum on security and other matters, such as preventative diplomacy, the encouragement of protection of human rights, and conflict resolution, besides the enhancement of security and stability. This means that it will promote co-operation between Member States to establish market-based economies. Membership includes countries of NATO, EFTA, the WEU, the EU, the North Atlantic Co-operation Council (NACC), the CIS, and the Black Sea Economic Council (BSEC).

Delegations from the member countries meet periodically, and may include representatives of business, as aims include the encouragement of improved economic relations between Member States, commercial exchanges, and industrial co-operation.

In 1990 the then CSCE states signed the Paris Charter for a new Europe, which includes statements on friendly relations between the Member States, security, the human dimension and human rights, social and scientific progress, environment and culture. The OSCE is entrusted with monitoring and administering the Pact on Stability in Europe 1995, which is aimed at promoting good neighbourly relations, and at resolving frontier and minority difficulties. It consists of a statement of willingness to overcome problems arising from the past, and to respect human rights. It includes a list of good neighbourly accords and agreements, and a list of measures taken by the EU to fulfil the Pact objectives, eg project assistance for education, transport and the environment.

In December 1994 the heads of state and government at the CSCE summit decided to change the name of the CSCE to the OSCE, and restated its objectives. It noted the continuing conflicts and discrimination against minorities in the area, and the increasing threat of terrorism. The OSCE is to be 'the primary instrument of early warning, conflict prevention and crisis management in the region'. There is a ratified convention on conciliation and arbitration within the OSCE. There is a new mandate to pursue measures of arms control, and commitment to the Treaty on the Non-proliferation of Nuclear Weapons. The OSCE secretariat is situated in Prague, Czech Republic.

The United Nations Organization

This was set up in 1945 with the aim of maintaining international peace and fostering good relations. It is described in more detail in Appendix 1. NATO frequently implements the UN Security Council Resolutions.

What has the EU done with regard to the proliferation of weapons?

There are various treaties under discussion, ratified or signed in this field, it being essentially a matter for individual countries. The treaties include: the Convention on Bacteriological and Toxic Weapons 1972, the 1990 Treaty on the Reduction of Conventional Forces in Europe (CFE), and the Nuclear Non-proliferation Treaty. Nuclear Test Ban Treaties were signed in 1963 and 1996, but the latter, banning all tests, has only been signed by a few of the 44 states with nuclear reactors that would be needed to bring it into effect.

What about the export of weapons or dual-use goods?

A Council Regulation 1994 controls exports of dual-use goods, ie goods that have both a civilian and a military use. It concerns the issue and recognition of export control licences. There is a decision on joint action under CFSP, which lists goods concerned, and closer co-operation is in hand following the Amsterdam Treaty. A common list is likely to be settled soon of the military equipment covered by the agreed common code of conduct on arms exports from the EU. Under the code, participants agree not to issue export licences for arms to countries where their use could lead to aggression or repression.

What about the satellite observation system?

The US and Russia wish to co-operate with the EU with regard to a space-based observation system, which could eventually be used to assist a European defence policy.

What conclusions can be drawn from the above?

There is a fear of instability in Eastern Europe, evidenced by recent difficulties, but the different forces of Europe have worked together successfully, not just in respect of peacekeeping but also humanitarian operations. With trouble so close to existing EU borders, and the escalating cost of military equipment, the realization that there is little option but to work together has undoubtedly helped political negotiations in this area.

The Stability Pact for South-East Europe, which was endorsed at an international summit in June 1999, has been supported by proposals for a stabilization and association agreement with the Former Yugoslav Republic of Macedonia (FYROM). This should incorporate political dialogue, co-operation in various areas, and work towards a free trade area between FYROM and the EU.

Civil protection policy

What is civil protection?

Civil protection has been defined by the Commission to include a wide range of areas connected with the protection of the public. The Commission promotes mutual assistance among Member States in the event of serious crisis and natural or human-made disasters such as floods, forest fires, oil spills and earthquakes.

What has the Commission done?

Besides producing studies and proposals, the Commission publishes a guide to civil protection, which is updated annually. It is intended as a practical manual for national authorities in charge of emergency planning and for those responsible for civil protection. The guide lists the main types of disasters it covers, and notes possible bilateral and multilateral agreements between Member States, the various categories of emergency planning arrangements at national, regional and local levels, and the resources available to assist people in the European Community.

The Commission has organized simulation exercises and training courses. Public awareness operations have been mounted and attempts made to achieve closer relations with relevant international organizations.

Are there any practical developments?

Useful developments include the listing of existing data banks, and an attempt to interconnect them, together with the progressive harmonization of multilingual terminology by producing a glossary of terms in all nine languages. A single Community-wide emergency telephone number (112) came into effect in all Member States except Spain and The Netherlands on 1 January 1993 (national numbers such as 999 in the UK continue where appropriate), and the Commission is trying to promote the use of space technology to improve telecommunications services and infrastructures.

The European Voluntary Service for the Young enables thousands of young people to participate in environmental or social action in other Member States.

The Commission has supported training workshops on combating forest fires, and other training programmes are being considered. Natural disasters, dangerous emissions and accidents do not respect borders, so it is certainly good sense to ensure that the whole of Europe can move together in the event of a disaster.

Further information may be obtained from the European Commission.

Appendix I
Institutions not to be confused with EC/EU institutions

Do not confuse EC/EU institutions with the following:

- The Council of Europe
- The European Free Trade Association (EFTA)
- The United Nations (UN)
- The General Agreement on Tariffs and Trade (GATT) and the World Trade Organization (WTO)
- The North Atlantic Treaty Organization (NATO)
- The Western European Union (WEU)
- The Organization for Security and Co-operation in Europe (OSCE), previously called the Conference on Security and Co-operation in Europe (CSCE)
- The Organization for Economic Co-operation and Development (OECD)
- The European Bank for Reconstruction and Development (EBRD)
- The Group of Seven (G7), now the Group of Eight (G8)
- The European Space Agency
- The Assembly of European Regions

The Council of Europe

The Council of Europe was set up in May 1949 with the aim of achieving a greater unity between its members for safeguarding and realizing the ideals and principles that are their common heritage and facilitating their economic and social progress.

The Council is now made up of about 40 countries, and membership is restricted to parliamentary democracies. The members of the Council of Europe's Parliamentary Assembly are drawn from members of national parliaments. The current members include all the members of the EU, Bulgaria, Cyprus, the Czech and Slovak Republics, Estonia, Hungary, Iceland, Liechtenstein, Malta, Norway, Poland, Romania, Russia, San Marino, Switzerland and Turkey.

The organization comprises a Committee of Ministers, which agrees on common action by governments, and is the main decision-making body; and a Parliamentary Assembly of about 286 members. The latter makes proposals for new activities and services, acting as a sort of parliamentary forum for Europe, but has no legislative powers. Its international staff are situated in Strasbourg.

The Council of Europe, which is seen as concentrating on human rights, culture and the environment, has concluded about 130 inter-governmental conventions and agreements, including the Social Charter, data protection, trans-frontier co-operation and the Convention on Human Rights, which is administered and enforced by the Commission on Human Rights and the Court of Human Rights.

The Council promotes a European identity and co-operation in education, environmental health and social services, youth activities, consumer protection and the general harmonization of law in Europe. Other subjects range from the Architectural Heritage of Europe Convention, to the Convention on Spectator Violence and Television without Frontiers. Its Convention for a European Charter for Regional and Minority Languages was opened for signature in 1992.

The Congress of Local and Regional Authorities, with the same number of delegates as the Assembly, is a forum for elected representatives of local authorities.

The European Free Trade Association (EFTA)

What is EFTA and when was it founded?

EFTA was founded in 1960. Its current member countries include Iceland, Liechtenstein, Norway and Switzerland.

Two of its founder members, the UK and Denmark, subsequently left to join the European Community, as did Austria, Sweden and Finland.

What are its aims?

Its main aim, to establish free trade in industrial goods between its members, was achieved by the end of 1966. The second objective was to establish a single market for industrial goods in Western Europe, and this was also achieved. EFTA's current objectives are to operate its free trade area, to co-ordinate the EFTA countries in relation to trade agreements with the EU, and to provide a useful forum in which members may consult with each other on international economic problems. It is directed by a Council, with twice-yearly ministerial level meetings, and has its headquarters in Geneva.

What is the relationship between EFTA and the EU?

The relationship is close. A 1984 joint declaration concerning a European Economic Space was followed by the European Economic Area (EEA) Agreement, signed in 1992 by all countries of EFTA and the EC. The Swiss electorate rejected it, so it was renegotiated to include the others but to exclude Switzerland and Liechtenstein, which still has customs union with Switzerland, but which joined the EEA in 1995 (and so free trade in agricultural goods was excluded from the EEA treaty with Liechtenstein). Since 1 January 1994 the EEA has extended to ratifying for EFTA countries the EC's free movement of goods, services, capital and people, and applied other provisions of the EC Single Market programme. It is specifically stated that any benefits to EFTA countries must be balanced by benefits to EU members.

What co-operation exists now?

So far there has been:

- adoption of a common transit procedure, and the validity of the Single Administrative Document (SAD) in EFTA countries as well as in the EU (see Chapter 8);
- improved co-operation on the approximation of technical standards;
- encouragement of EFTA countries to increase links with and participate in the Community technical and research programmes.

A new institution, the Joint Consultation Committee, deals with problems, but its findings must not conflict with the rulings of the ECJ, and it may refer matters to the ECJ. The EFTA Court of Justice is situated in Luxembourg.

What has been the effect of the EEA?

The EEA has encouraged trade within what is effectively a very large trade bloc, which is estimated to account for more than 40 per cent of world trade.

Further information may be obtained from EFTA (see Appendix III) or the European Commission.

The United Nations (UN)

The UN was first established by Charter on 24 October 1945. Its aim is to maintain international peace and foster good relations. There were 51 founder members, but most countries of the world have now joined. Its headquarters are in New York, but some of its other agencies are administered from different countries.

The General Assembly, within which each member country has one vote, meets for three months every year, and makes recommendations. The UN Secretariat, under the Secretary General, is responsible for administration. The UN has various divisions:

- The Security Council is concerned with the maintenance of international peace.
- The Economic and Social Council (ECOSOC) – not to be confused with the Economic and Social Committee of the EC – co-ordinates, through regional commissions, the economic and social activities of the UN.
- The International Court of Justice (sometimes called 'the World Court') sits at The Hague and has jurisdiction to consider disputes between states, provided parties have agreed to submit to it. It may also advise the UN and its members on international law.
- The United Nations Development Programme (UNDP) encourages the economic growth of developing countries.
- The United Nations Industrial Development Organization (UNIDO) promotes industrial development in developing countries.
- The United Nations Conference on Trade and Development (UNCTAD) promotes international trade to assist the economic development of developing countries.
- The United Nations Environment Programme (UNEP) promotes international co-operation in environmental protection.
- The International Bank for Reconstruction and Development (the World Bank), which produces useful reports, is the expert on, and assists, developing countries and has proposed a global social-policy code for them. It should not to be confused with the EBRD.

There are other specialized departments and agencies including the International Labour Organization, the International Monetary Fund, the UN FAO (Food and Agriculture Organization), the World Health Organization, and the United Nations International Children's Emergency Fund (UNICEF), besides the United Nations Educational, Scientific and Cultural Organization (UNESCO) promoting international co-operation in these areas. There are also two bodies for assisting refugees.

The General Agreement on Tariffs and Trade (GATT) and the World Trade Organization (WTO)

On 1 January 1995 the GATT was restructured and called the World Trade Organization (WTO). As an institution it was set up in 1947, with a secretariat based in Geneva. GATT itself is composed of a series of trade agreements, which, since 1947, have established strict procedures and reductions in tariffs for international trade.

Over 134 countries are contracting parties to the WTO, and more, eg China, are negotiating membership. These include all the industrialized (OECD) countries, over 70 developing countries, and some East European countries. It covers over 80 per cent of world trade. The underlying principle of the WTO is that members should enjoy favourable tariffs between themselves, providing home producers are not thereby disadvantaged, and often developing countries are given preferential treatment. Its aim is to ensure that open markets and fair competition are secured through the rules and disciplines of the Agreement. The WTO encourages member states to achieve the expansion of multilateral trade, to reduce to a minimum import tariffs and quotas, and to achieve the abolition of preferential trade agreements. Agreement is by consensus, and negotiation rounds therefore take a long time. Members are committed to multilateralism and a disciplined approach towards solving trade difficulties, and there is a dispute settlement procedure. Member states have to undertake not to introduce trade restrictions or take other action inconsistent with WTO principles set out in around 30 multilateral agreements, which together make up the WTO Treaty. The WTO can make findings against members infringing its rules, eg in June 1999 it found against the EU in respect of tariffs imposed on New Zealand spreadable butter.

The rounds of talks are seen as more than traditional trade concession negotiations, and are regarded as an attempt to organize the basis of economic relationships between countries and cover trade concessions for developing countries. The Uruguay Round texts signed in 1994 extended markets, and increased its geographical and sectoral coverage, to include trade in services and trade-related intellectual property (TRIPs). The latter had been much needed due to the enormous losses sustained due to piracy and copyright infringements, and the need to strengthen patent protection, particularly for pharmaceutical and chemical patents. Changes in agricultural subsidy and export rules and trade protection provisions also resulted from the Uruguay Round Agreement, which revised many import restrictions and rules, anti-dumping provisions and anti-subsidy measures, and provided for a mechanism to enable enterprises to make formal complaints of infringements.

The Agreement on Public Procurement 1994 covers a number of countries, and not only government contracts, but in some cases regional and local government contracts, for products, and for construction and services. Rules cover five utility sectors: airports, ports, water, electricity and urban transport, although not all countries have agreed to such a wide coverage. The rules reflect the EU public procurement provisions, and are based on reciprocity. Discussions continue on liberalization of financial services world-wide. The Information Technology Agreement 1996 is expected to cover 90 per cent of world trade. The Telecommunications Agreement 1997 will have enormous impact, with liberalization from 1 January 1998 of markets in data transmission, radio communications, voice telephony, mobile phones, paging systems and leased lines.

The new round of WTO trade talks, started in November 1999 in Seattle, collapsed almost immediately. They are likely to be restarted in 2000.

Further information may be obtained from the WTO, the European Commission, and the Department of Trade and Industry.

The North Atlantic Treaty Organization (NATO)

The North Atlantic Treaty was signed in Washington, DC, on 4 April 1949. For further details, see Chapter 20.

The Western European Union (WEU)

For further details, see Chapter 20.

The Organization for Security and Co-operation in Europe (OSCE), previously called the Conference on Security and Co-operation in Europe (CSCE)

For further details, see Chapter 20.

The Organization for Economic Co-operation and Development (OECD)

The OECD was founded in 1961 and took over from the OEEC, intended to administer the post-Second World War Marshall Plan for European economic recovery. The OECD's objectives went far beyond those of the original organization. Today it consists of around 30 member countries including the EU, the US, Canada, Japan, New Zealand, Switzerland, Turkey, and some Eastern European countries such as Hungary and Poland. The number of members is growing.

The OECD's objectives are to achieve high, sustainable economic growth, full employment and rising standards of living in member countries. It has three main tasks: economic policy co-ordination, expansion of trade, and the provision of aid to developing countries. On the last item, it tries to promote increased assistance by its members. Its headquarters are in Paris.

In 1990 the OECD Council agreed to reinforce its inter-governmental co-operation, in particular as regards economic and environmental policy-making, ie working towards creating an integrated world economic system. It has published valuable studies, and work continues to achieve further agreements.

The European Bank for Reconstruction and Development (EBRD)

The EBRD formally came into existence on 28 March 1991. There are nearly 60 participating countries, including Australia, the US, Japan, the CIS and the EFTA countries, plus the European Commission and the European Investment Bank, which, between them all, hold the major stake of 51 per cent of the ECU 10 billion authorized capital. The purpose of this bank is to finance priority projects, contributing both to the development of the private sector and to necessary infrastructure in Eastern European countries.

The seat of the EBRD is London and each member (or shareholder) is represented on the board of governors. It should not be confused with the International Bank for Reconstruction and Development (IBRD), known as the World Bank, which is a specialized agency of the United Nations and whose members must belong to the International Monetary Fund.

It is interesting to note proposals to set up an entity similar to the EBRD for the EU to assist some Mediterranean countries.

The Group of Seven (G7), now the Group of Eight (G8)

These are the seven major industrialized countries: Canada, France, Germany, Italy, Japan, the United Kingdom and the United States, and they have now been joined by Russia. The heads of state and government with the ministers of foreign affairs and finance meet periodically at economic summits. In June 1999 they all pledged to support the EU-led Stability Pact, specifically with regard to reconciliation in the Balkan countries.

The European Space Agency

This organization is aimed at co-operation in space research for peaceful use by its members, which include Austria, Belgium, Denmark, France, Germany, Ireland, Italy, The Netherlands, Norway, Spain, Sweden, Switzerland and the UK. Canada and Finland are associates. It processes and distributes data from over 50 space satellites monitoring the earth, eg as to pollution and weather.

The Assembly of European Regions

This is an assembly of 400 representatives of 282 regions in 23 Western, Central and Eastern European countries. It should not be confused with the Committee of the Regions (see Chapter 3). There are many more international and other organizations, but they are beyond the scope of this book.

Appendix II
The Statistical Office of the
European Communities
(EUROSTAT)

What is the role of EUROSTAT?

The role of this satellite department of the Commission is to supply up-to-date, reliable statistics Community-wide. These are needed by the Commission, the Council, and others involved in formulating policy, as well as those who need to monitor and analyse developments, both in the Community and world-wide.

Does EUROSTAT produce online information?

Yes. EUROSTAT provides updated information using electronic media, on all the economic and social activities of Community states, and their main trading partners. This is available to the public.

What sort of material is available?

The material offered includes:

- general statistics;
- economics and finance;
- population and social conditions;
- energy and industry;
- agriculture, forestry and fisheries;
- foreign trade;
- services and transport.

Does EUROSTAT have any input into what statistics are collected?

Yes. EUROSTAT assists in the formation of policy, and encourages harmonization of the statistical collection systems throughout the EU. It is a useful organization producing valuable data.

The European Advisory Committee on Statistics was formed in 1992 to avoid duplication of effort and improve the effectiveness of surveys. It includes both academics and scientists.

A 1997 Council Regulation is aimed at organizing the standard compilation, both as to standards and methodology, of Community statistics with closer co-ordination between national statistical bodies and EUROSTAT. The regulation adopted a five-year programme for listed statistics, which may be added to as requirements are agreed.

Useful publications EUROSTAT has published include: *A Portrait of the Islands*, describing the 440 uninhabited islands of the EU; *Facts through Figures: A Statistical Portrait of the European Union*; *The European Union: Key Figures*; *Basic Statistics of the European Union*; *Women and Men in the European Union*; and the *EUROSTAT Yearbooks*.

Not all the statistics produced are trade-based. A statistical pocketbook on living conditions in Europe, published in 1999, includes such statistics as percentages of people living alone, getting married or divorced, and of sole parents.

Further details of available information and databases can be obtained from EUROSTAT (see Appendix III).

Appendix III
Sources of additional information

This Appendix gives various sources of extra information and advice referred to in the text. Anyone trying to find information about the EU will probably be swamped by the sheer volume of material available.

Throughout the book I have given an idea of where further information is available. Much of this is available on hard copy, and often the easiest way to find out what can be obtained is by telephoning or faxing the Commission, one of its European Information Centres (EICs), or national representations, or a government department concerned. However, the first approach is increasingly by use of the Internet. Information about the EICs is on: http://www.euro-info.org.uk.

The Commission has a strategy to improve access by the public to information collected or held by government departments or public sector bodies, so as to enable EU citizens or enterprises to know and so enforce their rights. Further information on this is given on: http://www.echo.eu/legal/en/access/access.htm.

Finding Europe on the Internet

The increased use of the Internet has also been seen as a way of cutting printing costs, so there is often considerable reluctance to send hard copy. It also means that the volume of information easily available has increased dramatically, but it is not always easy to find what is wanted.

The Commission has produced a useful directory of electronic databases, and I listed what I felt to be the most useful of these in another book (*The European Union: A Guide Through the Maze*, also published by Kogan Page), and they are included with the information given there. I would also refer you to that book to give you an indication of the scope of publications available from the Commission, and for details of the telephone numbers and towns of information relays in the UK. You should also be able to get these from your local library. Your local European

Information Office is a good starting place for seeking information about Europe.

The UK Representation of the European Commission site on the World Wide Web is: http://www.cec.org.uk.

Useful contact details

Anti-Counterfeiting Group
PO Box 578
High Wycombe
Buckinghamshire HP13 5FY
Tel: (01494) 449165

Anti-fraud Hotline in the UK
Freephone: 0800 963 595

Association Européenne des Industries de Produits de Marque (AIM)
Rue de l'Orme 19
B-1040, Brussels
Belgium

Association of British Chambers of Commerce
Manning House
22 Carlisle Place
London SW1P 1JA
Tel: (020) 7565 2000
Fax: (020) 7565 2049

Bank of England
Threadneedle Street
London EC2R 8AH
Tel: (020) 7601 4878
Fax: (020) 7601 5460

British Bankers Association
Pinners Hall
105–108 Old Broad Street
London EC2N 1AP
Tel: (020) 7216 8800
Internet: http://www.bba.org.uk

Bootlegging Information Line/ Schengen Information System (SIS)
UK Freephone: 0800 901 901

British Copyright Council
29–33 Berners Street
London W1P 4AA
Tel: (020) 7580 5544

British Railways Board
24 Eversholt Street
London NW1 1VS
Tel: (020) 7928 5151

British Standards Institute
(harmonizing standards and health and safety)
389 Chiswick High Road
London W4 4AL
Tel: (020) 7629 9000

CEDEFOP
European Centre for the Development of Vocational Training
PO Box 27 Finikas
GR-55102 Thessaloniki
Greece
Tel: (00 30) 31 49 01 11
Fax: (00 30) 32 49 01 02
Internet: http://www.cedefop.gr

CEN/CENELEC (Joint European Standards Institutions; European Committee for Standardization; European Committee for Electrotechnical Standardization)
35 Rue de Stassart
B-1050 Brussels
Belgium
CENELEC:
Tel: (00 322) 519 6871
Fax: (00 322) 519 6919
Internet: http://www.cenelec.be
CEN:
Tel: (00 322) 550 0811
Fax: (00 322) 550 0819
Internet: http://www.cenorm.be

Central Bureau for Educational Visits and Exchanges
10 Spring Gardens
London SW1A 2BN
Tel: (020) 7389 4697

Centre for Development of Industry (CDI)
52 Avenue Herrmann
Debroux
B-1160 Brussels
Belgium
Tel: (00 322) 679 1811

Chartered Institute of Patent Agents
Staple Inn Buildings
High Holborn
London WC1V 7PZ
Tel: (020) 7405 9450

Chamber of Shipping
Carthusian Court
12 Carthusian Road
London EC1M 6EB
Tel: (020) 7417 8400

Citizens First
(the information initiative to tell citizens of their rights)
The telephone numbers for Citizen First are:
Austria: 0660 6811
Belgium: (Flanders) 0800 920 38
Belgium: (Wallonia) 0800 920 39
Denmark: 800 1 0201
Finland: 0800 1 13191
France: 0800 90 9700
Germany: 0130 860 400
Ireland: 1 800 553 188
Italy: 167 876 166
Luxembourg: 0800 2550
Netherlands: 06 8051
Portugal: 0505 329 254
Spain: 900 983 19
Sweden: 020 794 949
UK: 0800 581 591

In one month (November–December 1996) these centres received almost 150,000 calls requesting information.

Civil Aviation Authority
CAA House
45–59 Kingsway
London WC2B 6TE
Tel: (020) 7379 7311

Committee of the Regions
Rue Belliard 70
B-1040 Brussels
Belgium
Tel: (00 322) 282 2211
Fax: (00 322) 282 2325
Internet: http://www.cor.eu.int

Consumers in Europe Group
20 Grosvenor Gardens
London SW1W 0DH
Tel: (020) 7881 3021
Fax: (020) 7730 8540

Council of Europe, Point i
F-67075 Strasbourg, Cedex
Tel: (00 333) 88 41 20 33
Fax: (00 333) 88 41 27 45

Council of the European Union
Rue de la Loi 175
B-1048 Brussels
Belgium
Tel: (00 322) 285 6111
Fax: (00 322) 285 73/97/81
Internet: http://ue.eu.int/index.htm

Court of Auditors
12 Rue Alcide de Gasperi
L-1615 Luxembourg
Tel: (00 352) 43 98 1
Internet: http://www.eca.eu.int

Court of Justice of the European Communities
Boulevard Konrad Adenauer
BP 96
L-2925 Luxembourg
Tel: (00 352) 43 03 1
Fax: (00 352) 43 03 25 00
Internet: http://europa.eu.int/cj

Department of the Environment, Transport and the Regions
2 Marsham Street
London SW1P 3EB
Tel: (020) 7276 3000

Department of Trade and Industry
There are so many departments dealing with different issues it is suggested that a preliminary enquiry be made by telephone to 020 7215 5000. Details can then be taken of the appropriate address or fax number.

Developing Countries Trade Agency
St Nicholas House
St Nicholas Road
Sutton
Surrey SM1 1EL
Tel: (020) 8643 3311

ECAS (Eurocitizen Action Service)
Rue Defacqz 1
B-1050 Brussels
Belgium

ECHO Information European Commission
3 Rue de Genève
B-1040 Brussels
Belgium
Tel: (00 322) 295 4400
Fax: (00 322) 295 4572

Economic and Social Committee Secretariat
Rue Ravenstein 2
B-1000 Brussels
Belgium
Tel: (00 322) 546 9011
Fax: (00 322) 513 4893
Internet: http://www.esc.eu.int

ERASMUS Bureau
70 Rue Montoyer
B-1040 Brussels
Belgium
Tel: (00 322) 233 0111

Eurochambres
Conference of European Chambers of Commerce
5 Rue Archimède
Box 4
B-1040 Brussels
Belgium
Tel: (00 322) 231 0715
Fax: (00 322) 223 0003 8
Internet: http://www.eurochambres.be

EUROCITIES
18 Square Meeus
B-1050 Brussels
Belgium
Tel: (00 322) 552 0888

Eurocontrol
Rue de la Fusée 96
B-1130 Brussels
Belgium
Tel: (00 322) 729 9011

The European Agency for Safety and Health at Work
Gran Via 33 48009
Bilbao
Spain
Tel: (00 34) 94 479 43 60
Fax: (00 34) 94 479 43 83

European Agency for the Evaluation of Medicinal Products
7 Westferry Circus
Canary Wharf
London E14 4HB
Tel: (020) 7418 8400
Fax: (020) 7418 8416
Internet:
http://www.eudra.org/emea.html

European Association of Securities Dealers (EASDAQ)
PO Box 2
B-1930 Zaventem
Belgium
Tel: (00 322) 27 20 78 70
Fax: (00 322) 27 20 83 06

European Bank for Reconstruction and Development (EBRD)
One Exchange Square
London EC2A 2EH
Tel: (020) 7338 6000
Fax: (020) 7338 6100

European Broadcasting Union (EBU)
Ancienne Route 17A
PO Box 67 CH1218
Grand Saconne
Geneva
Switzerland
Tel: (00 41) 22 717 2111

European Business and Information Centre Network (EBN)
Avenue de Terveuren 188A
B-1150 Brussels
Belgium
Tel: (00 322) 772 8900

European Central Bank
Kaiserstrasse 29
D-60311 Frankfurt am Main
Germany
Tel: (00 49) 69 27 22 70
Fax: (00 49) 69 27 72 27
Internet: http://www.ecb.int

European Commission *(for advice on matters under the control of particular Directorates, please refer to the listing in Chapter 3)*
Rue de la Loi 200
B-1049 Brussels
Belgium
Tel: (00 322) 299 1111
Internet:
http://europa.eu.int/comm/
index.htm

European Commission (UK Representation)
8 Storey's Gate
London SW1P 3AT
Tel: (020) 7973 1992
Fax: (020) 7973 1900
Internet: http://www.cec.org.uk

European Commission (Northern Ireland Representation)
9–15 Bedford Street
Belfast BT2 7EG
Tel: (01232) 240 708
Fax: (01232) 248 241

European Commission (Scotland Representation)
9 Alva Street,
Edinburgh EH2 4PH
Tel: (0131) 225 2058
Fax: (0131) 226 4105

European Commission (Wales Representation)
4 Cathedral Road
Cardiff CF1 9SG
Tel: (029) 2037 1631
Fax: (029) 2039 5489

European Council of Ministers Secretariat
Justus Lipsius
Rue de la Loi 175
B-1048 Brussels
Belgium
Tel: (00 322) 285 6111

European Disability Forum
4 Rue de la Presse
B-0140 Brussels
Belgium
Tel: (00 322) 227 1121
Fax: (00 322) 227 1116

European Environmental Agency
Kongens Nytorv 6
DK-1050 Copenhagen
Denmark
Tel: (00 45) 33 36 71 00
Fax: (00 45) 33 36 71 99
Internet: http://www.eea.eu.int

European Food and Veterinary Office
Trident House
Rockhill Main Street
Blackrock
County Dublin
Ireland
Tel: (00 353) 1 2064 711
Fax: (00 353) 1 2064 700

European Free Trade Association
Rue de Varembé 9–11
CH-1211 Geneva 20
Switzerland
Tel: (00 41) 22 749 1111
Internet: http://www.efta.int

European Foundation for the Improvement of Living and Working Conditions
Loughlinstown
County Dublin
Republic of Ireland
Tel: (00 353) 1 204 3100
Fax: (00 353) 1 282 6456
Internet:
http://www.eurofound.eu.int

European Information Centres (EICs)
(there are many)
London City EIC
33 Queen Street
London EC4R 1AP
Tel: (020) 7248 4444
Fax: (020) 7489 0391

European Institute for Training in Fisheries and Agriculture (IEFPA)
Rue de la Science 23/25
B-1040 Brussels
Belgium
Tel: (00 322) 230 4848

European Investment Bank
100 Boulevard Konrad Adenauer
L-2950 Luxembourg
Tel: (00 352) 43 79 31 22
Internet: http://www.eib.org

European Investment Bank
68 Pall Mall
London SW1Y 5ES
Tel: (020) 7343 1200

European Movement
158 Buckingham Palace Road
London SW10 9JR
Tel: (020) 7824 8388

European Ombudsman
1 Avenue du President Robert Schuman
BP 403
F-67001 Strasbourg Cedex
France
Tel: (00 333) 88 17 23 13
Fax: (00 333) 88 17 90 62
Internet: http://www.euro-ombudsman.eu.int

European Organization for Safety of Air Navigation – Eurocontrol
Rue de la Loi 72
B-1040 Brussels
Belgium

European Parliament
Avenue de l'Europe
BP 1024
F-67000 Strasbourg
France
Tel: (00 333) 88 17 40 01
Fax: (00 333) 88 17 48 60
Internet:
http://www.europarl.eu.int/sg/tree/
en/default.htm

European Parliament
Information Office
2 Queen Anne's Gate
London SW1H 9AA
Tel: (020) 7222 0411

European Patent Office
Erhardstrasse 27
D-80298 Munich
Germany
Tel: (00 49) 89 23 990
Fax: (00 49) 89 23 99 44 65

**European Plant Variety Rights
Office**
Rue de la Loi 102
B-1040 Brussels
Belgium
Tel: (00 322) 299 1944
Fax: (00 322) 299 1946

European Road Safety Federation
179 Avenue Louise
B-1050 Brussels
Belgium
Tel: (00 322) 646 6230

**European Trade Union
Confederation (ETUC)**
Rue Montagne aux Herbes
Potagères 37
B-1000 Brussels
Belgium
Tel: (00 322) 309 2411
Fax: (00 322) 218 3566

European Training Foundation
Villa Gualino
Viale Settimo Severo 65
I-10133 Turin
Italy
Tel: (00 39) 011 630 2222
Fax: (00 39) 011 630 2200
Internet: http//www.etf.it

Europe Direct
Freephone: 0800 581 591
Internet: http://europa.eu.int/
citizens

EUROSTAT Publications
The Statistical Office of the
European Communities
Bâtiment Jean Monnet
Rue Alcide de Gaspari
L-2920 Luxembourg
Tel: (00 352) 43 01 33 01 2
Fax: (00 352) 43 01 32 68 9
Internet:
http://www.europa.eu.int/en/comm/
eurostat/eurostat.html
Eurostat Data Shop:
Tel: (0171) 533 5676

Force Technical Assistance Office
34 Rue du Nord
B-1000 Brussels
Belgium
Tel: (00 322) 209 1311
Free EU information service: *see
Europe Direct*

GLOBE
Globe International
50 Rue du Taciterne
B-1040 Brussels
Belgium
Tel: (00 322) 230 6589

Health and Safety Commission
Rose Court
2 Southwark Bridge
London SE1 9HS
Tel: (020) 7717 6000

Institute of Trade Mark Agents
4th Floor
Canterbury House
2–6 Sydenham Road
Croydon
Surrey CR0 9XE
Tel: (020) 8686 2052

Interact News
Ambiorix Square 32
PO Box 47
B-1040 Brussels
Belgium

International Court of Justice
Peace Palace
2517 KJ
The Hague
The Netherlands
Tel: (00 31) 70 302 2323

International Credit Assurance Association
PO Box 16
7018 Flims-Waldhaus
Switzerland
Tel: (00 41) 81 39 36 39
Fax: (00 41) 81 39 36 28

International Road Freight Office
Westgate House
Westgate Road
Newcastle-upon-Tyne NE1 1TW
Tel: (0191) 201 4000

Lingua Bureau
10 Rue de Commerce
B-1040 Brussels
Belgium
Tel: (00 322) 511 4218

London Chamber of Commerce and Industry
33 Queen Street
London EC4R 1AP
Tel: (020) 7248 4444

London Chamber of Commerce and Industry Examinations Board
Athena House
112 Station Road
Sidcup
Kent DA15 7BJ
Tel: (020) 8302 0261
Fax: (020) 8302 4169

Ministry of Agriculture, Fisheries and Food
Whitehall Place
London SW1A 2MH
Tel: (020) 7270 8080

Office for Harmonization of the Internal Market (Trade Marks and Designs)
Avenida de Aguilera 20
E-03080 Alicante
Spain
Tel: (00 34) 65 13 91 00
Fax: (00 34) 65 13 91 73
Internet:http://oami.eu.int

Office for Official Publications of the European Communities
2 Rue Mercier
L-2985 Luxembourg
Tel: (00 352) 29 29 1
Fax: (00 352) 49 57 19

Organization for Economic Co-operation and Development (OECD)
2 Rue André Pascal
75775 Paris
Cedex 16 France
Tel: (00 33) 1 45 24 82 00

Patent Office
Concept House
Cardiff Road
Newport
Gwent NP9 1RH
Tel: (01633) 3930
Fax: (01633) 813 600

PETRA, INFAPLAN
2/3 Place de Luxembourg
B-1040 Brussels
Belgium
Tel: (00 322) 511 1510

Road Haulage Association
Roadway House
35 Monument Hill
Weybridge
Surrey KT13 8RN
Tel: (01932) 841515

**Royal Commission on
Environmental Pollution**
Church House
Great Smith Street
London SW1P 3BZ
Tel: (020) 7276 2080

**Technical Centre for Agricultural
and Rural Co-operation**
De Rietkampen Galvinstraat 19
Ede
The Netherlands

Tenders Electronic Daily
Echo Customer Service
117 Rue d'Esche
L-1471 Luxembourg

The Treasury
*(economic and monetary union and
taxation)*
Parliament Street
London SW1Q 3AQ
Tel: (020) 7270 3000

**Union of Industrial and
Employers' Confederates of
Europe (UNICE)**
40 Rue Joseph II
B-1040 Brussels
Belgium
Tel: (00 322) 237 6511

**World Intellectual Property
Organization**
PO Box 18
34 Chemin des Colombettes
1211 Geneva 20
Switzerland
Tel: (00 41) 22 730 9428

World Trade Organization
154 Rue de Lausanne
CH-1211 Geneva 21
Switzerland
Tel: (00 41) 22 739 5019
Fax: (00 41) 22 739 5458
Internet: http//www.wto.org

Youth for Europe
The European Community Youth
Exchange Bureau
2/3 Place de Luxembourg
B-1040 Brussels
Belgium
Tel: (00 322) 511 1510

Other useful web sites
*Information to assist purchasers to
buy cars:*
http://europa.eu.int/en/comm/dg4/
aid/en/car.htm

*Dialogue with Citizens and
Business* (help to people to take
advantage of the Single Market):
http://citizens.eu.int/originchoice.
htm

*List of contact points for the
Internal Market across Europe for
citizens and business*:
http://europa.eu.int/comm/dg15

*Free one-stop information shop for
companies needing practical information on the Single Market, eg
funding opportunities and technical
standards*:
http://europa.eu.int/business

European grants (information free through Information Relays): http://www.cec.org.uk

Euro Web site: http://europa.int/euro

Accession negotiation Web site: http://europa.eu.int/comm/tfan/ index_en.html

European Consultative Forum on the Environment and Sustainable Development: http://europa.eu.int/comm/dg11/ forum/home.htm

Bathing water: http://europa.eu.int/waterbathing/ index_en.html

Consumer information (CEG Web site): http://www.ceg.co.uk

Database of EU law: http://europa.eu.int/eur_lex/en/ index.html

LCCI Examinations Board: http://www.lccieb.org.uk

Appendix IV
The development of the Single Market: measures listed in the 1992 Programme

The Single Market Programme

On 1 January 1993 the (then) 12 Member States officially became a Single Market. The 265 measures listed in the 1985 White Paper were aimed at eliminating from that date:

- physical barriers;
- technical barriers;
- barriers to the movement of goods and services;
- barriers to the free movement of persons;
- fiscal barriers.

In 1994, and again in 1997, the Commission noted that the Single Market, while close, was still not a reality in some areas because Member States were not always implementing Community provisions properly. There was a need for a procedure to enable speedy dispute resolution; and there were gaps in Community legislation, particularly in relation to taxation.

The TEU enabled Member States to be brought before the ECJ for infringement of Community legislation and fined, and although this is giving some impetus to compliance, difficulties of ensuring a level playing field remain. Efforts continue to address these problems, to achieve a uniform application of Community law, with penalties for violations, and greater encouragement for the mutual recognition of national rules. Increased liberalization of telecommunications and energy, the development of trans-European networks and the information society, and the drive towards creating a globally competitive business environment where jobs can be created, have been priorities. Global trade developments, particularly in electronic commerce and the information society, have made significant changes.

What about transposition into national legislation?

By March 1997 273 provisions in the Single Market Programme were in force. In 10 of the 15 countries, 97 per cent of measures had been transposed correctly. It was agreed that out-of-date measures should be removed or updated, and in 1997 the Commission adopted an outline action plan to ensure the effective working of the Single Market by 1 January 1999 (the intended date for the introduction of the Euro).

What about recent Commission action to ensure the functioning of the Single Market?

The Commission's first Report on the Functioning of the Goods, Services and Capital Markets in the EU was published in January 1999. This makes useful reading, and covered such matters as the efficiency of markets, their weaknesses and the reforms needed. It also provided general recommendations – suggesting, for example, that improvements could be made in the areas of the current framework for public procurement, in the mutual recognition of national standards and structures in the financial services market. It was also reported that some trade barriers still remained in the EU despite the Single Market Programme, and that these should be tackled. The whole document is set out at: http://europa.eu.int/comm/dg15.

In October 1999 the Commission issued a communication setting out a strategy for the development over the next four years of the Single Market, with the aims of:

- improving the quality of life of EU citizens;
- improving the business environment;
- enhancing the efficiency of markets in the different areas;
- exploiting the achievements of the Internal Market in a changing world.

The text of the communication is at: http://europa.eu.int/comm/dg15/en/update/strategy/strategy/1.htm.

What kinds of subjects were included in the 1992 Single Market Programme?

It is interesting to list some of these provisions, and to divide them by subject.

- *Control of goods (11 provisions)*. These covered such matters as simplification of transit procedures, the single administrative document, and abolition of customs presentation charges.

- *Veterinary and phytosanitary control provisions (72 proposals).* These accounted for a large part of the Internal Market Programme, covering such matters as eradication of classical swine fever, antibiotic residues, health problems relating to minced meat and similar products, and trade in the embryos of farm animals.
- *Food, ethical drugs and chemicals (40 provisions).* These dealt with such matters as materials and articles in contact with food and food additives, price transparency and the prices of medicines, social security refunds, and the restrictions on the marketing and use of PCBs (poly-chlorinated biphenyls).
- *Motor vehicles (11 provisions).* These related to such matters as roll-over protection structures for agricultural and forestry tractors and gaseous emissions.
- *Standards and general technical barriers (22 provisions).* These related to, for example, the safety of toys and gas appliances, certification in metrology, construction products and protection of hotels against fire.
- *People (19 provisions).* These included provisions on travel, employment, and such matters as recognition of diplomas.
- *Banking, credit institutions and insurance (19 provisions).* These related to matters such as the accounts of banks, freedom to provide insurance services and the recommendation for a European code of conduct relating to electronic payment.
- *Transactions in securities, capital movements, company law and direct taxation (22 provisions).* These concerned such matters as insider trading, liberalization of capital movements, the regulation on the control of concentration between undertakings, and an arbitration procedure concerning the elimination of double taxation.
- *Excise duties and VAT (18 provisions).*
- *Intellectual property and new technology (14 provisions).* This area (ie patents, trade marks and copyright, and new technologies) concerned such matters as the approximation of trade mark legislation in Member States, and pan-European mobile telephones.
- *Transport (11 provisions).* These related to, for example, passenger capacity-sharing and market access for air transport, and freedom to provide road transport services by non-resident carriers.
- *Public procurement (7 provisions).* These concerned the award of various types of contracts in the public supply and works contracts area, including energy and water.

In compiling this list I am indebted to the *Business Journal*, produced for the British Chamber of Commerce for Belgium and Luxembourg.

What about new provisions?

New proposals are being introduced all the time, although their number has intentionally dropped dramatically, as new measures must be scrutinized to ensure they comply with guidelines, ie that they are needed, that they do not fall at the fence of subsidiarity (in other words, that they would be better legislated for at a national rather than Community level), are commensurate with the need addressed, and take into account, for example, environmental considerations.

The Dialogue between Citizens and Business can help to form policy, as it not only provides information via the Internet and telephone, but it also provides feedback to the Commission, on attitudes and problems, and can indicate where new measures are needed, eg to reduce bureaucratic controls, or to create a level playing field for enterprises.

I have mentioned many new provisions in the body of this book, but for obvious reasons have not tried to list all the standards and other detailed provisions that are of particularly sectoral interest. Increasingly not only EC/EU legislation, but also international provisions and standards (eg formulated within the WTO) have to be taken into account.

The European Commission Information Centres hold constantly updated lists of EC proposals and legislation, which are also available on the Internet (http://www.cec.org.uk).

In November 1999 the Commission put forward a five-year strategy to link the internal market to four EU aims: to improve quality of life, the efficiency of product and capital markets, and the business environment; and to exploit globally the internal market achievements. The proposed measures are wide ranging, and can be accessed on http://europa.eu.int/comm/dg15/en/update/strategy/strategy2.htm.

Appendix V
List of Commissioners and their responsibilities

There are 20 Commissioners, including a President and two Vice-Presidents.

The 'new' Commission, appointed in 1999, is greatly stream-lined, with the number of departments reduced from 42 to 36. There are new departments for enterprise, justice and home affairs, and education and culture. This Commission was approved by the EP in September 1999.

The information set out below is largely taken from the Commission's Web page on: http://www.europa.eu.int/comm/commissioners/index_en.htm.

In each case the responsibilities of the Commissioner are set out below his or her name.

1. Romano Prodi (Italy): President

Secretariat General: Registry; Horizontal matters (institutional matters; application of Community law; information co-ordination); Relations with the Council of the European Union; Relations with the European Parliament, the Economic and Social Committee, and the Committee of the Regions; Monitoring the Amsterdam Treaty; Activities relating to justice and home affairs; Office for in-service trainees; European Group on Ethics in Science and New Technologies.

2. Neil Kinnock (UK): Vice-President for Administrative Reform

Personnel and Administration Directorate General; Inspectorate General; Joint Interpreting and Conference Service; Translation service.

3. Loyola de Palacio (Spain): Vice-President for Relations with the EP, and for Transport and Energy

Transport Directorate General; Energy Directorate General.

4. Michel Barnier (France): Commissioner for Regional Policy

Regional Policy Directorate General (with responsibility *ad personam* for the Inter-Governmental Conference).

5. Frits Bolkestein (Netherlands): Commissioner for the Internal Market

Internal Market Directorate General; Taxation and Customs Union Directorate General.

6. Philippe Busquin (Belgium): Commissioner for Research

Research Directorate General; Joint Research Centre.

7. David Byrne (Ireland): Commissioner for Health and Consumer Protection

Health and Consumer Protection Directorate General.

8. Anna Diamantopoulou (Greece): Commissioner for Employment and Social Affairs

Employment and Social Affairs Directorate General.

9. Franz Fischler (Austria): Commissioner for Agriculture and Fisheries

Agriculture Directorate General; Fisheries Directorate General.

10. Pascal Lamy (France): Commissioner for Trade

Trade Directorate General.

11. Erkki Liikanen (Finland): Commissioner for Enterprise and Information Society

Enterprise Directorate General; Information Society Directorate General.

12. *Mario Monti (Italy): Commissioner for Competition*

Competition Directorate General.

13. *Poul Nielsen (Denmark): Commissioner for Development and Humanitarian Aid*

Development Directorate General; Humanitarian Aid Office (ECHO).

14. *Viviane Reding (Luxembourg): Commissioner for Education and Culture*

Education and Culture Directorate General; Publications Office.

15. *Michaele Schreyer (Germany): Commissioner for the Budget*

Budget Directorate General; Financial Control Directorate General; European Anti-Fraud Office.

16. *Pedro Solbes Mira (Spain): Commissioner for Economic and Monetary Affairs*

Economic and Financial Affairs Directorate General; EUROSTAT.

17. *Chris Patten (UK): Commissioner for External Relations*

External Relations Directorate General; Common Service for External Relations.

18. *Gunther Verheugen (Germany): Commissioner for Enlargement*

Enlargement Directorate General.

19. *Antonio Vitorino (Portugal): Commissioner for Justice and Home Affairs*

Justice and Home Affairs Directorate General.

20. *Margot Wallstrom (Sweden): Commissioner for Environment*

Environment Directorate General.
Further details are listed on Europa server at:
http://europa.eu.int/comm/newcomm/index_en.htm.

Appendix VI
Qualifications for Europe

In 1992 the Council of Ministers adopted conclusions on the development of a European dimension in higher education in open and distance learning, education and training, networking information on education generally, and on health education in schools.

Euroqualifications have now been offered by the Examinations Board of the London Chamber of Commerce and Industry for several years, and the level of entries for examinations has been encouraging.

These Euroqualifications examinations have been developed specifically to meet the perceived need for those doing business in the European Union, and to promote and ease mobility of labour in Europe. The aim of these qualifications is to show that the successful candidates have the necessary skills to operate in a business environment in at least two languages.

The awards provide candidates with certificates to show a proficiency that is recognized throughout Europe in the skills covered by the awards, which are structured in a series of modules. Since January 1992 these examinations have been available world-wide on demand.

Euroqualifications were originally piloted in Germany, and they are already enjoying a growing popularity around Europe. This book is on the list of recommended reading for the European Union module (Part IV).

The highest qualification, the Diploma in European Business Administration, is awarded after the successful completion of four (or five) modules covering written and oral language skills, knowledge of the European Union, computer/office skills and management.

For the European Executive Assistant Certificate, written and oral language skills are tested, as are computer/office skills and a knowledge of the European Union.

At Commercial Language Assistant Certificate level, written and oral language skills are tested, as are computer/office skills.

Further information is available from the London Chamber of Commerce and Industry Examinations Board, Athena House, 112 Station Road, Sidcup, Kent, DA15 7BJ, United Kingdom. Their Web site is at http://www.lccieb.org.uk.

Appendix VII
Supplementary information on EC and EFTA member countries

In writing this Appendix, I am indebted particularly to Eurostat, and the *Europa World Year Book*, published by Europa Publications, to which I would refer you for further detailed and useful information and statistics.

I have rounded up percentages in some cases – and have put them in as an indication only of the relative importance of various sectors to the particular country. I have also added some supplementary information that I feel to be interesting. It should be noted that the Gross Domestic Product (GDP) figures used for the EU and EEA are from Eurostat, providing estimated 1998 GDP at market prices. For the EFTA countries, GDP figures are from the *Europa World Year Book*. Population figures are the most recent I can find, and most are from the *Europa World Year Book*. The comments are my own.

EC/EU Member States

Austria

1. Population

8.068 million.

2. Geographical dimension, location and climate

83,858 square kilometres. Austria is situated in Central Europe and is landlocked. The climate varies according to the topography.

3. Constitution/political system

Austria is a democratic federal republic with nine provinces, each of which has its own provincial assembly, but legislative power lies in the Federal Assembly. This is bicameral, consisting of the Nationalrat (National Council), with 183 members directly elected by proportional representation, and the Bundesrat (Federal

Council), with 64 members elected by the provincial assemblies. The Federal President, directly elected for six-year terms, is head of state and acts on the advice of a Council of Ministers led by a Federal Chancellor responsible to the Nationalrat.

4. Gross Domestic Product

ECU 189.8 billion.

5. Main industries

In 1995, agriculture, including forestry, fishing and hunting, contributed 1.5 per cent to GDP, and produced around 90 per cent of Austria's food requirements. Industry contributed about 31.6 per cent of GDP (1996), employing about 31 per cent of the work-force. Within industry, manufacturing contributed 20.6 per cent of GDP (1996), with the main sectors being machinery, metals and metal products, food products, wood and paper, and chemical products. Services continue to employ the majority of the work-force (61 per cent in 1996, contributing 66.9 per cent of GDP).

6. Major imports and exports

Austria's main imports are chemicals and related products, mineral fuels and energy, machinery and transport equipment. The principal exports include machinery and transport equipment, basic manufactures and crude materials. Austria's principal trading partner is Germany, which took 37 per cent of exports, and provided 43 per cent of imports in 1996. The bulk of its trade is with EU countries.

7. Languages

The language is German (99 per cent) with small minorities speaking Slovene and Croat.

8. Religions

Almost all are Christian: 77 per cent Roman Catholics, 5 per cent Protestants. There are some Orthodox Christians and about 10,000 Jews.

9. Capital City

The capital city is Vienna (Wien).

10. Currency

The Austrian Schilling. However, Austria has joined the Eurozone, and so is moving towards the Euro.

11. Comments

Austria provides a strong base for West European countries wishing to diversify into Eastern Europe. In 1991 Austria set up a risk protection fund for companies doing business in East Europe. On 1 January 1995 it became a member of the European Union, having resigned from EFTA. There is a comprehensive social insurance system covering around 99 per cent of the people. In 1995 there was one hospital bed per 105 inhabitants, and in the same year, 59 per cent of total government expenditure was for health, social security and welfare. Unemployment in December 1996 stood at 4 per cent. Education is free and compulsory between the ages of 6 and 15 years, after which there are good facilities for further education and training.

The Kingdom of Belgium

1. Population

10.2 million.

2. Geographical dimension, location and climate

Belgium lies in North-West Europe and has a temperate climate. The geographical dimension is 30,528 square kilometres.

3. Constitution/political system

Belgium is a constitutional hereditary monarchy with a bicameral parliament, consisting of the Senate and a Chamber of Representatives, each with its own President elected by the House. The Senate presently has 72 Senators. It has 40 directly elected members (by proportional representation), and 21 members elected by the legislative assemblies of the three language communities, 10 members co-opted by elected members, and one representative of the royal family. The Chamber of Representatives has 150 members directly elected by proportional representation. The King appoints the Prime Minister and, on his advice, the Cabinet. The regions and communes also have limited legislative powers.

4. Gross Domestic Product

ECU 223.6 billion.

5. Main industries

Manufacturing industries including mining and quarrying, manufacturing, power and construction accounted for over 31 per cent, and agriculture for around 1.7 per cent. The services sector contributed 67.3 per cent of GDP in 1994, and employed about 70 per cent of the labour force in 1992.

6. Major imports and exports

Major imports are machinery and transport equipment, chemical and related products, food and animals. The principal exports are basic manufactured products including diamonds, iron and steel, machinery, vehicles and transport equipment, food products, clothing, textiles and chemicals. The Belgo-Luxembourg Economic Union (BLEU)'s main trading partners are Germany, The Netherlands and France, which together accounted for 52.2 per cent of total imports and 53.4 per cent of exports in 1994.

7. Languages

There are four linguistic regions: Flanders, where Flemish is the main language; Wallonia, where French is the main language; Brussels, which is officially bilingual; and a German-speaking area. Flemish and French are the two official languages.

8. Religions

The great majority of the population are Christians, with most of those Roman Catholic (about 80 per cent). There are 250,000 Muslims and 35,000 Jews.

9. Capital city

The capital city is Brussels.

10. Currency

The currency is the Belgian Franc, but Belgium has joined the Eurozone and is moving towards use of the Euro.

11. Comments

Belgium gains significantly from the numbers of international organizations sited there. Social welfare is seen as important, with a high proportion of total expenditure by central government allocated to social security and welfare. In 1994 they had one hospital bed per 106 inhabitants. Unemployment in June 1997 was 9.6 per cent. Education is also seen as important. Students are required to be in full-time education from 6 to 16, then part time for two years.

The Kingdom of Denmark

1. Population

5.295 million (1998).

2. Geographical dimension, location and climate

43,094 square kilometres. It consists of the Jutland Peninsula, five large islands and 401 smaller islands. It is in Northern Europe with a temperate climate and a high rainfall.

3. Constitution/political system

The Danish Constitution was revised in 1953 and provides for a hereditary constitutional monarchy (with no personal political powers) and a unicameral Folketing (parliament) with 179 members elected by proportional representation, including representatives from the Faroe Islands and Greenland. The monarch, through the Prime Minister and Cabinet, exercises executive power. It should perhaps be noted that while Greenland is part of the Kingdom of Denmark, and joined the EC as part of Denmark, the Faroe Islands in fact retain home rule, and have not joined the EC. They retain their own parliament, although they send two representatives to the Danish Folketing, which is responsible for their defence and foreign policy.

4. Gross Domestic Product

ECU 150.9 billion.

5. Main industries

Agriculture (including fishing and forestry) provided 3.3 per cent of GDP in 1997, using 55 per cent of Denmark's land area and 3.7 per cent of the working population. Industry, including power, construction, mining, manufacture and water, provided about 25.4 per cent of GDP in 1997. Besides agricultural products, the most important manufacturing industries are food processing, steel and metals, chemicals and pharmaceuticals, printing and publishing, machinery, electronic goods and transport equipment.

6. Major imports and exports

The main trading partner is Germany, for imports (21.5 per cent in 1995) and exports, followed by the UK and Sweden. Denmark made 64 per cent of its exports to EC countries in 1995. The main exports are food and food products, industrial machinery, chemicals and basic manufactures (iron, steel and paper). The EU provided nearly 70 per cent of Denmark's imports in 1995.

7. Languages

The main language is Danish, with German spoken in some areas and Faroese spoken in the Faroe Islands (although Danish must be taught in all schools). Greenlandic and Danish are the official languages in Greenland.

8. Religions

Nearly all the population is Christian, with around 87 per cent
Evangelical Lutheran.

9. Capital city

The capital city is Copenhagen. (The capital city of the Faroe
Islands is Torshaun and the capital city of Greenland is Nuuk.)

10. Currency

The currency is the Danish Krona. Denmark does not intend to
join the Eurozone at this time.

11. Comments

The Danish economy has encountered difficulties, with a significant budgetary deficit and high social welfare costs, but is improving. Average annual unemployment in January 1998 was 7.4 per
cent. Social welfare remains a high priority, with an allocation of
24 per cent of total budget expenditure in 1996. There were
21,900 hospital beds in 1994. Education accounted for about 6.7
per cent of budget spending, but education is only compulsory for
nine years (7–16) with a possible exemption after seven years.

The Republic of Finland

1. Population

5.147 million (1997).

2. Geographical dimension, location and climate

338,144 square kilometres. Situated in Northern Europe, the climate varies and is warm in summer and cold in winter, varying
with the latitude.

3. Constitution/political system

Finland has a republican constitution with a President (directly
elected) and a unicameral Parliament (Eduskunta) with 200 members elected by proportional representation. The President has
executive power, and appoints a Prime Minister and a Council of
State (Cabinet), responsible to Parliament, which exercises legislative power. There are 12 separate provinces.

4. Gross Domestic Product

ECU 111.5 billion.

5. Main industries

Agriculture, including hunting, forestry and fishing, accounted for

3.9 per cent of the GDP in 1997, and employed 7.1 per cent of the work-force. Industry contributed 34.8 per cent of GDP and employed 27.4 per cent of the work-force. Of this, manufacturing, mostly paper and food products, provided 25.7 per cent of GDP in 1997, employing 20.1 per cent of the work-force. Services provided 62.2 per cent of GDP in 1996, and employed 64.2 per cent of the employed work-force in 1995.

6. Major imports and exports

The main imports are machinery and transport equipment, mineral fuels and chemicals, paper and paper products, wood and pulp. The chief exports are forestry products, which produced 31 per cent of export earnings in 1997. The main trading partners are Germany (taking 11 per cent of exports and providing 14.5 per cent of imports in 1997), Sweden and the UK.

7. Languages

There are two official languages: Finnish (spoken by over 93 per cent) and Swedish (spoken by 5.9 per cent). There are some Lapps in the north.

8. Religions

Almost all the population are Christian. About 85.4 per cent are Evangelical Lutherans. There are some Roman Catholics, Methodists, Jews and Muslims.

9. Capital city

The capital city is Helsinki.

10. Currency

The currency is the Markka, but Finland is part of the Eurozone and so is moving towards the Euro.

11. Comments

Finland suffered in the recession with a budgetary deficit, and recovery is slow. Social security, health and welfare accounted for about 24 per cent of total general budget expenditure in 1997, following various austerity measures. There were 46,400 hospital beds in 1994. Finland became a member of the EU on 1 January 1995. Unemployment reached 12.6 per cent in 1997. Education is compulsory for nine years, from 7–16, and is free.

France

1. Population

58.9 million.

2. Geographical dimension, location and climate

544,000 square kilometres. Corsica is part of metropolitan France with special status. The climate is temperate in mid and northern France, but Mediterranean in the south.

3. Constitution/political system

France is a republic and under its constitution of 1958 has a bicameral parliament, a Senate (321 members) and a National Assembly (577 members). The President has executive power and is elected for seven years. He or she appoints the Council of Ministers, headed by the Prime Minister, which administers the country. There are 21 administrative regions with significant administrative and financial powers.

4. Gross Domestic Product

ECU 1,274.5 billion.

5. Main industries

Finance, insurance, business services and real estate account for a significant part of GDP. In 1994 agriculture accounted for about 2.5 per cent of GDP. Industry, including power, construction, manufacturing and mining, accounted for 27.6 per cent and employed 26.6 per cent of the work-force in 1994. The largest manufacturing sectors included food (14.3 per cent) and transport equipment (13.5 per cent), followed by chemicals, other manufactured products and metal and metal products.

6. Major imports and exports

France's main trading partner is Germany (18.5 per cent imports and 17.7 per cent exports in 1995), and 60.6 per cent of exports are to, and 59.5 per cent of imports are from, EC countries. The principal exports are machinery, transport equipment and vehicles, basic manufactures, chemicals and chemical products, and wine. The principle imports are machinery and transport equipment, basic manufactures and manufactured articles.

7. Languages

French is the main language with various regional dialects. Breton and Basque are spoken in those regions, as well as French.

8. Religions

The great majority of the population are Christian, with about 81 per cent Roman Catholic, 950,000 Protestants and 200,000 Russian and Greek Orthodox. There are small Muslim and Jewish communities.

9. Capital city

The capital city is Paris.

10. Currency

The currency is the French Franc, but France is part of the Eurozone and moving towards the Euro.

11. Comments

The French economy is affected by the need to comply with the convergence criteria for EMU, with significant budgetary restrictions being applied. France has a comprehensive social security system that is considered a priority in terms of government spending. There was one hospital bed per 107 inhabitants in 1993. Unemployment in December 1996 was 12.4 per cent. Education is seen to be important. There is compulsory full-time education from 6 to 16, with the aim that 80 per cent of all schoolchildren should achieve the Baccalauréat or equivalent qualification on leaving school. Around 83 per cent of children attend state schools.

Germany

1. Population

82.012 million (1996).

2. Geographical dimension, location and climate

357.021 square kilometres. Germany is in Central Europe. The climate is temperate, but varies considerably between the north and the south and with the topography.

3. Constitution/political system

Germany is a bicameral parliamentary democracy. There are 16 Länder or states, each with its own legislature, government and constitution. Each sends representatives to the Upper House, which is the Federal Council or Bundesrat of 69 seats. The Lower House, the Federal Assembly or Bundestag, has 669 members elected by a mixed system of direct voting and proportional representation. The Federal Chancellor heads the Federal Government, which has executive authority. He or she is elected by the Bundestag and elects other ministers. The Federal President, who is a constitutional head of state only, is elected by a special Federal Convention. The Federal Government has power in respect of national matters such as defence, foreign affairs and finance.

4. Gross Domestic Product

ECU 1,910.3 billion.

5. Main industries

Agricultural production including wine, sugar beet, barley, wheat and potatoes employed 2.9 per cent of the work-force in 1995, and provided 1 per cent of GDP in 1997. Industry including power, manufacturing and construction then employed 34.3 per cent of the work-force, producing about 33.2 per cent of GDP in 1997. Manufacturing employed 23.7 per cent of the working population in 1997 and produced 24.6 per cent of GDP (mainly non-electric machinery, food products, metal and metal products and chemicals). Services employed 62.8 per cent of employees and provided 65.8 per cent of GDP in 1997.

6. Major imports and exports

Germany has a broad trading base, the most important in manufacturing being vehicles and transport equipment, electrical and non-electrical machinery and chemical products. A large proportion of trade is with other countries in the EU. In 1997 Germany had a trade surplus. France was its major trading partner, taking 10.6 per cent of its exports, and supplying 10.5 per cent of imports in 1997.

7. Languages

The language is German, although there is a small minority (about 100,000) of Serbian-speaking people. There are significant numbers of Turkish 'guest workers', who are on temporary contracts.

8. Religions

The majority of people of West Germany are Christians, almost equally divided between Protestants (mostly evangelical) and Roman Catholics. In East Germany about 35 per cent are Protestants and 7 per cent Roman Catholics. There are about 47,000 Jews and 2.6 million Muslims.

9. Capital city

The capital city is Berlin, but the Upper House remains in Bonn. The rest (except for some federal ministries) is gradually being transferred to Berlin.

10. Currency

The currency is the Deutschmark, but Germany is part of the Eurozone and so is moving towards the Euro.

11. Comments

The economy remains under some strain as the dominant economy in the Eurozone. The reunification of Germany put a strain on the German economy. Germany puts a very high priority on social benefits. In 1996 the number of hospital beds was 593,743. The general level of unemployment in December 1996 was 9.3 per cent (but in the Eastern Länder this was 18.7 per cent in January 1997). Education is seen as important, with government allocation for education accounting for 9.2 per cent of total government spending in 1997. There is free primary education followed by elementary and secondary schooling. Compulsory schooling is from the age of six for 9 or 10 years (depending on the Land). Until 18 years all young people must attend full or at least part-time (possibly vocational) school.

Greece – the Hellenic Republic

1. Population

10.49 million (1997).

2. Geographical dimension, location and climate

131,957 square kilometres. Greece lies in South-Eastern Europe. It consists of a mountainous peninsula and many small islands. The climate is Mediterranean with hot summers and relatively mild winters.

3. Constitution/political system

The 1975 Constitution provides that the President, elected by Parliament for a five-year term, is head of state. He appoints the Prime Minister on whose recommendation he appoints other Cabinet members. The unicameral Parliament consists of 300 members directly elected by a form of modified proportional representation. The legislature holds executive power. Local councils also have some powers. Greece comprises 10 regions with 51 administrative divisions.

4. Gross Domestic Product

ECU 107.8 billion.

5. Main industries

Agriculture, including forestry and fishing, contributed 8.1 per cent to GDP in 1997, employing 19.8 per cent of the labour force in 1997. Industry contributed 23 per cent to GDP in 1997 and employed 22.5 per cent of the work-force, with manufacturing accounting for 13.3 per cent of GDP in 1997, and employing 14.5

per cent of the work-force. Food products, textiles and petroleum products, metal and metal products, electrical machinery and beverages constitute the most important manufacturing industries. Services contributed 68.6 per cent of GDP in 1997, and employed 57.7 per cent of the work-force.

6. Major imports and exports

Germany is Greece's main trading partner, taking about 18 per cent of exports and providing about 14.4 per cent of imports in 1997. The major exports are clothing and textiles, fruit and vegetables, and petroleum products. Tourism is an important industry in terms of earning foreign currency.

7. Languages

The language is Greek, of which there are two forms: formal Greek (Katharevoussa) and colloquial Greek (Demotiki), which is the most commonly taught and spoken.

8. Religions

The population is 97 per cent Greek Orthodox Christian, with over 9 million adherents. There are about 59,000 Roman Catholics, around 5,000 Jews, 5,000 Protestants and some Muslims.

9. Capital city

The capital city is Athens.

10. Currency

The currency is the Drachma. Greece is not presently part of the Eurozone, as it did not achieve the convergence criteria required.

11. Comments

The general economic situation is not good. Greece suffers from an increasing public sector deficit. In 1995 the cost of servicing the public external debt equalled 33.6 per cent of earnings from the exports of goods and services. The average level of unemployment was an estimated 10.2 per cent in 1996. Greece continues to receive significant funds from the EU, and infrastructure investment, which should help the economy. It was admitted to the ERM in March 1998. There is a state social insurance scheme, and in 1988 there was one hospital bed per 193 inhabitants. Education is free at all levels, and compulsory from the ages of 6 to 16.

Republic of Ireland

1. Population
3.7 million.

2. Geographical dimension, location and climate
70.285 square kilometres. The Republic of Ireland has 26 counties. The remaining six counties on the island form Northern Ireland, which is part of the UK. Ireland is in Western Europe, and the climate is mild.

3. Constitution/political system
It is a republic with a bicameral National Parliament: the Upper House or Senate (Seanad Eireann) with 60 members, which has restricted powers, and the House of Representatives (Dail Eireann), with 166 members, who are elected by a single transferable vote (a form of proportional representation) for a five-year term. The President is the constitutional head of state, directly elected for seven years. The Prime Minister, nominated by the Dail, is appointed by the President, as are the other ministers to the Cabinet, who are nominated by the Prime Minister with the approval of the Dail. The Senate includes 11 members nominated by the Prime Minister. The Cabinet holds executive powers.

4. Gross Domestic Product
ECU 76 billion.

5. Main industries
Agriculture employed over 10 per cent (estimated) of the work-force and contributed 6.3 per cent of GDP in 1997. Industry employed about 28.8 per cent of the work-force and provided 37.2 per cent of the GDP in 1997. Peat, lead, zinc ore and coal are mined. Service industries including finance, transport, communications, public administration and commerce employed 61.1 per cent of the work-force in 1997 and contributed 56.6 per cent to the GDP in 1997. International banking and tourism are significant sectors.

6. Major imports and exports
Machinery and transport equipment, beef and dairy produce and chemicals are significant, as is the manufacture of high-technology products. The UK is Ireland's main trading partner, followed by the USA, Germany and Japan (a significant source of imports).

7. Languages
The languages are Irish and English.

8. Religions

The majority are Roman Catholic (73 per cent) with 297,205 Presbyterians, 58,659 Methodists, and 370,000 Church of Ireland members. There are an estimated 9,000 Muslims, and 1,200 Jews (1996).

9. Capital city

The capital city is Dublin.

10. Currency

The currency is the Irish Punt, but Ireland has joined the Eurozone and is moving towards the Euro.

11. Comments

The difficulties arising out of a divided Ireland and the threat of terrorist activities should not be ignored. As to the economic situation, Ireland is doing well. It is still benefiting from EU funds. It is now reputed to be the world's second-largest exporter of computer software. Social welfare benefits vary in scope depending on whether they are non-contributory (for persons of inadequate means) or contributory (compulsory for self-employed people and employees). Equally, health services vary in cost (free to low-income groups, but with fewer free services to the two higher income bands). In 1995 there were 13,557 hospital beds. Unemployment in December 1996 was 11.8 per cent. Education is compulsory in Ireland from the ages of 6 to 15, and academic or vocational schools offer courses to the ages of 17 or 18. Education accounted for 15.4 per cent of total budget expenditure in 1998.

Italy

1. Population

57.6 million.

2. Geographical dimension, location and climate

301,341 square kilometres. Italy consists of a peninsula from South Europe into the Mediterranean Sea and various islands, the largest of which are Sardinia and Sicily. The climate is generally temperate, but changing to Mediterranean in the south.

3. Constitution/political system

Legislative power is vested in a bicameral parliament elected until now by a system of proportional representation, but the system is to be changed as it is felt to have caused problems of political uncertainty. Under the new system, 75 per cent of the Senate will be elected by majority vote. The Senate has 315 elected members (seats allotted regionally) and 10 life senators. The Chamber of Deputies has 630 members. The President is elected by an electoral college of the two Chambers. As head of state, he appoints the Prime Minister, who is the President of Council, and on his recommendation other ministers. A Parliamentary Commission on constitutional reform has recommended further changes with a reduction in the number of delegates. There are 20 regions with considerable executive power, some having special status and considerable regional autonomy. It should be noted that the Vatican City is a separate sovereign state under the jurisdiction of the Pope.

4. Gross Domestic Product

ECU 1,046.7 billion.

5. Main industries

Agriculture contributed 2.9 per cent of GDP in 1996, and wine is a significant sector in terms also of exports, employing 6.8 per cent of the work-force in 1997. Industry contributed 32.5 per cent in 1996, and state assistance of heavy industry is significant. Italy has mineral reserves. Manufacturing industries are significant, the largest being machinery and transport equipment, and including vehicles, textiles, clothing and chemicals. Services accounted for 65.6 per cent of GDP in 1996 employing 61.2 per cent of the work-force.

6. Major imports and exports

The major trading partner is Germany for imports and exports. In 1993, 61.7 per cent of Italy's exports were to other EU members. Machinery and transport equipment, and basic manufactures, constitute the major exports. Tourism is a significant currency earner.

7. Languages

The main language is Italian, but German and Lodin (on the Austrian border), French (near the French and Swiss borders) and Greek and Albanian (in the south of Italy) are spoken among minorities. A Catalan-type language is spoken in the north of Sardinia.

8. Religions

Almost the whole population are Christian, with about 90 per cent Roman Catholic and about 50,000 Protestants. There are some 40,000 Jews.

9. Capital city
The capital city is Rome.

10. Currency
The currency is the Lira, but Italy is part of the Eurozone, and moving towards the single currency.

11. Comments
A continuing high level of public debt (122 per cent of GDP in 1997) has led to emergency measures to reduce budgetary deficits, including public sector reforms and cost-cutting measures. Italy managed to join Stage III of EMU, but economic problems remain. There is a social security system and a comprehensive national health service. In 1996 there was one hospital bed per 175 inhabitants. Unemployment in December 1996 was 11.9 per cent. Education is free, and compulsory only from the ages of 6 to 13. Secondary education is streamed. In 1995 the total enrolment at primary and secondary schools together was only 92 per cent; and 88 per cent in respect of secondary school only (which shows a great improvement on previous figures). Government expenditure on education was about 5.4 per cent of GDP in 1992.

The Grand Duchy of Luxembourg

1. Population
0.429 million.

2. Geographical dimension, location and climate
2,586 square kilometres. Luxembourg is set in Western Europe, and is landlocked. It has a temperate climate.

3. Constitution/political system
Luxembourg is a constitutional, hereditary monarchy. There is a unicameral parliament (the Chamber of Deputies), which has 60 directly elected members on the basis of proportional representation, and exercises legislative power. The Council of State consists of 21 life members appointed by the Grand Duke, who also appoints the ministers, who are led by the President of Government (Prime Minister). The Council of Ministers is responsible to the Chamber of Deputies. Luxembourg has 12 cantons (administrative regions).

4. Gross Domestic Product
ECU 15.5 billion. (GNP is among the highest in the world.)

5. Main industries

In 1995 agriculture constituted 1.1 per cent of GDP; and industry about 21.8 per cent (employing over 26 per cent of the workforce in 1996), with manufacturing contributing about 16.5 per cent (1995). Iron and steel, chemical, rubber, plastic, metal and machinery products, paper and printing are all important sectors, as are financial services. The service sector contributed 77.1 per cent (estimate) in 1995, and employed 70.7 per cent of the employed labour force in 1996.

6. Major imports and exports

Major imports are mineral products, basic manufactures, transport machinery and chemicals. Foodstuffs and petroleum products are significant. Main exports are basic metals and manufactures, plastics, rubber and machinery, but financial services must be taken into account, due to the favourable legislation in this regard. Luxembourg's principal trading partners are Belgium (providing 39.4 per cent of imports in 1996), Germany and France.

7. Languages

The official language is Letzeburgish, but French is used for administrative purposes and German for the press and commerce.

8. Religions

Around 96 per cent are Christians, with 95 per cent Roman Catholics and 1 per cent Protestants.

9. Capital city

The capital city is Luxembourg-Ville.

10. Currency

The currency is the Luxembourg Franc, but Luxembourg is in the Eurozone and moving towards the single currency.

11. Comments

Luxembourg is a small country with a prosperous economy and low unemployment – 3.3 per cent in 1996, 2.8 per cent in May 1999. Its social welfare system is comprehensive, albeit not operated by the government itself, but by semi-public bodies by way of a contributory comprehensive social insurance scheme. In 1992 there was one hospital bed per 87 inhabitants. Education is compulsory from 6 to 15, with various vocational and educational courses available thereafter. Government spending on education was 9.9 per cent of total government spending in 1995.

The Netherlands

1. Population

15.7 million.

2. Geographical dimension, location and climate

33,939 square kilometres. The Netherlands is in Western Europe and is bordered to the north and west by the North Sea. The climate is temperate.

3. Constitution/political system

The Netherlands is a kingdom with a hereditary monarchy and a constitution with a bicameral state government. The 12 provincial councils elect the 75 members of the First Chamber. The Second Chamber (150 members) is directly elected by a form of proportional representation for a four-year term. The Prime Minister is appointed by the monarch who, on the Prime Minister's recommendation, also appoints the other ministers to the Council of Ministers, which has executive power. There are 12 provinces, each with a Provincial Executive, a Sovereign Commissioner and an elected council.

4. Gross Domestic Product

ECU 336.7 billion.

5. Main industries

Agriculture, including forestry and fishing, accounted for about 3.4 per cent of the GDP in 1993. The Netherlands is a net exporter of food and live animals. Industry contributed 38.6 per cent to GDP, and employed 22.8 per cent of the working population in 1994, with manufacturing contributing 18.4 per cent of GDP in 1993 and employing 16.1 per cent of the work-force in 1994. Services contributed 68.1 per cent of GDP in 1993, and employed 70.4 per cent of the work-force in 1995.

6. Major imports and exports

The main exports are machinery, transport equipment, chemicals, basic manufactures, horticulture, food and live animals. Natural gas reserves are a useful resource. The main import is mineral fuels. Germany is its main trading partner, taking 29.1 per cent of exports and providing 23.5 per cent of imports in 1993.

7. Language

Dutch is the official language.

8. Religions

About 67 per cent of the population are Christians, of which 33 per cent are Roman Catholics. Many profess no religion.

9. Capital city

The capital city is Amsterdam. The Hague is the seat of government.

10. Currency

The currency is the Netherlands Guilder, but the Netherlands is part of the Eurozone, and moving towards the single currency.

11. Comments

The Netherlands has a relatively strong economy, but efforts continue to control public expenditure. Unemployment in June 1997 was 5.6 per cent, and 3.3 per cent in April 1998. Social welfare spending in the Netherlands is high, and was allocated over 37.7 per cent of total central government expenditure in 1996. There was one hospital bed per 314 people in 1995. Full-time education is compulsory from 5 to 16 years, schools are fully subsidized, and 98 per cent of four-year-olds also attend. Part-time education for a further two years is also compulsory. The provisional budgetary allocation for education and culture in 1997 was 18.5 per cent of total government expenditure.

Portugal

1. Population

9.9 million.

2. Geographical dimension, location and climate

92,345 square kilometres. Portugal is situated in Western Europe and includes two archipelagos in the Atlantic Ocean, namely the Azores and the Madeira Islands. It has a mild temperate climate.

3. Constitution/political system

Portugal is a republic. Its head of state is the President, who is directly elected for a five-year term. The President appoints the Prime Minister and, on his or her recommendation, the other members of the Council of Ministers. The Assembly of the Republic is unicameral with 230 directly elected members. The Council of State consists of 17 members and is a consultative body. Proposals to reduce the numbers of deputies and to make other reforms were agreed in 1997.

4. Gross Domestic Product
ECU 95.7 billion.

5. Main industries
Agriculture, including forestry, wine and fishing, employed nearly 14.4 per cent of the working population in 1997, and contributed 6.4 per cent of GDP in 1994. Industry then contributed 35.6 per cent of GDP, and employed 31 per cent of the work-force in 1995, with manufacturing and mining contributing 25.8 per cent to the GDP in 1993 and employing 23.5 per cent of the work-force in 1994. Ceramics, textiles and clothing and footwear manufacture are also significant. Services provided 60.3 per cent of GDP and employed 56.8 per cent of the work-force in 1997.

6. Major imports and exports
Clothing accounted for an estimated 16 per cent of total export earnings in 1995. Other manufactured goods include footwear, paper, ceramics and electrical appliances. Tourism was a significant source of earnings. Petroleum is the chief import. Germany, France and Spain are its main trading partners, between them supplying over 40 per cent of total imports, and taking 50 per cent of exports in 1996.

7. Language
Portuguese is the official language.

8. Religions
Most of the population are Roman Catholics, but there are also some Protestants, and an estimated 15,000 Muslims and 2,000 Jews.

9. Capital city
The capital city is Lisbon.

10. Currency
The currency is the Portuguese Escudo, but Portugal has joined the Eurozone, and is moving towards the single currency.

11. Comments
Portugal has pursued a tight fiscal policy and achieved significant improvements, and so is moving towards the Euro. Portugal does benefit from EU funding. Unemployment in December 1996 was 7.1 per cent and remains high, but there has been a job-creation drive. Although Portugal allotted about 10.5 per cent of total

expenditure to health services in 1993, some social welfare services are not as developed as elsewhere. Pre-school education from 3 to 6 is free. School is compulsory between the ages of 6 and 15. Education is free, although private schools exist. Supplementary courses for students over 14 are available. Access to higher education is subject to quotas. Education accounted for 12.9 per cent of budget expenditure in 1994, and in 1993 total enrolment in basic and secondary education was 99 per cent.

Spain

1. Population

39.4 million.

2. Geographical dimension, location and climate

504,782 square kilometres. Spain is situated in South-Western Europe, and includes the Balearic Islands in the Mediterranean Sea, the Canary Islands in the Atlantic Ocean and some small enclaves in Morocco. The climate is Mediterranean, with hot summers and cold winters, varying with the topography.

3. Constitution/political system

Spain has a hereditary monarchy, and the King is head of state. He appoints the President (Prime Minister) and, on his recommendation, other members of the Council of Ministers. The Council of State is the supreme consultative body with 23 members. Legislative power is vested in the Cortes Generales, which is bicameral, with the Congress of Deputies consisting of 350 members directly elected by proportional representation, and the Senate consisting of 208 elected members, plus 48 regional representatives. Spain has 50 provinces, each with a council and government delegate. There is considerable regional self-government. Parliament is elected for a four-year term.

4. Gross Domestic Product

ECU 507.7 billion.

5. Main industries

In 1996 agriculture, forestry and fishing together made up 3.7 per cent of GDP. Industry provided 33.2 per cent of GDP, and employed 30.1 per cent of the work-force in 1995. Manufacturing, particularly of motor cars and ships, footwear, textiles, chemicals and steel, is significant. Tourism contributes significantly. Services contributed 63.1 per cent of GDP in 1996, and employed 60.7 per cent of the work-force in 1995.

6. Major imports and exports

Major exports are cars, machinery, iron and steel goods, and agricultural products. The main imports are mineral fuels, petroleum and chemical products, machinery, electrical equipment and vehicles. In 1995 France and Germany between them provided 32 per cent of imports, France then taking about 20 per cent of exports.

7. Languages

The principal language is Castilian Spanish, with Catalan being spoken in the north-east, Galician in the north-west and Basque in the north.

8. Religions

There is no official state religion, but a large percentage are Roman Catholics. There are almost 300,000 Muslims, 30,000 Protestants and 15,000 Jews.

9. Capital city

The capital city is Madrid.

10. Currency

The currency is the Peseta, but Spain has joined the Eurozone, and is moving towards the single currency.

11. Comments

Spain has had to make great efforts to be able to qualify to join in Stage III of EMU, and a continuing battle is being waged against inflation, corruption and tax evasion. There is a high level of unemployment – 22.2 per cent in December 1996 – and job creation remains a target. Government cut-backs have been made, including reductions in social benefits. In 1995 Spain had 168,048 hospital beds. Strong economic growth continued through 1998. Education is compulsory and free from the ages of 6 to 16. Vocational and other courses are available, and there are also some private (mostly Roman Catholic) schools. The government's draft budget allocation in 1998 for educational and cultural purposes was 6.1 per cent of total expenditure.

Sweden

1. Population

8.8 million.

2. Geographical dimension, location and climate

449,694 square kilometres. Sweden is in North-Western Europe and about 15 per cent of its area lies north of the Arctic Circle. Summers are warm and winters are cold. Temperatures vary with the latitude.

3. Constitution/political system

Sweden is a constitutional monarchy, but the King, although head of state, has limited powers. There is a unicameral parliament (the Riksdag), with 349 members directly elected by proportional representation for a four-year term. The Prime Minister is nominated by the Speaker and confirmed by the House. The Cabinet is responsible to the Riksdag. There are 24 counties, and local governments have significant powers, particularly in respect of administration.

4. Gross Domestic Product

ECU 202.6 billion.

5. Main industries

In 1996 agriculture contributed 2.5 per cent and industry 33.7 per cent to GDP, with manufacturing contributing 24.6 per cent. The most important products were foodstuffs, paper, motor vehicles, machinery, chemicals, electrical goods, and printing and publishing. The services sector contributed about 67.3 per cent of GDP, and employed about 70.9 per cent of the employed workforce in 1996.

6. Major imports and exports

The principal exports are machinery, transport equipment, and wood and wood products (which accounted for 16.7 per cent of total merchandise exports in 1994). The principal imports are machinery and transport equipment, mineral fuels and foodstuffs. Germany is its main trading partner, providing 19.6 per cent of imports and taking 12.6 per cent of exports in 1995, followed by the UK, the USA and Norway. The EU provided 70.5 per cent of imports, and took 59.9 per cent of exports in 1995.

7. Language

The national language is Swedish, but small Finn and Lapp minorities continue to speak their own languages.

8. Religions

Most inhabitants are Christians, and 86.5 per cent are Evangelical Lutherans. There are over 100,000 Muslims and around 20,000 Jews.

9. *Capital city*

The capital city is Stockholm.

10. *Currency*

The currency is the Krona.

11. *Comments*

On 1 January 1995 Sweden became a member of the European Union. It has encountered economic difficulties, particularly due to the decline in the steel and shipbuilding sectors. The government is committed to reducing the budgetary deficit, and cutbacks are affecting state benefits. Job creation is a target, as unemployment in December 1997 was estimated to be 13 per cent. Sweden has a highly advanced system of social security schemes. In 1995 there was one hospital bed to every 165 inhabitants. In 1997, 28.8 per cent of total government spending was allocated to health and social welfare. Education is compulsory for nine years between the ages of 7 and 16. At the end of this period a student may enter the integrated upper secondary school. About 4.9 per cent of total expenditure was for education in 1996.

The United Kingdom of Great Britain and Northern Ireland

1. *Population*

59.2 million.

2. *Geographical dimension, location and climate*

241,900 square kilometres. The UK is situated in North-Western Europe. The climate is temperate.

3. *Constitution/political system*

The UK is a constitutional and hereditary monarchy, and the Queen is head of state. The bicameral parliament consists of an upper house or House of Lords, the members of which are hereditary or life peers and peeresses, and a lower house or House of Commons, which consists of 651 directly elected members. The House of Lords may delay, but not prevent, legislation from being passed by the House of Commons. Executive power is held by the Cabinet, which is led by the Prime Minister and answerable to the House of Commons.

4. *Gross Domestic Product*

ECU 1,220.4 billion.

5. Main industries

In 1996 agriculture (including forestry and fishing) contributed 1.8 per cent of GDP. Industry in that year contributed 30.2 per cent, and in 1995 it employed 23.6 per cent of the work-force, with manufacturing contributing 20.4 per cent of GDP and employing about 16.3 per cent of the work-force in 1996. Services (mostly business and financial services) contributed 68.1 per cent of GDP in 1996, employing 73.5 per cent of the work-force in 1997 (excluding Northern Ireland).

6. Major imports and exports

Business services are important, as is tourism. Main exports are machinery and transport equipment, basic manufactures, chemicals and related products, generators, and telecommunications equipment. Major imports are road vehicles, machinery, office equipment, petroleum, paper, manufacturing and textiles. The principal trading partner for imports (14.8 per cent) and exports (12.3 per cent) in 1996 was Germany. Other major trading partners include France, The Netherlands, the USA and Japan.

7. Languages

The language is English, with Welsh spoken by a fifth of the population of Wales.

8. Religions

The established church in England is the Church of England, with a membership of about 7 million, but there are large numbers of other Christian denominations: Roman Catholics (4.23 million), the Church of Scotland (702,000), and Quakers (18,000). There are Jews (about 300,000), Muslims (1.5 million), Buddhists (25,000), Sikhs (400,000) and Hindus (350,000). These numbers are all estimates.

9. Capital city

The capital city is London.

10. Currency

The currency is Sterling.

11. Comments

The government has maintained a tight control on the economy, which remains stable. Stringent measures have been taken to control government spending and the level of inflation. Unemployment in December 1996 stood at 7.5 per cent, and job creation remains a target. There is a comprehensive social welfare system with a National Health Service that has been subject to significant reforms. There was one hospital bed per 217 people in England and Wales, and per 110 in Scotland in 1993/4. Education is compulsory and free from the term following a child's fifth birthday until age 16. There is a significant private education sector.

EFTA member countries

The Republic of Iceland

1. *Population*

0.275 million (December 1998).

2. *Geographical dimension, location and climate*

103,000 square kilometres. Iceland consists of one large island and many smaller ones. It is located near the Arctic Circle in the North Atlantic Ocean, 800 kilometres north of Scotland. It is cold but affected by the Gulf Stream so the temperature varies between 1 °C in the winter and 50 °C in summer.

3. *Constitution/political system*

Iceland is an independent republic, with an elected President who appoints the Prime Minister and Cabinet, under a bicameral system. The Althing (parliament) has 63 members directly elected by a form of proportional representation for a four-year term, and these are divided into an Upper House (one-third of members) and a Lower House. There are seven administrative districts. In practice the Cabinet holds executive power, and the President and Althing hold legislative power.

4. *Gross Domestic Product*

524.419 million Kronur in 1997.

5. *Main industries*

Agriculture, including forestry and fishing, contributed over 12 per cent to GDP in 1992. Industry, including mainly manufacturing, construction and power, accounted for 30.2 per cent of GDP in 1992. Hydroelectric and geothermal power are useful but under-exploited resources.

6. *Main imports and exports*

Fisheries products accounted for 71 per cent of exports in 1997, and mineral fuel and lubricant exports were significant. Iceland's principal trading countries are Norway, Germany and Denmark (for imports) and the UK, Germany and the USA (for exports). In 1997, 59.5 per cent of imports were from EU countries, and 59.5 per cent of exports were to EU countries (with the USA taking 13.9 per cent of its exports).

7. Languages

Icelandic is the official language.

8. Religions

Almost all the population are Christians, with 90 per cent being Evangelical Lutherans, and 1 per cent Roman Catholics.

9. Capital city

The capital city is Reykjavik.

10. Currency

The currency is the Icelandic Krona (plural: Kronur).

11. Comments

Iceland is a member of EFTA and the Nordic Council. Fishing is very important to Iceland's economy, which is affected by conservation measures over fishing and depleted fish stocks. The government have been taking action to increase the competitiveness of Iceland's manufacturing and financial services industries, and to reduce the significant budgetary deficit, with the cost of debt servicing equivalent to 28.8 per cent of export earning in 1995. An overall growth of 5.2 per cent GDP was achieved in 1998. Unemployment is low, and was about 2.2 per cent in 1998. The social security system is comprehensive, and in 1992 health and welfare accounted for 36.7 per cent of central government expenditure. Education is free, and compulsory from age 6 or 7 to 15, with three years of secondary education starting at 16 taken up by about 89 per cent of students. There are day schools in towns, but children from remote areas can attend state boarding schools. Education accounted for 11.9 per cent of total government spending in 1995.

Liechtenstein

1. Population

0.031 million (December 1994).

2. Geographical dimension, location and climate

160 square kilometres. Liechtenstein is in Central Europe, and is

landlocked, but on the east bank of the Upper Rhine River. Its climate is alpine and relatively mild.

3. Constitution/political system

Liechtenstein is a hereditary principality with a unicameral parliament (the Landtag) of 25 members directly elected by proportional representation for a four-year term. The Landtag elects a five-member government, confirmed by the sovereign. Women were only given full voting rights in 1986.

4. Gross Domestic Product

2,250 million Swiss Francs (1995).

5. Main industries

Agriculture is not important, employing an estimated 1.5 per cent of the work-force in 1996. Industry accounts for a high proportion of GDP, employing 46 per cent of the work-force in 1996, while the services sector, including banking, employed 52.5 per cent of the working population in the same year.

6. Major imports and exports

Liechtenstein exports include artificial teeth and dental products, metal, machinery and precision instruments, and furniture. Liechtenstein's main trading partner is Switzerland, which took 14.5 per cent of exports in 1996, and with whom it has a customs union.

7. Languages

The official language is German, and the spoken dialect is Alemannish.

8. Religions

Almost all the population are Christian, and about 80 per cent Roman Catholic.

9. Capital city

The capital city is Vaduz.

10. Currency

The currency is the Swiss Franc.

11. Comments

Liechtenstein is a member of EFTA, and joined the EEA in 1995. Like Switzerland, Liechtenstein is very rich in terms of GNP per head, and is the site of many foreign enterprises taking advantage of banking secrecy. Over one-third of its population are not nationals. There is a comprehensive social welfare system. Unemployment is low, and was 1.5 per cent at the end of 1993. Education is compulsory from the ages of 7 to 16 years. There is no university, but children at 12 may choose either a four- or six-year course. Many students continue their studies in Austria, Germany or Sweden.

The Kingdom of Norway

1. Population

4.392 million (1997 official estimate).

2. Geographical dimension, location and climate

323,758 square kilometres. The Kingdom of Norway is situated in Northern Europe, and part of it is within the Arctic Circle. The temperature varies, warmer on the coast and in the south, and colder inland and in the north.

3. Constitution/political system

A constitutional monarchy, Norway has a unicameral parliament (the Storting) holding legislative power with 165 members elected by proportional representation. The Storting itself is divided into two houses, for legislative proposals: an upper house (Lagting) with a quarter of its members, and a lower house (Odelsting). The State Council, or Council of Ministers, is appointed by the sovereign on the recommendation of the Storting, and is led by a Prime Minister. Norway is divided into 19 counties.

4. Gross Domestic Product

ECU 130 billion.

5. Main industries

Agriculture, including forestry and fishing, contributed an estimated 2.5 per cent of GDP in 1996. About 60 per cent of Norway's land area is forested. In 1996, industry contributed 36.1 per cent of GDP, with hydrocarbons being the most important sector, and employed over 22 per cent of the work-force. Mining contributed 16.7 per cent and manufacturing about 12.9 per cent in 1996. The services sector used 71.8 per cent of the employed work-force, and contributed 61.5 per cent to GDP in 1996.

6. Major imports and exports

In 1993 Norway started exporting hydroelectricity. Norway's

main trading partner is the UK, which took 24 per cent of exports and provided 9 per cent of imports in 1992. Sweden and Germany are also important trading partners. The principal exports are petroleum and natural gas, and the principal imports are machinery, chemical products and transport equipment. Shipping remains important.

7. Languages

There are two forms of officially recognized Norwegian: Bokmal (80 per cent), the old form, and Nynorsk (20 per cent), the new form. Lappish is spoken by the Sami minority in the north.

8. Religions

Most Norwegians are Christians. In 1997 about 86 per cent were Evangelical Lutherans (the State Church is Evangelical Lutheran). There were about 42,000 Roman Catholics, 42,000 Muslims and 1,048 Jews.

9. Capital city

The capital city is Oslo.

10. Currency

The currency is the Krona.

11. Comments

Norway is a member of EFTA, the EEA and the Nordic Council, but did not become a member of the EU in 1995, as its electorate rejected membership. The Norwegian economy is dependent on hydrocarbons, and was beneficially affected by difficulties in the Middle East supplies. There are attempts to diversify, for example, fish farming is being encouraged, and hydroelectricity developed. Average unemployment in 1996 was 4.9 per cent. There is a comprehensive social welfare system. Over 50 per cent of total government funding in 1996 was on social expenditure including health. There was one hospital bed per 199 people in 1995. Education is compulsory from 7 to 16 years, and accounted for 13.3 per cent of total government expenditure in 1996.

Switzerland

1. Population

7.081 million (31 December 1996 official estimate).

2. Geographical dimension, location and climate

41,284 square kilometres. Switzerland lies in Central Europe and is landlocked. The climate is temperate, but varies with the topography.

3. Constitution/political system
Switzerland is a confederation, with 23 cantons and three half-cantons. Legislative power is vested in a bicameral Federal Assembly consisting of the Council of States (with 46 elected members representing the cantons and half-cantons) and the National Council (with 200 members directly elected by proportional representation for a four-year term). The Federal Council (seven members including the President elected by the Federal Assembly) holds executive power. The President acts as head of state. The cantons hold considerable powers.

4. Gross Domestic Product
ECU 225 billion.

5. Main industries
Agriculture provided about 2.7 per cent of GDP, and employed 4.6 per cent of the work-force, in 1996. Industry provided 29.6 per cent of GDP in 1993, with manufacturing industry providing 21.3 per cent. The services sector provided about 76 per cent of GDP in 1993, employing 67.2 per cent of the work-force in 1996 (estimated figures).

6. Major imports and exports
Switzerland's earnings in respect of international financial transactions are significant. Tourism is also a useful source of earnings, equivalent to about 11.2 per cent of export earnings from goods in 1996. The principal exports are machinery, metal, pharmaceutical and chemical products, precision instruments such as watches, agricultural and forestry products, and textiles. Principal imports are energy, machinery, metal products, motor vehicles and chemicals. Germany is its principal trading partner for imports and exports. Switzerland imported 72.9 per cent of its imports from, and exported 56.8 per cent of its exports to, EU countries in 1994.

7. Languages
The three official languages are German (73.4 per cent in 1990), French (20.5 per cent) and Italian (4.1 per cent). Raeto-Romansch is also spoken in eastern Switzerland.

8. Religions
Most of the Swiss are Christian, of which about 45 per cent are

Roman Catholics and 40 per cent Protestants. Muslims make up 22 per cent of the population, and Jews 3 per cent.

9. Capital city

The capital city is Bern (or Berne).

10. Currency

The currency is the Swiss Franc.

11. Comments

Switzerland is a member of EFTA. Its GNP per head is one of the highest in the world, and the proportion of resident non-nationals was 26.2 per cent in 1992. Inflation is under control, and economic growth is expected. As to social welfare, a Federal Insurance law applies, and almost everyone is medically insured. Insurance is not compulsory, although unemployment, medical care and pension insurance for employees is compulsory. There is no national health service as such. In 1995 there was one hospital bed per 183 inhabitants. In 1995, 25.2 per cent of total spending of the Federal budget was on social welfare. Education is mainly controlled regionally, so 26 different systems apply, but education is compulsory between the ages of 7 and 15 years, in some areas 16 years. There is a strong emphasis on vocational training. There are many private schools, and a significant number of foreign children attend them.

Appendix VIII
Revised Co-decision Procedure

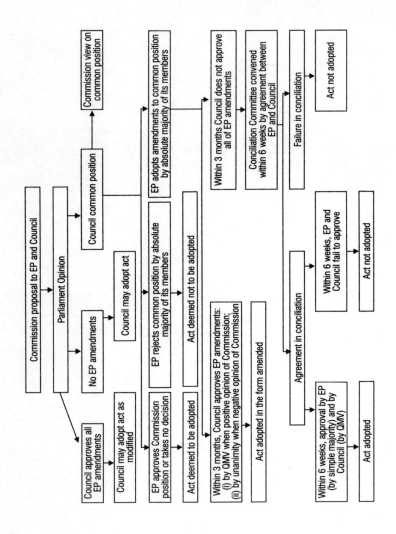

Index